DR SIAN WILLIAMS

THE POWER OF Anxiety

How to Ride the Worry Wave

ALLEN&UNWIN

First published in trade paperback in Great Britain in 2026 by
Allen & Unwin, an imprint of Atlantic Books Ltd.

Copyright © Sian Williams, 2026

The moral right of Sian Williams to be identified as the author of this work has been asserted by her in accordance with the Copyright, Designs and Patents Act of 1988.

All rights reserved. No part of this publication may be reproduced, stored in a retrieval system, or transmitted in any form or by any means, electronic, mechanical, photocopying, recording, or otherwise, without the prior permission of both the copyright owner and the above publisher of this book.

No part of this book may be used in any manner in the learning, training or development of generative artificial intelligence technologies (including but not limited to machine learning models and large language models (LLMs)), whether by data scraping, data mining or use in any way to create or form a part of data sets or in any other way.

Every effort has been made to trace or contact all copyright holders. The publishers will be pleased to make good any omissions or rectify any mistakes brought to their attention at the earliest opportunity.

p. 107: Excerpt from A NEW EARTH: OPRAH'S BOOK CLUB: AWAKENING TO YOUR LIFE'S PURPOSE by Eckhart Tolle, copyright © 2005 by Eckhart Tolle. Used by permission of Dutton, an imprint of Penguin Publishing Group, a division of Penguin Random House LLC. All rights reserved.

p. 161: "CREEP"
Words and Music by Albert Hammond, EDWARD JOHN O'BRIEN,
PHILIP JAMES SELWAY, COLIN CHARLES GREENWOOD, Jonathan Greenwood,
THOMAS EDWARD YORKE and MIKE HAZELWOOD
WARNER CHAPPELL MUSIC LTD (PRS)
All rights on behalf of WARNER CHAPPELL MUSIC LTD
administered by WARNER CHAPPELL MUSIC LTD.

p. 255: "The Summer Day" by Mary Oliver
Reprinted by the permission of The Charlotte Sheedy Literary Agency as agent for the author. Copyright © 1990, 2005, 2008, 2017 by Mary Oliver with permission of Bill Reichblum.

Some names and identifying characteristics have been changed to protect the privacy of those individuals.

10 9 8 7 6 5

A CIP catalogue record for this book is available from the British Library.

Trade Paperback ISBN: 978 1 80546 503 4
E-book ISBN: 978 1 80546 504 1

Printed in Great Britain

Allen & Unwin
An imprint of Atlantic Books Ltd
Ormond House
26–27 Boswell Street
London
WC1N 3JZ

www.atlantic-books.co.uk

Product safety EU representative: Authorised Rep Compliance Ltd., Ground Floor, 71 Lower Baggot Street, Dublin, D02 P593, Ireland. www.arccompliance.com

'Such a clear-sighted and informative read. It demystifies anxiety and offers a way through it. Invaluable.' Kaye Adams, presenter

'What if we made friends with anxiety? If we stopped trying to fight it? In this brilliantly counter-intuitive book, Williams gives us the tools to do just that.' Rachel Kelly, *Sunday Times* bestselling author of *The Gift of Teenagers*

'Wonderfully insightful and constantly fascinating – a must-read.' Rt Hon Sir Norman Lamb, former Minister of State for Care and Support and mental health campaigner

'Calming, helpful and timely.' Richard Madeley, presenter

'Dr Sian Williams has written a book that many of us need.' Nick Midgley, PhD, Professor of Psychological Therapies with Children and Young People, UCL and Anna Freud, London

'A delightfully warm and human book.' Dr Lucy Maddox, author of *A Year to Change Your Mind*

'Informative and engaging.' Gwendoline Smith, author of *The Book of Overthinking*

'A must read and a great companion. Full of helpful tools, reading this book will make you feel less lost and alone with your anxiety.' Zoe Ball, broadcaster

'It's terrific and so very helpful. If I could eat a book it would be this one.' Derren Brown, mentalist

'A warm and comforting bundle of science, case studies and evidence-based tips.' Professor Catherine Loveday, cognitive neuroscientist

'The perfect Anxiety Tool Kit. Sian's advice is accessible, soothing and spoken from the heart.' Julia Bradbury, presenter

'A wise, warm, compassionate guide to living well *with* anxiety.' Emma Freud, broadcaster

'It's a chill pill in book form.' Kathy Lette, author

'A brilliant, thoughtful, generous human.' Tim Minchin, comedian, actor, composer

Dr Sian Williams is a Chartered Counselling Psychologist practising in the NHS. She helps emergency service staff manage anxiety, stress and trauma and has worked with the Royal Foundation to bring attention to mental health in first responders. Sian also has her own private clinic delivering psychology and coaching to on- and off-air media professionals and business leaders. She's worked with the *Guardian*, BBC, ITN, Sky, ITV and Google and has written on mental health for major newspapers and publications including the *Daily Mail*, *Daily Telegraph* and *Good Housekeeping* magazine. Sian is an Associate Fellow of the British Psychological Society and a Research Fellow at City St George's, University of London.

Sian is also an award-winning broadcaster, having spent a quarter of a century presenting some of TV's most popular shows, including over a decade at the helm of BBC *Breakfast* and hosting many prime-time series on the BBC, ITV and Channel 5. She now presents BBC Radio 4's *Life Changing* which has had around twenty million downloads and presents a daily morning show on BBC Radio 3 Unwind. Her first book *Rise: Surviving and Thriving after Trauma* was described by the *Daily Mail* as 'the book every woman MUST read'. Anxiety is her lifetime companion.

To Paul, with love, always.

'You can't stop the waves, but you can learn to surf'

Jon Kabat-Zinn
Wherever You Go, There You Are

Contents

Preface	xi
Introduction	1

Part One

1. Dandelion or Orchid?	23
2. Anxiety – a Life Sentence?	48
3. The Happy Trap	74

Part Two

4. Understanding the Inner Voice	107
5. High-Functioning Anxiety, Perfectionism and… Procrastination	134
6. Imposter Syndrome, Performance and Social Anxiety	161

Part Three

7. How to Soothe our Anxious Body	197
8. How to Calm Our Anxious Thoughts	230
9. How to Manage Our Anxious Behaviours	255
10. And Finally… Four Extra Tips for Tending the Orchid	286
Epilogue	312
Acknowledgements	325
Appendix	328
Helpful Reading	331
Notes	334
Index	366

Preface

This is a book about anxiety. You'll probably know a lot about it already. That feeling of fear that can grip your guts and start the worries whirring. Perhaps you've tried pushing it away, ignoring it, hiding from it. Yet still it persists, heckling your every move, hijacking your every thought. You may have tried loads of tricks and tools (and maybe therapy) to deal with your anxiety, but here it is. Stopping you from doing things or being things. Like an angry passenger telling you you're driving down the wrong road, or going too slowly, or will never reach your destination.

I get it. I was an anxious child, and anxiety has been my lifelong companion. In my first year of high school, a teacher wrote in my report: 'Sian Williams is a small girl with thin powers of concentration, who tries hard and is keen to please.' Harsh, but he got it right, and I'm not sure much has changed. I *do* try hard; I *am* keen to please. My concentration is still a bit ropey and I haven't grown much either. But that small, people-pleasing, rather anxious child became a national BBC TV presenter – perhaps a strange profession for someone who feels self-conscious in the spotlight, who would rather stay in and read a book than face a party, or a room full of people or, horror, a red-carpet event.

THE POWER OF ANXIETY

I was a TV newsreader for a quarter of a century before I became a counselling psychologist, mainly working in the NHS – and anxiety has come with me. A kind of daily exposure therapy. Are you an overthinker who fears judgement and criticism? Let's see what happens when we put you in front of millions of people. It was both a brilliant job and one which could occasionally propel me into a spiral of worry and doubt.

The reason I kept going and loved it – and, as a BBC radio presenter, still do – is because when the camera is on, when the microphone is live, you can't see the audience looking back at you. They get in touch during the show or afterwards – via emails, texts or social media – kindly pointing out how tired you look, or that you asked the wrong question, but when you're in the flow and news is being thrown at you, it's the best job in the world. You use that stress and thrive on the adrenaline and cortisol rush. It's the buzz of hearing the director in your earpiece telling you to get ready, because you're about to interview the prime minister, or a Hollywood film star, or break a big news story, or reveal the outcome of a general election.

That's when the body and brain click into gear and the nerves are useful. When they're not so useful is afterwards, when that comment comes in that tells you that you are rubbish, a failure, that the job should go to someone else.

People are lovely when you bump into them in the supermarket, and when I left *BBC Breakfast* after eleven years there was a warm and emotional response from viewers who had quietly watched and loved the show, and they got in touch to say thank you, which moved me to tears. But the thing about the brain is that it always gets stuck on the negative comment. Then panic and anxiety set in and you begin to question yourself or lose faith or think people are just confirming what you already know about yourself – and that perhaps they're right, this job just isn't for you. If you've ever received a piece of crushing feedback, you'll know how that feels.

Very occasionally, the job itself could become overwhelming, when body and brain would go into fight-flight-freeze-faint-fawn, the common reactions to threat. When any of us sense we are under attack by something or someone – real or imagined – everything comes together fast, to help us survive it. We might try to confront it, or escape it. We may become immobilized, or pass out, or do what we can to appease or placate it. I'm a freeze-fainter. We rarely choose our own threat response. There have been serious life-and-death situations where I've reacted by shutting down to get through, but I've also fainted twice, live on air. I'll let you into the story of one of those occasions, one that I haven't told before.

It's 6 July 2004 and the Queen is opening the Diana, Princess of Wales Memorial Fountain in London's Hyde Park, a £3.6 million monument that is actually an oval stone ring containing water and has been drenched in controversy. It's the first time Diana's two families, the Windsors (Charles, the then Prince of Wales, and Princes William and Harry) and the Spencers (Charles, the 9th Earl Spencer) have been together publicly since Diana's funeral in 1997. I've been chosen as the BBC's anchor for the special programme, which is to be broadcast simultaneously on BBC One and BBC World.

I've done national events like this before, and there is always a feeling of anxiety. I have over-prepared, as usual. Like the crowds that have come to witness the event, I arrived early in the day. It's now mid-morning, the programme is underway and I'm on an incongruously high barstool, in a marquee overlooking the fountain. It is blazingly hot and I've been on this stool and talking for what seems like forever, until at last, my director tells me, 'The royals are on their way.' I'm to commentate over their arrival, in that slow, sonorous tone we presenters use for Big Occasions.

I'm looking at a feed of pictures on a TV screen by my feet, and it's my job to talk, continuously, as the royals get out of the cars, greet one another and move towards the fountain. Their cars still haven't turned into Hyde Park, so I am 'sustaining broadcasting'. In other words, talking out of vision and over pictures, while we all wait for them to arrive. Just before they do so, the feed on the little telly by my feet suddenly stops.

I have no idea what's happening. 'Keep talking,' my director says. I do but can't see what I'm supposed to be talking about. And then, my brain starts to swim, my heart seems to slow, my tongue fills up my mouth, my words become incomprehensible. Just as I start to keel over and fall off the stool, I hear the director shouting to our royal correspondent, Nick Witchell, who's standing by in his position next to the fountain: 'Fill! Fill! Fill!' *Thump*. I land on the floor.

For a few moments I am unconscious before a producer runs up to me and gives me three custard cream biscuits. 'Eat them. Now,' she commands. I stuff the biscuits in, get back on the stool, reassure the director, and with pictures restored, start commentating again. Low blood sugar? A hot day? Sat in the same place for hours? Stress levels overwhelming my resources to cope? Probably all of the above. But for a while after that day, anxiety set in about whether it would happen again – and, crucially, who would find out about it.

No one did. In fact, Nick told me recently he'd had no idea what was going on. Told to talk, he just 'wittered away'. Those expert witterings saved me. But at the time, I felt sure word would get out somehow. It's testament to the producer and director that it didn't.

Think back to a situation which makes you wince. It might be a presentation in front of colleagues where your brain froze, or you may have been at an event and said or done something embarrassing that you instantly regretted. Whatever it is, when the next presentation or social occasion comes up, our brain tries to protect us by reminding us of what went wrong last time and then predicting numerous ways it can go wrong again. 'Remember that disaster and how all those people judged and laughed at you?' says the brain. 'It could be even worse this time, so let's think through all the possible ways you might let yourself down.'

While the mind is ruminating, catastrophizing and distorting this unpredictable future meltdown, the emotions are throwing up dread, worry, fatigue; the body becomes tight, tense, uncomfortable, and the only way out of all of this is to escape, avoid and withdraw. 'I won't go to the event,' you say. 'I will procrastinate and not get round to writing the presentation.' There's short-term relief perhaps, in sending off that cancellation email, or hunkering down for a binge and a box set, but longer term we're in for problems. Because we know we'll blame and shame ourselves for our instinctive avoidance habits, we know that the more we hide, the harder it'll be to go out the next time an invite comes in, or to deliver the speech we've been dreading. It's all perfectly natural and understandable, and yet really hard to live with.

Anxiety is there for a reason. It tries to prepare us for a future where that feared situation might happen, or happen again, to give us command and control over the uncontrollable. It plugs the gap of terrifying uncertainty by keeping us on our guard, scanning the horizon for the next danger, making sure we are emotionally highly charged, priming us to escape. We convince ourselves that the harder we think and the more disasters we imagine, the more prepared we'll be if something awful does happen, or if we're rejected, or if we lose what we love.

The core of anxiety is trying to control an uncertain, imagined future. It is not the uncertainty *itself* that causes anxiety; it is the intolerance of that uncertainty. We are not able to control or predict what will happen to us, and that creates a vacuum of knowledge – into which slides worry, the thinking part of anxiety. Anxious thoughts are a natural response to a perceived danger. But when anxiety becomes severe, overwhelming and persistent, when it inhibits how we function day to day, affecting our choices and changing our behaviours, that's when it might be diagnosed as a disorder.[1] If we have been affected by trauma, or had an unpredictable childhood, or are naturally sensitive, we can be more prone to anxiety, and we'll look at that later too.

Twenty years after that spectacular fall from a TV barstool – or pedestal, as my husband calls it – and now with a master's in psychology, a doctorate and thousands of therapy practice hours under my belt, I still haven't eliminated anxiety from my own story, nor would I want to. I have learned how to stop struggling with it though, to stop trying to protect myself from an uncertain future and instead to start living a life here, in the present, guided by values, not by fear. Because values are the things that give life meaning. They are close to our heart, uniquely ours and act as our guiding star. They can help us navigate towards what is truly important and away from anxiety's powerful, terrifying, exhausting hold. If you have been fighting anxiety and are tired and wrung out, if you want to try a different way of living with it – welcome. I hope you'll find things here to help.

Dr Sian Williams

Before we dive in. Or the Introduction

Some myth-busting about anxiety first.

Anxiety is not your fault. It's there to protect you. But sometimes it misreads the room.

Anxiety lives in the body as well as the mind, and affects our behaviour too.

Anxiety thrives on the toxicity of social comparison, the illusion of control and the demand to be happy.

Anxiety has a harsh, self-critical voice which gets louder if you try to run away from it.

Anxiety fights back, the more you struggle with it.

If you have tried and 'failed' to get rid of anxiety in the past, then I want you to know that many, many people feel the same. Professor Oliver Robinson, head of the Anxiety Lab at University College London, tells me that – for most people – the first thing they try for anxiety won't work for them. After that he says, 'The meds work for a third to a quarter of people and therapy can work for something like a half. You put those together, you maybe get to 75 per cent, but even then, you're going to have at least a quarter to a third of people who think nothing works at all.'

Medication can work for some, therapy can work for others, both may work together, but if you have tried those and still find yourself plagued by anxiety, perhaps it's time to think of living with it differently. Not fighting, blocking or avoiding it, but starting to notice when it's helpful and when it's harmful, so you can exert more of a choice over what it does to you.

We're going to look at what the struggle with anxiety is costing you and how to stop fighting it and start regaining power over your life. The way to do that is to try to remember the Four Pillars of CARE. You don't have to memorize them now, this instant; you can let these little seeds of thought float through your mind, and they'll settle and take root as we go through this book together:

C is *curiosity*. Learning to be an interested observer when anxiety shows up.

A is *acceptance*. Accepting anxiety is part of us, and appreciating when it's helpful.

R is *relating*. Developing a new relationship with anxiety, so it's no longer our enemy.

E is *empathy*. Allowing for self-compassion. This one can be tricky.

The stories we tell shape our world

Because we are all shaped by our narratives, in this book I'll be using stories to help illustrate how anxiety can affect us. Stories give structure and meaning to our lives and experiences, and if you've been wrestling with worry, it's good to hear from others and know you're not alone. Often, the way to understanding an issue is to hear from those caught up in it and see how they've coped. That's what I've been doing as a journalist and presenter for the past four decades and it's been helpful for me, for those I talk to and for the audience watching and listening. A story helps us relate to and show compassion for those who are going through something difficult. An experience which might look a bit like ours.

We'll hear from a range of people who have had or still experience anxiety. Some you may recognize – including a member of a band which has sold more than 30 million albums, an author with ten books and a sell-out play under her belt, and another (current) national TV newsreader. Other stories will be a mix of experiences from both my NHS and my private clinics – and there will be advice and guidance too, from experts and other psychologists who specialize in anxiety.

Journalism and psychology both rely on storytelling to help make sense of something difficult. One does it on a big public scale; the other is personal and private. In my years as a producer, news correspondent and presenter, I've reported on huge, life-changing events which have impacted both individuals and communities. I first understood what a responsibility that was in 1989, covering the Hillsborough football stadium disaster, where a crush on the terraces resulted in the deaths of ninety-seven Liverpool fans. Then, in a catalogue of tragedy and misery,

I was sent to cover rail crashes, earthquakes, tsunamis, terror attacks. Always turning up on someone's worst day ever. The job means witnessing people in immense pain – seeing them emerge from the flames, or the rubble, blinking and unsure and then using their account to show the world what's happening. To try to make sense of it, even when that suffering seems incomprehensible.

One of my last big news jobs was presenting from the scene of London's Grenfell Tower fire in June 2017, which killed seventy-two people. A few years later, I joined the NHS as a counselling psychologist and began working with the first responders who ran into that building to try to rescue the survivors as the tower threatened to collapse around them. I've also worked with couples, families, students and people living with a cancer experience, and anxiety runs through many of them. I won't use the terms 'case studies' or 'patients', because they are like you and me. Humans, going through something horrible, trying to make sense of it and get through it in one piece. And whatever their experience, we've all had to do that. Some of what they say about what part anxiety plays for them may resonate and help you. Later, I'll talk about the importance of the story you tell yourself.

How this works

I've divided this book into three parts:

Part One: How and why we make ourselves anxious

BEFORE WE DIVE IN. OR THE INTRODUCTION

Part Two: How to stop beating ourselves up

Part Three: How to live better with our anxious body, brain and behaviour

First, we'll look at what anxiety is and why some of us are naturally more anxious than others (and why that can be a good thing). Then, how we allow anxiety to have power over us and why it can be so hard to let go of. And finally, how we can change how we think, feel and act, to allow ourselves to thrive with it.

I invite you to travel with me through these parts bit by bit, rather than jumping to the end, because this is not about handing out advice. It's about you getting to know yourself better and bringing a curiosity and compassion to what you've probably lived with for a long time, not just acquiring a set of tasks, structures and processes to 'get rid' of anxiety.

If you're anything like me and you love a plan, you'll be itching to start something new – because then there's a possibility of success. Perhaps your bookshelves are groaning with self-help manuals and yet, despite filling in the worksheets and committing yourself to an anti-anxiety strategy, you're still struggling.

There are exercises in this book too, but they're designed to help clarify thinking, to allow you to take a good look at yourself and what your anxiety is doing for you and to you. You may be reluctant to let your anxiety go, and I'm not asking you to. There are times when we need it, because it can both protect us and propel us.

Anxiety is a funny one – or a parasite

As Professor Oliver Robinson tells me, anxiety is 'a funny one', because 'more than any other mental health problem, it is a clinical problem but is also clearly an essential function. You need to be anxious, right? You need to, when you're in a situation that can cause you harm, be primed to detect those harms, avoid those harms and get back to safety, and that's all anxiety is. It is just that process of turning on a mode that can get you back to safety. What's not helpful is when that mode is turned on at times when you don't need it to be turned on, or it's turned on all the time and gets in the way of your life.'

Ultimately, this book is about recognizing the power of anxiety, hence the title. When it's helpful, when it isn't, what keeps it going, why it proves so hard to get rid of, and most importantly, how we might live with it – and live well.

I should say here, I don't have all the answers. If you want that certainty, you will find it elsewhere, with someone full of brio and confidence and promises. But my guess is, you've already tried that. Perhaps the reason you're here is because you know it's incremental, learning about yourself like this. You understand that it can be mucky and difficult to live alongside something as gnarly as anxiety, and hard to reacquaint yourself with it, because it forces you to ask questions. *What is it saying? What can it teach me? How can I use it to grow and transform?* It isn't easy, I know. I've counselled people through panic attacks and had a couple myself, and it can honestly feel, in that moment, as if you're dying. We'll have a look at panic in more detail in Chapter 7.

The thing about anxiety is that, even if you deal with that panic or the underlying thought that may have got you there, it's like whack-a-mole. You bash it down and it pops up somewhere else. Or as the journalist and lifelong anxiety sufferer Flic Everett writes: 'Anxiety is a parasite willing to attach itself to any host. When one issue dies away, it just leaps to another.' Like many of us, Flic accepts that her anxiety will not vanish – but equally, she is not trying to chase it away. 'It lives with and inside me,' she says.[1]

This book, then, is about trying to live with anxiety better, and what that looks like will differ for everyone. But I hope there is something in these pages you can use – as you learn from others, as you find out about the latest research, as you hear about the things that can help. Perhaps, by the end of this book, you'll have acknowledged what the struggle with anxiety has cost you and discover a different, healthier, more positive and hopeful way to live with it. A new story. One you get to tell.

The 'artist of anxiety'

The master storyteller and film director Alfred Hitchcock once said, 'There is no terror in the bang, only in the anticipation of it.'[2]

Hitchcock was masterful in lots of ways, but partly because he was so good at manipulating our emotions. He understood how terrifying it can be to wait for something, not knowing whether it will happen. Described by fellow director François Truffaut as neurotic, fearful, vulnerable and an 'artist of anxiety',[3] Hitchcock put both his fears – of strangers, heights, police, falling over and almost everything else[4] – and his understanding of the anxious, terrified mind into films like *Psycho* and *The Birds*.[5] Those swarming, pecking, screeching things that get caught up in helpless Tippi Hedren's hair, and which you know are going to besiege the town and leave no safe space to hide.

Hitchcock knew it was the waiting, the suspense and the not knowing that create the tension. The horror lies in the time spent in uncertainty, even more than if or when the thing happens. That's been backed up in a recent study showing that our 'hazard rate' is higher if we predict something dreadful will happen, but we don't know or can't know when.[6]

The expectation of something fearful can induce more terror and anxiety than the thing itself – and that makes sense, in evolutionary terms. It's a primal response, a hangover from when we needed to scan the horizon for predators, to prevent us from being taken by surprise and eaten. And the reason we still have it is because the world is full of threat and danger, even if they now look different.

BEFORE WE DIVE IN. OR THE INTRODUCTION

If you're going into the dark, remember to take a torch

There is a way of managing this threat and danger, but only if we are willing to shine a light and look at it. Because light makes the feared object smaller, or even non-existent. Take Stephen King's novel *It*, in which a shapeshifting, evil clown lures children into the sewers and cellars in which it lurks. Cellars are a key feature of horror, because they are dark, the light switch never works and there is always, always something down there.

George, one of the children, is told to go into the cellar to get some paraffin, a bowl and some matches. He doesn't like going into the basement because he imagines something will get him, something with a 'horrible clawed paw', jerking him into the dark, where it smells of dirt and rotting vegetables. Of course, the light switch fails, his heart hammers, his eyes get hot, his hands go cold and the hairs on the back of his neck stand on end. He grabs what he needs and races up the stairs to get back into the light, sure that the thing will grab his shirttails before he does. This time, he makes it.[7]

What a perfect metaphor for anxiety. What exists in the dark are your worst fears, and they can shapeshift. They can give you goosebumps and make your heart race and your palms sweat and bring up all the 'what if?' questions. *What if it's down there? What if it gets me? What if I can't cope? What if I never escape?* You can close your eyes and think about what shape it will take for you if you'd like, but you can also turn the light on. Remember, if you're going into the dark, take a torch. Things are always less frightening in the light.

Terms and conditions

Worry, stress and anxiety are all slightly different.

Worry is in your head. It's the term for all those negative thoughts that fill the uncertain spaces in life. Whether the niggle in your back is something serious, whether you've left the gas on, whether you have enough money for the rest of the month. Worry is the brain's way of keeping you safe. Yes, you need to go to the doctor, or check the oven, or look at how you'll spend your remaining pay packet. It's only when those thoughts become repetitive and stuck that they turn into something called rumination, a pattern of worrying that is no longer functional or productive.

Stress is an emotional response to a trigger, which also shows up in the body. It's what happens when you're presented with something that you need to pay attention to. If you're driving and a child suddenly crosses the road in front of you, your brain sends signals to the rest of your body, telling it to act. Hormones like adrenaline and cortisol send a burst of energy through your system, your heart rate accelerates and blood sugar is released to prime the muscles to slam on the brakes. Although you might be a little shaken up, afterwards everything usually settles down and you return to how you were before – perhaps with more awareness of that stretch of road, and perhaps slowing down next time. Chronic stress is what happens

BEFORE WE DIVE IN. OR THE INTRODUCTION

when the body reacts like this every time you get behind the wheel, when you are constantly in a state of alertness and when the amount of stress exceeds the resources that you have to cope. This kind of stress, sometimes experienced in long-term illness, or because of work and family issues, can lead to an increased risk of heart disease, a weakened immune system, irritability, fatigue and digestive problems.[8]

Anxiety is when lots of stress and worry come together. It happens in your mind and your body, and it's different from fear. Fear is based on a current threat, which sparks intense alarm and heightened energy. Anxiety involves something that hasn't happened and may never do so, but still brings excessive thought-loops and a heart-grip of panic, affecting the way we think, feel and act. While the brain tries to find a reason for being in fight-flight, thinking through all the things that might be out there, the body stays primed to deal with the unknown threat, riding a wave of hormones to keep us wired, just in case.

Bad things do happen. Many of us experience loss, abandonment or rejection, we stumble and fall, we live with illness or heartache or grief, and we understand that it's all part of life. Anxiety can have a real and obvious root cause too: financial worries, health concerns, the climate crisis, relationship problems. Sometimes, though, anxiety is a creeping sense of nameless dread that brings with it restless nights and hypervigilant days.

Everyone will experience and deal with it differently. As Professor Robinson puts it, 'There are as many different types of anxiety as there are people in the world.'

But it can show up in similar ways, often as an embodied thrum of threat and disquiet, like a wire twanging throughout our body and brain. The good news is that, once we start to understand that and observe how we are reacting to anxiety, we create a space where we can begin to assert some choice and control over it. Just noticing introduces a pause into which curiosity and compassion can start to come. And that changes the power that anxiety has over us.

When worry is a habit

I'm with the psychotherapist and bestselling author Philippa Perry. We are sitting on the bed in her spare room because the light is lovely today, and it feels snug as we wedge cushions between our backs and the wall. It's like being a teenager again, except instead of pop and biscuits, we are drinking tea and eating sponge fingers. And talking about worry and anxiety. Or 'shop', as we call it.

'Worrying can become a superstition,' she says. 'If you're a worrier and things are going right, your brain makes a connection between the worrying and things going right. So, you feel like you need to worry *in order* to get things to go right. Productive worrying is when you worry about something because you're looking for a solution – that's problem-solving. And then there's habitual worrying. Because it's a habit. It's just a habit.'

We need the productive worry. We need our mind to scan for danger, telling us something's not right so we can do something about it. Superstitious worrying is where we worry to protect ourselves, even when that threat or danger doesn't exist. We've done it once, our worry-mind thinks, and the bad thing didn't happen, so it must have worked, and we must keep doing it. That kind of worry can become something we do regularly, meaning our brain learns this pattern of worrying thinking, forming new neural pathways.

The more regularly we do it, the more those pathways become entrenched and the easier they are to access – and the quicker the brain gets to worrying next time. As the saying goes, 'neurons that fire together, wire together'. That's when anxiety becomes a habit.

How do you distinguish between helpful and unhelpful worry? We'll get on to that. But the basic purpose of worry is to protect you, even if your brain doesn't read the room right. We can retrain our minds to distinguish between the real threat and the one that feels real but is not, though.

Worry is the 'thought' part of our anxiety. Anxiety is the whole thing; it's felt bodily, and can affect all aspects of our behaviour. Often in unhelpful, unproductive ways.

When to let anxiety go

In both my NHS and private clinics, many of those who arrive with anxiety have lived with it for years, and are often desperately low too. We know that anxiety and depression can walk hand in hand, and nearly half of those presenting with a depressive disorder live with an anxiety disorder.[9] They are worn out and tired of trying to get rid of something which keeps grabbing hold of them and pulling them under. Sometimes the thought of losing their anxiety makes them even more nervous, because they think they'll become lazy, inattentive or unproductive.

They believe that if they let it go, complacency – and worse, danger – will sneak in and it'll be their fault for not paying attention. I spent two years counselling those with cancer, and many of them believed that their repetitive worry and catastrophic thinking kept them vigilant to the cancer returning or getting worse. Anxiety was the thing that kept them alert, and losing it became the threat.

I felt that myself when I had breast cancer. After my surgery, there was too much uncertainty and lack of control for my liking. I'd had a double mastectomy, but after a conversation with my brilliant oncologist, Glen Blackman at University College London, we decided I wouldn't have radiotherapy, even though the surgeons hadn't got rid of all the cancer cells. What, I wanted to know, was the percentage risk of the cancer returning, based on the available empirical evidence? How did I stop it returning? What was the likelihood of it doing so? What would happen if it did come back?

Mr Blackman smiled as he listened to my questions. 'Sian,' he said. 'If you're stuck in a maelstrom of anxiety about the worst happening and then it does, then you have lived through it twice. You need to learn to live with uncertainty. I have a heart condition and could drop dead at any moment. If I spent life worrying about it, I would never leave the house.'

Easier said than done, I know. But none of us has certainty and control. We need to aim for 'safe uncertainty', as we used to say in the family therapy practice I worked in. We need to tolerate and be with uncertainty and yet still feel safe. We need to relinquish control of the things we can't control, but control the things that are in our power. That goes for anxiety too. Understanding which bits we can let go of and which we can hang on to.

What I learned from my first client

My first-ever client had anxiety. Or rather, they had lots of different anxieties. The children might die, their partner might leave, the boss might sack them. They were anxious about their health, their finances, being late, the household chores and letting everyone down. They worried about being worried.

I was an anxious trainee counselling psychologist. One who, in her journalist's role, was used to researching, evaluating and problem-solving. As they sat reeling off their terrors, I thought: Right. Let's sort this. We'll reality-check all these assumptions one by one; we'll tick off every likelihood of something catastrophic happening.

But every time I thought we'd got one of the worries nailed, a new one would slot right into its place. We never seemed to reduce the overall burden. And the more

I thought I was failing at helping, the harder I tried, and the more effort and thinking I'd throw at it.

They left therapy after the six sessions they were allocated, perhaps no better than when they'd walked in. My supervisor told me they probably had 'generalized anxiety disorder', where daily life feels like being in a constant state of dread. Probably. But giving it a name might not have helped either.

I was in training and it was a long time ago. Now, I would treat them very differently. Not trying to solve their worries for them, but helping them to understand how their feelings, thoughts and behaviours were driving the bus and how they could take back control of the wheel.

Don't be a back-seat driver

It's good to have an idea of where you want to be, and be willing and committed to have a go at getting there. I know that isn't easy and there's no satnav to guide us through the confusing landscape of an anxious mind. I hope this book will help you to understand what fuels your anxiety and how it serves you, and when it doesn't. Then how to identify the drivers of change – your values – so you can start to head off on a different path.

That first client was trying to be all things to all people, and wanted to get it right for everybody but wasn't thinking about where *they* wanted to go. They were so busy trying to be the perfect parent, partner and worker that they'd forgotten what they wanted. And I was so busy trying to be the best therapist that I perhaps wasn't encouraging them to get into the driving seat and take control. If you have spent your life pleasing others, worrying what they might think, making sure everyone else is happy and hoping things will change if you sit in the back seat – well, perhaps it's time to change seats. You need to get into the driving seat and grab the steering wheel. I can help navigate, but it's you who'll have a sense of which direction you want to go in. We just need to work out the 'how' of getting there.

Stop struggling

We'll look at self-criticism, perfectionism and people-pleasing later, but now I just want to expand on that thought about trying to worry the future bad things away. When terrible things happen – and they inevitably do – we deal with them, however difficult. If we spend time worrying about the likelihood of them happening, we risk ending up living in a constant tumble dryer of negative thinking and in a crippling vortex of psychological pain.

The way I was helped, and the way I hope I help others, is to look at anxiety differently. To acknowledge, accept and learn from it, rather than trying to fight it. As the Swiss psychiatrist Carl Jung said: 'What you resist not only persists, but will grow in size.'[10] Telling anxiety that we can't cope with it and pushing against it, however forcefully, only makes it stronger. All of us who have fought, struggled with, avoided or resisted anxiety know that trying to fix it or get rid of it doesn't work.

There are big social, economic and political issues at play which can feed into our anxiety – like climate despair, poverty and global insecurity. These can lead to stress, alienation and hopelessness. We can wait for politicians and companies to do the right thing to alleviate anxiety's societal causes, but in the meantime it's us who experience it. What can we do as individuals to live well, alongside it? To acknowledge when it serves us and when it punishes us?

We need to look at anxiety differently, because for many it's a vital sensitivity, an intense and important set of feelings and thoughts to recognize, rather than try to quash. We *can* learn to make peace with it and even embrace the sensitivity, rather than battling it. We can learn to drop the struggle – and in doing so, redress the power imbalance, allowing ourselves to have more awareness and acceptance of our anxiety, rather than having it dominate and bully us.

That means tuning in to what anxiety is saying, bringing a curious and compassionate sense of enquiry to it and using a different framework of understanding. Instead of allowing it to keep us stuck and lonely – chastising ourselves for not having beaten it, berating ourselves for failing – I suggest we turn towards it, ceasing to see it as a problem to solve and instead as a truth to acknowledge, accept and work with.

If we let anxiety have power over us, we are fixed and static, with no flexibility for questioning, no opportunity for change and renewal. But if we recognize anxiety as our alert system that tells us that something isn't right

BEFORE WE DIVE IN. OR THE INTRODUCTION

instead of allowing it to destabilize us, if we listen to what it is telling us rather than quietening it, then it can propel us towards action. It's about letting our intuition guide us, instead of our fear.

It's seeing anxiety as a tool, not a trap.

Part One

1

Dandelion or Orchid?

'Sensitivity is a sign of life. Better hurt
than hardened.'

Jeff Brown

Nearly a decade ago I was recording a programme for the BBC called *The Science of Resilience*, when I was told by Professor Michael Pluess, a leading expert in sensitivity, that I might not be as resilient as I'd thought. At least, not in the way I understood resilience. I'd just completed a battery of tests on my thoughts and feelings, my childhood and concerns. I'd dealt with cancer OK, I thought, but I'd been lucky. I had a good job, a loving husband and five gorgeous kids. My growing-up years had been broadly happy. The questions focused on what I had experienced, my 'life events' and who I turned to for support.

As I typed out the answers, I knew there was a flaw in the belief I was strong and capable in all circumstances. Yes, I'd had difficult experiences, yes, there were people I could talk to, and no, I hadn't let them help me. Was I very sensitive? Were there occasional emotional crashes and periods of burnout? 'Umm, I think I'll finish this questionnaire at home,' I said as the tape recorder rolled. 'It's quite personal, isn't it?'

Without needing to know the outcome, I thought I'd probably failed the first test of resilience, just by the way I'd answered the questions.

There was anxiety, sensitivity and a reluctance to seek help running through everything like a seam. How embarrassing. The journalist doing a programme on resilience, who'd worked in high-pressure environments all her adult life, revealed as a super-sensitive people-pleaser. Someone who might be described by some psychologists as an 'insecure over-achiever', who was striving, driving and goal-driven while riding a wave of anxiety and sensitivity.

But Professor Pluess told me I'd been thinking about resilience in the wrong way. The strongest among us, he argued, aren't those who appear unbreakable. The resilient ones are those who are reactive to changes in conditions and adapt to them. They sense when the storm is coming, and if they've learned how, can bend with it.

Professor Pluess then mentioned the brilliant 'orchid hypothesis', a theory originally developed by the American paediatrician W. Thomas Boyce, who suggested some children are more sensitive than others. Boyce came up with the idea after hearing the Swedish idiomatic expressions for a 'dandelion child' (*maskrosbarn*) and an 'orchid child' (*orkidebarn*).[1]

Dandelion children survive and thrive through whatever life throws at them, much like the yellow flowers that burst through cracks in the pavement, or on a dry lawn, or in a field after rain. Whatever the soil, whatever the weather, they keep growing.

Orchid children can wilt and decline with neglect, but can flourish and become magnificent given the right environment. These early life experiences can programme and shape an individual's sensitivity, meaning the orchids might be more reactive in later life.

Ten years later and I'm chatting with the professor again, because he and his colleagues have developed an adult version of the orchid test, called 'The Highly Sensitive Person Scale – Revised'. It has six different sections which measure overstimulation, how we react to emotion, our sensitivity to details around us, our sensitivity to positive experiences, our depth of thinking or processing and our social sensitivity.[2]

The original scale measured negative aspects of sensitivity; this one brings in the positive too. So, as well as testing how quickly you become overwhelmed by your environment, how anxious and emotional you become and how disturbed you are by subtle changes, it also measures how the positive aspects within your environment affect you, how deeply you think and feel about them, and your levels of empathy towards others.

Think you're sensitive? Have a go, it's here…

Exercise: The Highly Sensitive Person Scale[3]

Instructions: Please answer each question below by circling the number between 1 = 'Not at all' to 7 'Extremely' that describes you best as a person overall. If a question can't be answered, please just leave it out and move on.

1.	Do you notice when things have been moved around?	1	2	3	4	5	6	7
2.	Are you easily affected by feedback (both negative and positive)?	1	2	3	4	5	6	7
3.	Are you easily overwhelmed by things like bright lights, strong smells, coarse fabrics, or sirens close by?	1	2	3	4	5	6	7
4.	Do you easily recognize what others are feeling?	1	2	3	4	5	6	7
5.	Do you notice and enjoy delicate or fine scents, tastes, sounds, works of art?	1	2	3	4	5	6	7
6.	Are you easily affected by the mood of people around you?	1	2	3	4	5	6	7
7.	Do you tend to reflect on things deeply?	1	2	3	4	5	6	7
8.	Are you good at anticipating how someone may feel about a situation?	1	2	3	4	5	6	7
9.	Are you bothered by intense stimuli, like loud noises or chaotic scenes?	1	2	3	4	5	6	7
10.	Do you generally react strongly to your experiences, whether you show it or not?	1	2	3	4	5	6	7
11.	Do other people tell you that you are good at understanding what they are feeling or thinking?	1	2	3	4	5	6	7
12.	Do you tend to get deeply immersed in music?	1	2	3	4	5	6	7

13. Do you find yourself thinking about philosophical questions?	1	2	3	4	5	6	7
14. Do you seem to notice changes in the weather more than others?	1	2	3	4	5	6	7
15. Do you become unpleasantly aroused when a lot is going on around you?	1	2	3	4	5	6	7
16. Are you deeply moved by the arts or music?	1	2	3	4	5	6	7
17. Do you tend to notice subtle signs of changing seasons (winter/spring etc.)?	1	2	3	4	5	6	7
18. Do you like deep conversations?	1	2	3	4	5	6	7

Calculating the Results

You can get your total sensitivity score by adding up all the scores for each question. Then divide the total by the number of questions to get your average score. An average score of greater than 5 indicates a tendency towards high sensitivity.

Total Sensitivity Score =

Average Score =

Subscales

The subscale scores provide an understanding of how core but different aspects of sensitivity contribute to your overall sensitivity. For each category, add up the scores of the relevant questions, then divide the total by the number of questions to get your average score.

Overstimulation - Questions 3, 9, 15

Total Score =

Average Score =

Sensitivity to Positive Experiences – Questions 5, 12, 16

    Total Score =

    Average Score =

Social Sensitivity – Questions 4, 8, 11

    Total Score =

    Average Score =

Depth of Processing – Questions 7, 13, 18

    Total Score =

    Average Score =

Emotional Reactivity – Questions 2, 6, 10

    Total Score =

    Average Score =

Sensitivity to Details – Questions 1, 14, 17

    Total Score =

    Average Score =

How did you do? You may have found more sensitivity in some areas than others. It might have told you something about yourself that, deep inside, you already knew. Perhaps you need to escape when the noise around you dominates and excludes your ability to think, or you may be the one at work who holds on to criticism when your colleagues seem able to let it go.

Whatever it might be – the texture of a blanket, the smell of someone's perfume, the sound that makes you wince – I wonder whether you have sometimes felt the world was just too harsh, too loud. Highly sensitive people can be overwhelmed by multiple demands and tasks, or struggle to deal with intense smells, sounds, sights or people. They also tend to be more introverted and emotional.[4] Dandelions sit at the other end of the sensitivity scale, and it used to be thought that they were the vast majority.

Enter the tulips. Those who fall in the middle. Orchids are now thought to make up 30 per cent of the population, dandelions 30 per cent and those with medium sensitivity, the tulips, are the remaining 40 per cent.[5] Sensitivity exists on a continuum, but the theory suggests that, broadly, people fall into one of these three distinct categories, with orchids scoring higher than tulips and dandelions in both neuroticism and emotional reactivity, and lower than both in extraversion.[6] In other words, orchids can worry more, react more emotionally and be more introverted and avoidant than tulips and dandelions. Not all the time, but typically.

Highly sensitive people are more likely to be affected by the negative stuff and react to it by becoming stressed and overwhelmed, especially in the wrong environment, than those with medium or low sensitivity.[7] We are all programmed to pay attention to threat because that's what helps us survive, but orchids will pick up signals around them faster than dandelions and tulips. The highly sensitive folks tend to be more neurotic, anxious and experience things more negatively, but Pluess says they are also the ones who sense changes quickly. And that can be very useful.

'You need people who are super sensitive,' Philippa Perry tells me. 'They are good at reading people. I mean, we need geniuses. I think my husband [the celebrated

British artist Sir Grayson Perry] is an orchid but I'm probably a dandelion. We need people who have got highly developed, rational brains who can do sums and that.' She laughs. 'We need all these different people to make a society, make a community. Sensitive people shouldn't be seen as a problem. They just need to be given the right kind of soil and sunlight to thrive.'

That means responding to sensitive people sensitively – understanding and validating their feelings, she adds.

Born this way

Were you born sensitive or made this way by experience? Have a think about what you were like as a child. Whether you were easily affected by loud noises, too many people, unusual textures or tastes. Whether you grew up reacting emotionally to books, films or people in ways others didn't. You might have been told you were over-sensitive, dramatic, emotional or fragile. You may have been told to be quiet when you alerted an adult to something you felt was wrong.

Some of that high sensitivity is down to your genes. In studies of twins,[8] Pluess and his team identified the heritability of sensitivity and put it at around 50 per cent. There's no one sensitivity gene, just like there's no one anxiety or depression or resilience gene; it's a complex interplay of many thousands.

But, if you are sensitive, half of that could be genetically set in stone before you even take your first breath.

Of course, just because you inherit a sensitivity trait, it doesn't automatically mean you'll develop anxiety – and equally, some of those who don't have that particular combination of genes can still be anxious. If you are highly sensitive, though, you are significantly more likely to develop anxiety and depression than those who are not.

If half of our sensitivity is down to our genes, which we can do nothing about, what's the other half? Our environment. And that makes perfect evolutionary sense. If you are born sensitive and then live in a family where your parents are absent or neglectful, or you grow up in extreme poverty, or are exposed to trauma or adversity, you must adapt by becoming vigilant to any new dangers to survive.

For a highly sensitive person, protecting themselves and staying safe means constantly scanning their surroundings and the people within it. Sensitivity serves them well if further threats are lurking, making them highly attuned to noticing the negative or predicting if bad things are likely to happen.

All the ACEs and none of the cards

'More people than we like to acknowledge simply don't grow up experiencing the kinds of relationships that deliver consistent safety, good physical nourishment, attention to how they feel and commitment to welfare that is love in action,' says the psychoanalytic psychotherapist Sue Gerhardt. Exploring and witnessing those harms caused in early life can limit some of the damage, but 'undoing the painful devaluations of an abusive childhood is rarely quick or easy'.[9]

Gerhardt references the importance of adverse childhood experiences, or ACEs, in our understanding of the effects of trauma on our mental health. ACEs are based on a concept devised by American doctors Vincent Felitti and Robert Anda. In the 1980s, Felitti was running a clinic in San Diego, California, for those trying to reduce smoking, obesity and stress. On questioning those who came in to the clinic, he noticed that more than half of his patients with obesity had experienced sexual abuse. He and Dr Anda developed a questionnaire based on various adverse childhood experiences, including being beaten, threatened, humiliated, abused, neglected, witnessing domestic violence and living with a mentally ill, depressed or addictive parent. They found that the more ACEs the person had experienced, the worse the outlook for both physical and mental health.[10]

Today, the ACE model is still used, with the ten most measured events or situations involving some kind of neglect, abuse or adversity. One long-term study following thousands of British children into middle age suggested that these kinds of early experiences affect adult health, impacting the hormonal, nervous and immune systems.[11]

There has been controversy about using ACEs as a tool to predict emotional wellbeing, however, because it relies on people remembering their experiences rather than following them in real time. There are also many children who have four or more ACEs who are coping well. But there are other studies which suggest that those who have experienced hostile, invalidating, humiliating, coercive or abusive parenting are more likely to experience various conditions including anxiety and depression.[12] And the higher the levels of emotional abuse in childhood, the more severe the anxiety in adolescence – something also seen in studies in adults.[13] That's hardly surprising.

Anxious child = anxious adult?

Say you grow up in a household where you are constantly put down or humiliated. You would need to be vigilant all the time, wouldn't you? How would you develop a strong and confident sense of self that could stand up to bullying if no one has shown faith in you, or allowed you to have faith in yourself? How would you learn to trust yourself and your instincts, try new things and fail without risking judgement or ridicule? How would you manage an unpredictable world if there is no one at home to show you how? How would you learn to deal with sadness, fear and anger if you weren't taught coping strategies by those closest to you?

If your emotional needs have never been met or if you have been condemned, laughed at or punished, if you do not know how to soothe yourself when frightened or anxious, you have to learn those things by yourself, and you must navigate a world which feels dangerous and exposing on your own.

That might mean developing techniques that make you feel safer, like remaining hyper-alert, avoiding uncertain situations, distracting yourself by blocking out uncomfortable feelings or thoughts, or withdrawing and hiding. Surviving in a difficult environment for a sensitive child means being alert to anything that might threaten their safety. That child becomes an adolescent, and then an adult, and all the while they carry these patterns of behaviour with them. Again, and I can't say this enough, some patterns of anxiety are not your fault.

Because sensitive people are, as Professor Pluess says, 'emotionally more reactive, more creative and process more deeply', if they think something is wrong but can't identify it, they will use their imagination, think through all the potential dangers and be biased towards the negative. The highly attuned, deep-thinking, creative and sensitive brain believes there's an increased likelihood of horrible things happening, either because they've previously experienced them or because they're preparing themselves for the possible worst thing that might occur. Which means more negative thoughts, more rumination and more anxiety, and more demands on the body to try to manage it all – including inflammation[14] and increased 'wear and tear' in midlife.[15]

Where is all the good news?

I'm sure you're thinking, where's the positive in all this? Well, there is a flip side. Professor Pluess says those who are sensitive and reflective are more likely to experience the good things positively. That might mean being profoundly moved by art, music and nature, or having a rich, deep, creative imagination. If you are born with a highly sensitive 'genetic load' and grow up in a supportive environment, or move to one, you're likely to respond more intensely to the good influences in your life, be more adaptable and think through alternative solutions to emerging problems.[16]

No matter your background, if you receive positive support and are offered ways of coping with your sensitivity, you can thrive. Schoolgirls in an economically deprived area of East London went through a twelve-week resilience-building programme that included cognitive behavioural therapy techniques to reduce depression. The students with high sensitivity showed a bigger drop in negative symptoms than those with low sensitivity, and they continued to feel those benefits a year later. Researchers suggested their sensitivity had helped them process the information more deeply and meant they continued to use the tools they had been given.[17]

Another benefit of the super-sensitive is that they pick up on signals in their environment and the people around them quickly, which means they can recognize emotions faster than those who are not sensitive – making them more empathic. If a situation demands a deep level of engagement and connection, a sensitive person is your go-to. Which is why, Professor Pluess says, they make good artists, authors and therapists.

And Australian therapist Dr Russ Harris says if there's a little self-doubt in there, all the better. Research suggests therapists who are reflective and questioning are much better at their jobs than those who are confident, as long as they are also self-compassionate.[18] We'll be getting on to how to moderate the self-doubt and boost the self-compassion later. But this goes for all of us. A little self-doubt is OK, because it makes us question ourselves and our motives and keeps us from falling into complacency. As long as it's balanced with self-kindness. This can be hard for those with a strong self-critical voice, but it is achievable. I'll be showing you how soon. There'll be more from Russ too. He's a trainer in acceptance and commitment therapy (ACT) and I'll be sharing a few of his – and other ACT – ideas later.

Exercise: For the sensitive

For now, here are some questions to ask yourself if you are sensitive:

- What is the role of my environment, and how can I use it to benefit me?
- What are the environments that are good/bad for me?
- How will I know when the environment is not suiting me and do something about it?
- What might my coping strategies be in those circumstances?

A highly sensitive person (HSP) is simply more open to stimuli in their environment. If that environment is busy and stressful, they may need to plan time away in a calmer place, like a walk in the park or reading a book in a peaceful spot, in order to reflect without being constantly bombarded by new information and competing demands.

The key for an HSP is not to allow other people to control or dominate their habitat but to shape it themselves, with space to recharge. For example, if you know you're often exposed to a challenging environment, make sure you schedule in breaks to allow your system to reset. If your life is socially crowded, plan a short period of solitude. If your home or work area is cluttered and noisy, create a safe area to retreat to.

You'll know if your environment isn't benefiting you, because you'll be on constant alert, with nerve endings humming, or you'll feel drained or depleted – or want to switch off or dissociate. Become curious about how you react in certain places and situations, and learn what works to rebalance you – like regulating your emotion through breathing exercises, which we'll explore in Part Three (see page 209). We all differ in our sensitivity levels, so our coping strategies will be unique too, but here are a couple of examples of how the environment can affect the sensitive.

Teachers on an on-the-job training scheme in the UK had their wellbeing levels tested before they started the course and throughout their first year. Those low in sensitivity saw no change in their wellbeing when they started training, but those who reported high sensitivity saw a significant drop.[19] They recovered OK, and it was a small study and more research needs doing, but if you are sensitive and something unfamiliar, challenging and potentially stressful is coming up, it makes sense to go into it armed with the knowledge of what you can do to support yourself through it. The changes you can make elsewhere in your environment. The things that make you feel better.

Like watching happy video clips. I kid you not. Undergraduates with sensitivity who watched a three-minute film of young Americans handing out gifts to the homeless saw a much bigger improvement in mood than the less sensitive folks who watched the same clip.[20]

Because highly sensitive people are affected by shifts in their environment, they benefit from plenty of rest and sleep because they need more time to process all the information that's coming at them. Movement helps, as does spending time in nature, simplifying life if possible, and making use of that rich, inner world with meaningful relationships and connections. More on what works for the super-sensitive can be found in Part Three.

Heightened sensitivity to the environment can make you self-aware, able to sense the moods of others by reading verbal and visual clues, and it can also bring with it a capacity for creativity and compassion – much-needed skills in today's world. We can use these tools both for ourselves and for others.

The world needs orchids

The orchids are the early-warning signallers, the ones more sensitive to change and danger, and they should be celebrated. They pick up on feelings, fast. They look into the deeper issues. They use their creative brain to call for solution-based change.

The former New Zealand prime minister Jacinda Ardern was known for stepping into crises during her premiership with compassion and sensitivity. After the March 2019 attack on the mosque in Christchurch, where fifty-one Muslims were massacred, she empathized with the families of the victims and passed strong gun control laws. At the start of the global Covid pandemic in March 2020, she closed the country's borders early, took a pay cut, and spoke to the nation daily with messages of reassurance. She was criticized for some of her decisions, and police say the recorded threats against her trebled over three years.[21]

It's not known what her final political legacy will be, but part of it will be as a leader who was kind, empathic and accessible. In her final address to parliament, Ardern said she wanted people to know that 'you can be anxious, sensitive, kind and wear your heart on your sleeve... You can be... a nerd, a crier, a hugger. You can be all of these things, and not only can you be here, you can lead, just like me.'[22]

The anxious among us live life with intensity, experience more vividly and feel more strongly. We wear our hearts on our sleeves, we cry, we hug – and yes, that can bring criticism. We know that, because we are the harshest critics of all. But be in no doubt, we can also use all that for the good of ourselves and others.

Anxiety can throw us into a vicious cycle of overthinking, worry and hypervigilance, and we can easily blame ourselves for all of the above. But there is a way of looking at this differently, of acknowledging, accepting and working with our anxieties and sensitivities, rather than allowing them to keep us trapped, wriggling like a worm on the hook. I know it might not feel like it now, but these very elements that we criticize and blame ourselves for are powerful agents of change, and we have a choice about what we do with them.

During the coronavirus pandemic, the ones who fared best were those who had equipped themselves to manage psychologically. Those with anxiety had already armed themselves with the tools they needed to cope with future distress. Research suggests they were mentally more able to manage, while the less anxious struggled.[23] The sensitive were alert to anxiety and were ready for action if the worst did happen.

That's not an argument for living in a state of perpetual catastrophizing. Quite the opposite. It's suggesting that if you are alive to your sensitivities and aware of how you might react to potential dangers, you can respond more thoughtfully. Think of how beneficial these sensitivities are in a world that feels like it's on fire, with constant political and economic instability and uncertainty.

The sensitive are the ones who will say, 'I'm feeling this. Are you? Shouldn't we do something about it?' Here's renowned podcaster and *New York Times* writer Glennon Doyle: 'Yes, I've got these conditions – anxiety, depression, addiction – and they almost killed me. But they are also my superpowers. I'm the canary in the mine and you need my sensitivity because I can smell toxins in the air that you can't smell, see trouble you don't see and sense danger you don't feel. My sensitivity could save us all. And so instead of letting me fall silent and die – why don't we work together to clear some of this poison from the air?'[24]

Yes, why don't we? Working together doesn't mean coming up with more definitions of anxiety disorders – there are already nearly a dozen of those in the big book of standard psychological problems, called the *Diagnostic and Statistical Manual of Mental Disorders*, or the *DSM*.[25] It means seeing anxiety differently.

It might be difficult, at this point, to see anxiety as some sort of 'superpower'. We are right at the beginning of exploring this stuff together, and I already feel you tensing with talk of how your sensitivity can benefit you and be your strength. It may even feel threatening, suggesting you live with your anxiety when you don't feel like you can. When ignoring it or fighting it feels like the only thing you can do to stay sane.

This stuff is hard. Change is tough. Anxiety might be something you can't ever imagine living comfortably with. Or it might have served a purpose for you, and it feels dangerous to give it up. I understand that. My own self-criticism and harsh judgemental voice have pushed me to achieve, kept me striving and driving, but they've also brought me close to burnout and I've had to ask difficult questions of myself about why I keep doing it.

Whose acceptance am I searching for? And how helpful is living on my nerves, and pleasing everyone else before looking after my own needs? We'll tackle some of that together later in this book, but before we do here's a quick exercise to get some energy back into the room after a lot of thinking.

Exercise: Your anxiety sculpture

Imagine what anxiety looks and feels like to you. It can be tricky to visualize the thoughts and feelings, but one effective way is to create a sculpture or statue of your anxiety. I've done this with clients, and it's a powerful way to understand what anxiety feels like. We close our eyes and imagine ourselves in a pose that best represents our anxiety. Then hold that image and capture it, like a mental snapshot.

Give it a try, preferably in a private place. Take your anxiety and live it. Be a living statue of it. Show it to the world, even if they're not looking. Be brave and demonstrate what it does to you. Strike a pose, hold it, take a mental picture.

Now, let it go. What did you look and feel like? Tight neck, hunched shoulders, wide, panicked eyes?

Whatever your anxiety looks and feels like when you do your sculpture – and it'll be different for everyone – the fact that it seizes both our body and our mind is the same for everyone. You're not alone.

I asked folks on social media what anxiety feels like to them, and I got hundreds of responses. Here are just a few:

- 'My stomach is doing somersaults, my chest is tight, my heart is pounding, and I'm shaking like a leaf.'

- 'My whole body is on edge, I'm trembling, and I'm tense like a coiled spring.'

- 'I feel like I'm wrapped up in a tight ball.'

- 'It's like a gripping feeling, like I'm shaking in my guts, and I can't stop.'

- 'I feel like I'm over-revved and paralysed at the same time, like I'm stuck in a never-ending loop.'

- 'I have a lump in my throat, I can't sleep, and it's an overwhelming feeling of doom.'

- 'It starts as a small nervous niggle in my chest and then turns into a full-blown opera singer sitting on my chest, starting a Mexican wave.'

- 'It's like being in a muddy ditch that I can't climb out of. No matter how hard I try, I keep slipping back.'

- 'That feeling when you're tipping back on a chair and you reach the point where you feel like you're about to go backwards.'

Anxiety felt different to all these people, but they used similar words to describe it – including *tension, tightness, knots, paralysis, sickness, exhaustion, fear, dread, fogginess, overwhelm, all-consuming*. They described feelings of *being trapped, lonely, uneasy, hopeless*. Someone said it was 'a feeling of impending doom, failure, criticism, disapproval, all rolled into one'. It was, another wrote, 'like something is coming to get me and I can't stop it, and it's my own fault'.

If there's one thing you take from everything so far, it should be this: it's not your fault.

An artistic impression

The free-thinking, remarkable Mexican artist Frida Kahlo lived in a world of pain, after a horrific traffic accident while still in her teens. A brilliant, revolutionary, creative woman, she also lived with anxiety and depression yet understood the futility of trying to block them out. 'I tried to drown my sorrows,' she once said, 'but the bastards learned to swim.'[26]

Kahlo wrote about being 'bizarre' and 'flawed', but recognized there were others in the world feeling the same, telling them 'I'm just the same as you'.[27] And she talked about the need to recognize both her sadness and her joy: 'There is nothing more precious than laughter and scorn – it is strength to laugh and lose oneself, to be cruel and light. Tragedy is the most ridiculous thing "man" has.'[28]

Kahlo believed we can endure more than we think we can. But 'endure' is a heavy word. I think we can learn to put the load down. We'll do lots of self-understanding and preparation before we do, and pick up lots of tools and techniques to help you live with your anxiety, but before I explain why you don't want to get rid of it completely,

I want to ask you a question. It's called the 'miracle question'.

Exercise: The miracle question

Imagine going about your life as normal and heading off to sleep. During the night, a miracle happens – and when you wake up the next day, whatever problem has been troubling you is no longer there.

- How do you know the miracle has happened?
- What would be the very first difference you would notice?
- What will others notice that makes them aware things are different or better?
- What will you do next?

The miracle question was first used in family therapy to get clients to imagine life without their problem existing, and it was later adapted to be a bit more realistic and hopeful.[29] Less a miraculous 'ta-da!' moment and more a sense of moving in the right direction.

Examples of answers given by a couple with relationship issues were to spend more time with and show a renewed interest in one another.[30] With anxiety, answers might be 'I'd start to feel lighter', 'I'd let worry consume me less', 'I'd take more time looking after myself, rather than trying to please everyone else', 'I'd act on what matters to me'. When answering the questions, watch out for unrealistic or perfectionist goals like 'my anxiety will be gone' or 'I'll stop worrying for good' or 'I won't make any more mistakes'. Good enough is good enough. Make your answers rooted in something achievable, even if that currently feels a long way off.

There's another version of this, called the 'dare question', with a slightly different approach – which also works well with high-functioning anxiety and self-criticism. It asks, 'What would you do, if you knew you could not fail?' This identifies what holds us back, and gives us a moment to reflect on who we believe we can be, if we can acknowledge our self-doubt and hold it more lightly.

It's time to stop struggling with anxiety and start living the values-led life you know you can lead. One based on the strengths and qualities that define and shape you; the actions that make life worth living. Because that's what values are. Words which describe what's most meaningful to us, which set the direction of travel. We'll look more at how to locate our values in Chapter 8.

Before we move on though, take that anxiety statue of you and – having answered the miracle and dare questions – do the exercise again. This time, as the 'you' that exists without being weighed down by fear or struggling with your anxiety and doubt. The anxiety is still there, but it's not the whole of you. It's no longer defining who you are and what you do. Hold the pose, and take a mental snapshot. How different does it look and feel?

Anxiety is not something to get rid of; it's something to listen to and be aware of. Hear what it's saying – rather than quietening it with busyness, sugar, alcohol, screens, avoidance, procrastination or withdrawal. If anxiety calls you, pick up and listen – don't let it ring and ring. Uneasy feelings are your allies, not your enemies. As the American motivational speaker and author Michael Singer wrote, 'You are not the voice of the mind – you are the one who hears it.'[31]

Chapter 1: A quick refresher

- Orchids are powerful – as long as they're given the right light and good soil.
- The super-sensitive react more strongly, feel more deeply and think more creatively.
- Resilience doesn't mean being tough, it means being adaptable and compassionate.
- You are not your past, but you can learn from it.
- You are not your thoughts, but you can learn to listen to what they're saying.

2

Anxiety – a Life Sentence?

'Remember, today is the tomorrow you
worried about yesterday.'

Dale Carnegie[1]

Years ago, my grandmother was described as someone who 'suffered with her nerves'. Unsurprising, when you hear what happened to her. Born in 1913, she was the youngest of seven children from what my Uncle David calls 'Welsh peasant stock'. When she was six years old, her father, a jobbing gardener, took his own life.

It was 1919, and his death left his wife and children with no money but with the stigma and judgement typical of the time, when poverty was shameful and suicide was still a crime.[2] Her older sister, Nell, then fell in love but was diagnosed with tuberculosis and had not long to live. The man she fell for, a local Presbyterian minister, married her anyway. Nell died soon after the wedding.

With no husband, no married daughter and no income, all prospects seemed lost to the family, and they were threatened with the workhouse in Bala where the paupers of the town, the single mothers and children were put to work in return for basic food and shelter.[3] The grieving widower stepped in to save them, by marrying his dead wife's sister – my grandmother, Mair. The family escaped the workhouse, a respectable future was secured, a good life lay ahead. You'd think. Except my nain (Welsh for 'grandmother') got soft tissue cancer in her thirties and had her leg amputated. Later, she lost an eye.

Too right she 'suffered from her nerves'.

She'd lost her father to suicide, she'd seen three of her siblings die of TB and the threat of poverty stayed with her for life. Even in her seventies, she was tormented by the terrifying thought of destitution returning. My uncle remembers his mother's constant refrain: 'You'll never get a proper job! We'll all be sent to workhouse!' Even decades after the workhouses closed, she was constantly fearful. Everything was always in crisis.

He feels sorry for her now and wishes he'd been kinder, but growing up it seemed like 'she was fucking crackers', constantly anxious and worrying about every tiny thing. Can you imagine living with all that threat, though? A family riven with disease, poverty, loss. Marrying a man who was grieving the death of his one true love, always thinking you're second best, while also trying to mourn the deaths of your father and siblings. And on top of all that, bearing the societal condemnation that came from suicide – shame which was not yours to carry, but which you shouldered nonetheless.

Nain came to live with us when her husband died. She was quiet and nervous, sad and withdrawn, would refuse the food my mum cooked for her and spent long periods alone in her room, banging on the floor with her walking stick if she needed something, or throwing it down the stairs with a clatter.

I was a child, probably with little interest in engaging her – wary of her, if anything. The narrative around her was that she was 'difficult' and 'emotional', but I only learned of her backstory recently and now there are so many questions I'd like to ask and can't. How did she cope? What did she do with all that anxiety? Why was she still so frightened?

Perhaps it was because society has a history of trying to suppress emotional distress, especially if showing it was risky and dangerous. Maybe Nain's withdrawal was learned behaviour, a means of survival, because she lived at a time where those who showed any intensity of feeling could find themselves locked up.

The undeserved stain of lunacy

Take the example of Rachel, a 48-year-old woman sent to an asylum on the advice of her family after a 'nerve rest cure' to the seaside was deemed to have failed. Her husband, a respected GP, had died of an overdose of opium – and Rachel was understandably anxious, depressed and grief-stricken. On arriving at the asylum, she was forcibly detained, after her sister signed committal papers preventing her release. The family left her there and never returned.

Rachel was locked in a room with up to ten other women. A room where the light was on all night and where she could hear the constant shouts and screams of the 'frenzied women' who were being beaten by nurses or 'ducked under' in cold baths. Rachel fought for twelve years to be released and was determined to try to clear her name of the 'undeserved stain of lunacy'.[4]

She wanted to be seen as 'perfectly right and normal' – which of course, she was. She had what all of us have: a healthy dose of what she called 'human frailty'. Eventually, she was freed and her writings were published in a book called *The Experiences of an Asylum Patient* in 1922, raising questions in parliament about the treatment of those locked up for life purely because they were struggling with basic human emotions.[5]

At the time, there were more than 100 'pauper lunatic asylums' in England and Wales, filled with women and shell-shocked soldiers, thousands of whom spent years there or who never came out at all.[6] When the asylums became mental hospitals, those living there were still being called 'lunatics' of 'unsound mind'.

And what about women being called 'hysterical'? The word comes from the Greek meaning 'womb', and was used to describe 'overemotional' or 'deranged' women – right up until the term was deleted from the official diagnostic manual in 1980.[7] In our recent history, society has been so frightened of conditions like anxiety, it has incarcerated those who have it or tried to quieten them with electric shock treatments – and, in extreme cases, frontal lobotomies.

Once seen as a miracle cure for mental illness – and, according to the media at the time, easier than curing toothache – a lobotomy meant drilling a pair of holes into your skull before a knife was inserted inside to sweep across the prefrontal cortex, severing the part of the brain which helps with decisions, planning and memories.

'It was based on this terribly crude, simplistic view of the brain, that the brain was a simple mechanism, and you could just sort of stick things into it,' says neuroscientist and surgeon Henry Marsh. 'The idea was that you had these thoughts running round and round, and by interrupting the circuit you would stop these distressing, obsessional thoughts.'[8]

The Portuguese neurologist who invented the lobotomy, António Egas Moniz, won a Nobel Prize in 1949. Those who experienced it were often left lethargic, unable to look after themselves and prone to fits of rage. Should we blame the medics for trying to cure distress in seemingly barbaric ways? Marsh says not. 'This business of dividing doctors into heroes and villains is wrong. We are all a mix of both, we are a product of our time, of our culture, of our training.'

The times, culture and sensibilities changed after lobotomies stopped being used. Language changed, a little. 'Unsound mind' and 'mental defectiveness' were replaced with 'mental disorder'; and in the 1960s, pills became the new way of quietening everything from anxiety to psychosis. Diazepam came on the market in the form of Valium, billed as 'Mother's Little Helper'. It became one of the most prescribed drugs of all time.[9] Decades later, different, better-tolerated drugs were used to target anxiety, like selective serotonin reuptake inhibitors (SSRIs), which work to increase the amount of serotonin in the brain. There is controversy about their effectiveness, however, together with questions about whether such medication is really meeting the needs of those who are struggling.[10]

A disordered world

Anxiety disorders are the world's most common mental health issue, affecting a third of a billion people, and yet we still don't seem to have truly effective and easily available ways of managing them. Medication takes a while to kick in and can cause side-effects; therapy can be hard to access. Globally, about a quarter of those with anxiety disorders will get treatment.[11] But even if you're lucky enough to get help, it doesn't necessarily mean you'll feel better. In England, only around half of those treated for anxiety and depression recover.[12]

In the US, the American Psychiatric Association says anxiety is increasing year on year, with the rise attributed to concerns about the economy, politics and gun violence.[13] Forty million Americans now live with an anxiety disorder – which is almost one in five of the adult population.[14] And Australia is getting close, with one in six reporting anxiety symptoms lasting up to a year.[15] This current state of play is not meant to be anxiety-inducing, but it may help you feel less alone to hear what's happening in the rest of the world. In the anxiety league tables,

Portugal is number one, followed by Iran, Brazil and New Zealand, but Canada, the US and much of Western Europe are up there too.[16]

As anxiety rises, so do ways of categorizing it. More people than ever are being diagnosed with generalized anxiety disorder (GAD),[17] which affects all areas of emotional, social and physical wellbeing – and where depression and panic come along for the ride.[18] There's a rise in social anxiety too,[19] paralysing the ability to get up, go out and face the world, as well as a reported increase in 'high-functioning anxiety', a non-diagnosable, whirring sense that something awful is about to happen, even among those who seem supremely organized and efficient. Like the novelist and playwright Daisy Goodwin, who says her 'anxiety comes in waves', attached to 'the threat of rejection'. She will plunge into a 'horrible spiral' worrying 'that there's a rule that everybody else knows, that I don't know'.

We'll hear later from the Radiohead drummer Philip Selway, who describes being on stage with his band in front of massive audiences, experiencing an anxiety that can 'feel very dangerous' yet not wanting to let anyone down. Neither might qualify as having an official anxiety disorder, but it doesn't stop anxiety affecting their lives. What Daisy and Philip do about it and how they live alongside it, we'll come to in Part Two. There's a way to go yet, though. They knew they had to notice and understand their anxiety before changing their relationship with it, and you're learning that too.

Disorderly conduct

A disorder simply describes several symptoms which have existed for a certain amount of time. Those who diagnose them do so with reference to that manual I mentioned earlier, the *DSM*, and there are loads of them in there – almost a dozen referring to anxiety alone.

The debate about the word 'disorder' is polarized. I know that some clients and my own family members have found being diagnosed with one validating. It can help those struggling with something they can't define, because it gives that feeling a shape, a name and an understanding. It can connect them with a broader community, where they can access support, medication and overcome stigma, and that can allow for a feeling of control over their condition.

But not everyone likes the 'disorder' label. Take neurodivergence. In the 1990s, a neurodiversity movement started among those with autism who were calling for civil and equal rights. They rejected the word 'disorder' as pathologizing, and began to shift the language away from deficits and symptoms towards acceptance. If you want to know more, read Steven Kapp's book tracing the history of the neurodiversity movement with perspectives from autistic activists and academics.[20]

In the medical model, autism is called autism spectrum disorder (ASD), and the word is also used in another form of neurodivergence, attention deficit hyperactivity disorder (ADHD). Neither are personality quirks. They are neurodevelopmental conditions which mean the brain is wired differently in key areas of reacting, relating and processing. This can affect relationships, work, emotions and self-esteem, which increases the risk of anxiety, and in Chapter 6 I'll introduce you to a client with autism whose socially anxious mind can easily go into overdrive.

You may find a diagnosis – any kind of diagnosis – useful, but you may not like the idea of calling it a 'disorder'. Or you might be fine with it. There is no right or wrong. Everyone is different, and when it comes to anxiety, we are all somewhere on the bell curve. Those really suffering will be at one end of the curve, and those who aren't suffering nearly as much will be towards the other end. It's less a question of where you draw the line for a disorder, and more about how much the anxiety is impacting your life. When someone feels unhappy and worried, a label can provide relief, but as consultant psychiatrist Dr Alastair Santhouse writes in *No More Normal*, it doesn't mean it's useful. 'Kindness and clinical utility are not the same,' he argues. 'Few things are more therapeutic than being listened to and understood.'[21]

And when it comes to anxiety disorders, Philippa Perry is concerned they are becoming 'another widening net, people are just craving diagnosis, and I think ordinary distress is getting commodified. If you make something into a disorder, then it can be monetized because Big Pharma can send you drugs for it. Get a diagnosis and then treat it like a physical illness and then you get the drugs for it. And people love that because it's validating for them to think, not "oh my God, I'm such a worrier", but to go

"I've got anxiety disorder". And then it's something that they can outsource rather than work on themselves.'

Philippa makes a comparison between physical and mental conditions. 'We never say "I've got diabetes disorder". We say we've got diabetes. We never say we've got measles disorder. We have measles. With some of these psychiatric disorders, you have to call them disorders because it makes them more real. We're pretending that we're abnormal for things like grief or like anxiety or sadness. It is so much easier just to look at the human and make sense of the story.'

You can have a raft of anxiety symptoms and they can feel as if they are ruining your life, yet you may not meet the criteria for a disorder. It doesn't mean you're not suffering. Categorization is helpful to some clinicians and clients, but when I meet someone with anxiety, the key question is not 'what kind of disorder is this?' but 'how does this affect your life?'

Sophia's story: where no diagnosis fits

This is the story of Sophia, a student at a prestigious university. Sophia had anxiety and wanted it gone. She worried about letting other people down and rejection. About failing and getting fat. She was having panic attacks, was binge-eating and was no longer going out. She described herself as lazy, disgusting and worthless and said she felt 'lonely, scared and overwhelmed'. Over time, she revealed extensive emotional and physical abuse, including school bullying, parents who were either absent, dismissive or critical, and a boyfriend who insisted on violent sex which she hated and tried to zone out from.

The institution I was working with liked counsellors to use measures, or questionnaires, to see a client's progress over time. With Sophia, I used a post-traumatic stress disorder (PTSD) scale, which assesses twenty symptoms and asks questions such as whether the individual has unwanted, distressing memories about an event.[22]

But Sophia did not score highly enough to show PTSD. Ah, I thought, it's the wrong measure. There's more than one trauma that's disrupting the sense of self and relationships with others, so it's more likely to be complex PTSD (C-PTSD). That questionnaire asks about the usual trauma symptoms plus issues around social or work life and managing emotions.[23] But again, Sophia did not 'meet criteria'. Other scales suggested there was no depressive disorder and only mild to moderate anxiety.

Can you see the issue here? Sophia's distress was impacting everything, from her understanding of who she was to her connections with others. She couldn't handle big emotions, she was self-judging and critical, and she distrusted herself and those around her. But if you based your judgement on whether she had a disorder, then she wouldn't have ticked enough boxes to be diagnosed with any of them. And worse, if her treatment *relied* on her having them, she might not get it. Thankfully, it didn't.

The way I worked with Sophia and the ideas I'll share with you here are based on being willing to accept difficulties in the past, to acknowledge any shame and blame that come with them, and to show some curiosity and self-compassion when uncomfortable thoughts, feelings and behaviours show up.

Some people, like Sophia, live with debilitating anxiety but won't be diagnosed with a disorder. Others can tick all the boxes but might be left with labels that don't really belong to them. Ann is one of those. I met her while working at a large London teaching hospital in the psycho-oncology department, the place where people with cancer go if they want emotional help with the disease.

Ann's story: all the diagnoses

Ann is consumed by worry. Understandably so, you might think, because she's recently been diagnosed with cancer. We're on a Zoom call because it's during the pandemic and neither she nor I can get to the hospital where she's being treated. She doesn't want to go anyway. When she was last there, she was furious with the medics for giving her the diagnosis and told them she wasn't going to have treatment.

They sent her to me for therapy, hoping that this agitated, distressed woman would respond well to emotional support and understanding. No chance. Ann turns up at our online sessions but angles her camera to the ceiling so I can't see her. I can feel her anger, though. 'Why me?

Why do I have this disease?' she says 'What's the point in going out? What's the point of living?'

And this one, after I ask a question about how she is coping: 'Why are all you people so fucking useless?' I can't see her face when she hurls her rage, but her aim is clear. I represent everything she cannot tolerate. 'I hate, hate, hate, hate, hate, hate, hate the lot of you,' she says. 'You all ask the most fucking inane questions.'

I probably have, in all fairness. Cancer stinks and I am part of a system that tells her she must manage it. If she were to engage with the doctors, they would explain that her tumour is treatable, that they have caught it at an early stage. But her brain is so full of threat and danger, her body and mind so taut with worry, that she can't concentrate.

Ann tells me that I can't possibly know what it's like to have the disease. I want to tell her that I do, but that is futile and unnecessary and not the point. I'm desperate to find something that works with Ann – to develop a trusting, engaging relationship with her. Perhaps I give more than I do to others, not wanting to be as incompetent as she claims, but each tentative connection skitters away.

Does she *really* hate the lot of us, and hate me? Maybe. Although I think she's been hurt and felt powerless before, and she's protecting herself in case it happens again. That shows itself in attacking anger, behind which is fear, behind which is sadness. But touching that sadness is unbearable. Instead, with me, she replays old relationship patterns with familiar feelings – a noisy tumult of rage and abusiveness.

She worries constantly, yet passively, not wanting to know about the progression of the disease, or possible treatments, or how she can help herself. Partly because she is in a system which she cannot control and wants to reject. She is powerless, scared and lonely, so hits out with language. I reel back, and then try harder.

Our patterns of behaviour in the face of threat are led by our experiences in trying to keep us safe. Ann rejects before she is rejected; I try to please and pacify before I am rejected. Ann is caught in a tangle of old relationship dynamics and new repetitive anxiety. So angry with her disease, and those telling her about it, that she stops listening or engaging and becomes alienated from herself and those around her.

Ann rates severe on both the anxiety and depression questionnaires we typically use in health settings. The Generalized Anxiety Disorder (GAD-7) Scale measures the fear of something awful happening, as well as irritability, restlessness, trouble relaxing, unstoppable and excessive worrying, and feeling nervous and on edge.[24] We also use a depression scale, the Patient Health Questionnaire (PHQ-9), which asks about lack of pleasure, feelings of hopelessness and fatigue, problems with appetite and concentration, having too much or too little energy, and thoughts of self-harm or suicide.[25] You'll find both at the back of the book.

If I were to test for it, Ann might also have borderline personality disorder (BPD) – in other words, being emotionally unstable. Or oppositional defiant disorder (ODD), which shows itself in hostility and defiance. As symptoms of these diagnoses are also found in C-PTSD and ADHD, she may meet criteria for those too. An alphabet soup of disorders.

They all add up to a long list of different symptoms and diagnoses, but they don't adequately describe what Ann is going through. That she's scared to death of the cancer and feels lost and lonely trying to deal with it. Add to that, all the past experiences that have made her scared and distrustful. Of course she's oppositional, defiant, angry, sad, bewildered and raging.

Once she acknowledges that these feelings are not her fault, but a reaction to uncertainty and lack of control, we start using easy breathing techniques to acknowledge the sharp pain of her suffering, to accept it's hard and frightening and to allow herself some kindness. Some of these, and the techniques used with Sophia, are included in Part Three.

Ann is often furious and frightened but continues to turn up on time, every week. We keep doing more of this acknowledging, accepting and allowing, even when my ideas are met with a contemptuous sniff.

Everyone's reaction to cancer will be different, based on our history, our sensitivities, our support structure. But anxiety, fear and rumination are common. Ann started using a cognitive behavioural therapy exercise to help define when to act positively on worry and when to try to let it go. This is the Worry Tree. There's one in our house, too.

Exercise: The Worry Tree[26]

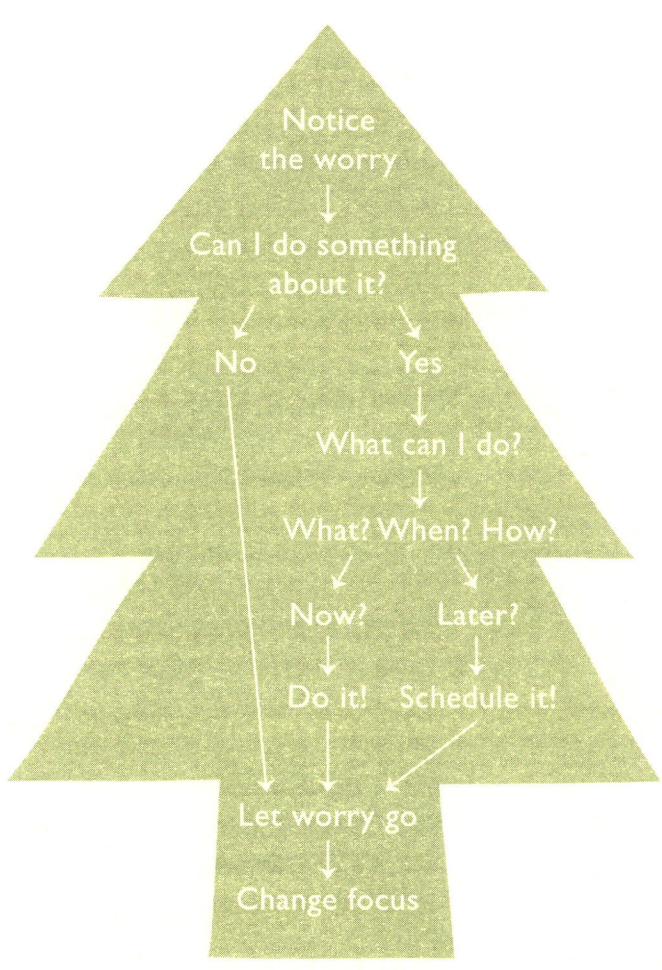

You'll see that the thought at the top of the tree is 'Notice the worry'. Noticing is important because it means you are pausing and tuning into what's happening with the worrying thoughts. The noticing creates a space from which you can start to acknowledge what's going on in your anxious body, brain and behaviour. We'll be looking at these in more detail in the next section, but briefly here's how anxiety might show up:

- The anxious body: heart rate changes, disruption to digestion causing butterflies or cramps, altered breathing, sweating.

- The anxious brain: worst-case-scenario planning, fear of embarrassment, rejection, feelings of fear, shame, blame, panic.

- The anxious behaviour: safety moves, including avoidance, withdrawal and the attraction of distraction.

Ann uses the worry tree regularly whenever a worry-thought appears. Is it about the cancer? Can she do something about it, like ring the cancer nurse? Or is she catastrophizing with little evidence? If so, can she try to let it go, or schedule a time to worry about it later in the day so it doesn't take up all her time?

At the beginning, Ann was hostile, a word that comes from *hostis* in Latin, meaning 'enemy'. It took time for her to see that although I'd never be her friend, I was not her enemy. Anger, I understand. Anger has energy; it's like a gateway to other feelings such as fear, sadness and anxiety. Once we'd identified and named that, her worry turned into something more adaptive and positive – actively reflecting, rather than endlessly ruminating.

Adding more diagnoses to the cancer one might not have helped Ann. What did was regaining control over what she could do to help herself, even if wasn't as much as she'd like. When the clinic opened, she began going to appointments and listening, rather than blocking and resisting. I don't know what happened to Ann, but I hope she knows herself, even likes herself, a little bit better. Less angry, less fearful, more accepting. I hope.

Stress and worry are understandable reactions to things that may happen in an uncertain future. The issue is when they start disrupting everyday life. A hundred years ago, we locked up people with anxiety, and now we have created our own internal prisons. When we rage against the bars, when we see anxiety as our jailer, something dangerous and bad, it becomes a bigger threat, and our brain responds accordingly. The greater the struggle, the harder it is to set ourselves free.

It's like a tug-of-war with a monster before it pulls you into a hole. Or fighting to get out of quicksand when the struggle pulls you further in. Or that toy in kids' party bags where you put your finger into a tube and can't pull it back out again, and the harder you pull, the tighter it becomes.

We have always been trying to get rid of what we don't like, and it puts power back into the hands of the very thing we fear. Have a think about what happens when anxiety has the power. How does it make you think? What does it make you feel? What do you avoid because of it? What gives it power – like your life experiences, self-beliefs, other people's expectations? What does it say to you? And then try this exercise. The first table shows you examples, and the second leaves space for you to fill in your own answers.

Exercise: When anxiety has the power

When **anxiety** has the power		When I have the power	
What does anxiety make you *think*?	Not good enough, stupid, small, worthless	What would I *prefer* to think?	I am good enough, loved and valued
What does it make you *feel*?	Tight stomach, headaches, fear, panic, frustration	How would I *like* to feel?	Calm, centred, content, optimistic, excited
What does it make you *do/avoid*?	Work too hard, avoid social situations and new experiences, overeat, binge-watch, constant phone checking	What do I want to *do* with my life?	Try new experiences, learn piano, write a book, spend more time with friends, start a course
What *external* things give it power?	Expectations of others, childhood experiences, demands of work, past traumas	What *external* things support me?	Exercise, yoga, friends and family, walking, dog, nature, music
What *internal* things give it power?	Perfectionism, running through worst-case scenarios, catastrophizing, ruminating on what-ifs	What *internal* strengths do I have?	Kindness to others, loyalty, persistence, resilience
What does your *self-critic* say?	I am...	What would my *kind voice* say?	I am...

ANXIETY – A LIFE SENTENCE?

When **anxiety** has the power		When **I** have the power	
What does anxiety make you *think*?		What would I *prefer* to think?	
What does it make you *feel*?		How would I *like* to feel?	
What does it make you *do/avoid*?		What do I want to *do* with my life?	
What *external* things give it power?		What *external* things support me?	
What *internal* things give it power?		What *internal* strengths do I have?	
What does your *self-critic* say?	I am...	What would my *kind voice* say?	I am...

I wonder how you're feeling having completed this. Perhaps the first column, about when anxiety has power, was much easier to complete than the second. That's because our brain jumps to the negative; we are primed that way. The self-kindness part might feel quiet, or even non-existent for you. We will get there, but it's early days. This section of the book is about seeing how anxiety might have trapped us, and what we'd like to do with our lives once we've freed ourselves. It might be hard right now to think about your strengths and resources, and much easier to think through what you can't achieve rather than what you can.

If you have anxiety, there is nothing wrong with you. You are not disordered, or defective. For too long, we've been asking 'what's wrong with you?' That locates the problem squarely with the individual and ignores all the other things that might feed into their anxiety – the experiences they've endured, the society and culture in which they live, the external pressures bearing down on them, their lack of agency.

Not 'what's wrong with you?' but 'how do I make meaning from this?'

A more helpful and hopeful way of managing anxiety is asking 'what has happened to me?' and 'how do I make sense of it?' and 'what did I do to survive?' That way, we look at past stories and experiences to see if our reactions are based on trying to protect ourselves from any further danger. Once we've noticed that and seen how we behave when we're anxious, we can start to focus on our strengths and find a new way of living with our anxiety.

Let's try it. This next exercise asks about the strategies you use to manage your anxiety, how it benefits you in the short term, and what it's cost you in the longer term.

Exercise: Going deeper, what have you tried so far?[27]

Anxious thoughts/feelings
e.g. *I'm worthless, not good enough, unlovable*

Strategy/treatment tried
e.g. *Not going out, not forming close friendships*

Short-term benefits
e.g. *Feel less anxious and worried*

Long-term benefits
e.g. *I'm safe, in control and never have to think about it again*

Short-term costs
e.g. *Not seeing friends, no fun*

Long-term costs
e.g. *Lonely, even more scared of going out*

Why did/didn't they work?
e.g. *It kept me inside, stopped me doing what I wanted to do and made me more nervous*

If you look at the examples, you'll see that trying to avoid situations that make you anxious can cut you off from other people and make you even more worried, because you're not testing your own, perhaps flawed, assumptions of what'll happen or what others may think of you. We'll look at this more when we talk about social anxiety.

Calling anxiety a disorder doesn't help move things on. Seeing how it affects us and then working with the exercises in this book, where we think about what we want from life, is more hopeful and workable. Here's the difference.

A medical model of anxiety identifies target symptoms, makes a diagnosis and intervenes to manage those symptoms. If you use a different framework, you start thinking about the role of anxiety in your life – and what sense or meaning you attach to it and what you have done just to stay alive and get through the day. And then you look at your own resources and start a new narrative. A forward-thinking, strengths-based story, not just a diagnostic one. One which acknowledges what has happened in the past but also makes way for a plan based on values and meaning and what you want from the rest of your life. How you want to act, what you want to do, who you want to be. Values work as a guide and motivator, whatever else is going on in life. More on them later.

'Know through' your anxiety

A label doesn't make the problem go away. Whether it's a disorder or a collection of symptoms, anxiety can disrupt life and there are things you can do now to live more peacefully with it, rather than keep fighting it. Diagnosis means to 'know through' in Greek. We'll be looking at social anxiety, panic, perfectionism and high-functioning anxiety in the next chapter, and although they differ, they have similar effects on our body, brain and behaviour. If we take a good hard look at those effects, if we 'know through' our anxiety – whatever it's called – we can start to relate to it differently.

Part of being able to live with anxiety is recognizing that those thoughts and feelings that you are trying to fight or escape from, the denial and avoidance behaviours you're using to find safety, are also those which are important to pay attention to. Then, you can understand their function. Anxiety tries to watch out for us, even when it vastly overestimates or imagines the threat, or keeps reminding us of past hurts and traumas.

If we acknowledge that, then we can tell a different story – one of meaning, witnessing and healing. We may start to feel differently and more compassionately towards our anxiety and focus instead on our strengths, values and goals, rather than just our problematic thoughts, feelings and actions.

Our childhood experiences and formative relationships have a lot to answer for, and we'll be looking at the role of early attachments and anxiety in Chapter 7. We can't change or undo these experiences. But we can react to them differently rather than allow them to continually hijack how we feel. As Philippa Perry says, 'If you want to be happy, there's really one main rule. Choose your parents really, really carefully.' Ah, happiness. Found it yet? If not, there may be a few reasons why, but that's for the next chapter.

Chapter 2: A quick refresher

- Being taught – and told – not to feel has kept anxiety alive.

- Fear, shame and stigma are heavy. Put them down – you do not need to shoulder their weight.

- Disordering anxiety won't make it go away. Work with it. Don't struggle with it.

- Worry can be a habit. Understand when it's productive and when it's punitive.

- 'Know through' your anxiety – see it as a teacher, not a tyrant.

3

The Happy Trap

'Some have happiness, everyone has summer'

100-year-old Finnish proverb

What can we learn from the happy Finns?

I'm in Finland, the world's happiest place for the past eight years. For context, the UK and the US are twenty-third and twenty-fourth respectively.[1] Visitors arriving at Helsinki airport are greeted by a confident sign that says: 'Welcome to your happy place'. When I pop to the loo, I hear tweeting and look around, confused, before I realize they are piping birdsong into the toilets. The soap and towel dispensers have pictures of trees, badgers and bears on them. It's charming, all this nature brought inside to the most utilitarian of places.

I've come to Finland with my third son, Seth, for an adventure before he leaves home for university and to celebrate our landmark birthdays. We're off to the Arctic Circle to see the Northern Lights. Hopefully. On the flight up to Saariselkä, 1,000 kilometres north of Helsinki, I look out of the window and see snow, forests and very little else. When I ask the flight attendant why Finns are so happy, she pauses. 'We have nature,' she says, 'and we like to be alone.'

Well, they get to experience both here. Three-quarters of Finland is woodland; urban areas don't even cover 2 per cent of the country.[2] Wherever you are, you are never more than ten minutes away from a forest, and they're very important to the Finns. For every tree chopped down to provide wood for homes, three more are planted.[3] It's enshrined in law that any Finn who wants to hike or camp or gather berries in the forest can do so, regardless of who owns the land.[4] Is happiness down to being close to nature, the fact that few people populate the land, or something else?

I know we are seeing a romanticized version of the Finnish lived experience on this break. When we get to our destination, we are taken to a wood cabin among the trees, with a roof that's half glass. It's tiny, like a Hobbit house, and inside everything is warm and cosy, while outside it's quiet and still. Living like this would make me happy, I think. This peace and isolation nestled among nature, unplugged.

My son flops on the bed, plugs in his earphones and picks up his Nintendo Switch. 'This is relaxing,' he says. At night, we watch for the aurora borealis, the dancing, magical Northern Lights, made by the sun's solar flares penetrating the earth's magnetic field, creating waves of colour according to the way they react with elements in the atmosphere. They usually only happen at the poles, North and South, although some years they can be seen in Europe. They were visible in the UK in 2024, but I missed them.

Saariselkä is a remote spot in the far north of Finland, 200 kilometres north of the Arctic Circle. Surely, we can't fail to see them here? We get an alert on our phones at 2 a.m. 'Northern Lights visible'. Jumping up, we go outside into the snow in our pyjamas and look up. A haze. Is there colour? Take a picture through the phone. Peer at it. Is that something? Or just a cloud? Disappointed, we get back into bed. That night, there are five or six pings and five or six times we jump up and head outside. We're exhausted in the morning and send our crappy pictures home. 'We think these are the Lights,' we say, without confidence.

The nature is astounding though. Seth grabs a pair of snowshoes and says he's off to wander in the forest alone, telling me there are no bears around here, just rabbits and foxes. And that he's a scout leader and can find his way home if he gets lost because he has his compass. Not much reassured, I wait, anxiously.

When he returns, he's flushed and excited. He's walked a few miles, with no one around, just snow and trees and silence. That night, we're taken on a trek through the forests to a teepee, where we sit and wait for the lights again. The skies are clear, and our guide points up to the constellations and down to the animal footprints in the snow. We return to our cabin, having seen beauty, but no light show.

I go to bed, he stays up listening to a podcast – and then, sometime after midnight, he shouts me awake and we look through our window and there they are. Green, spiralling, wispy, floating, glorious lights. We run outside and I point my old phone up to take a picture. 'Just look at it with your eyes, Mum,' he says.

It's been an amazing few days, and we are treated again the following night. I'm happy, he's happy. But we'll go home tomorrow and I have programmes to record and clients to see and emails to answer and he has exams. What can we take from here to boost our happiness levels? This is a holiday, not real life. If we were living here, we'd have to find real jobs, and deal with −25 degree temperatures. Finland's happiness can't all be down to nature and the Northern Lights, surely?

It's not. There are quite a few good reasons to love the place. Finland was the first country in the world to allow women the right to vote and to stand in elections. It offers generous maternity and paternity leave, good state-run schools, and high-quality health and social support.

And it's the best country in the world to lose your wallet. In an experiment where people were asked if they expected a dropped wallet to be returned, Finland and the Nordic countries said 'yes'. When that experiment went further and had researchers actually drop a wallet, it was more likely to be returned in those countries, too.[5] People tend to be happier living in areas where they know others are likely to help them.

Like any country, though, Finland has complexities. One man tells me they are bored and frustrated by their country topping the happiness rankings. 'No one talks about the darker side of living in a country where it's cold and isolated. Alcoholism and domestic violence are high here.' Alcohol plays a part in the homicide rate too, which is triple that of other Nordic countries.[6]

Antidepressant use is among the highest in the world,[7] and in a study of more than forty countries, Finnish parents rated as the seventh-most burnt-out.[8] It's a beautiful country, with amazing scenery and wonderful people, and once home I'll be planning to come back – but what is it about Finland that puts it at the top of the happiest nations, year after year?

Hauling yourself up the Happiness Ladder

Every year, residents of around 140 countries are polled by Gallup for the World Happiness Report.[9] That's the one where Finland has come top for eight years in a row. The main source of happiness data is based on a question, asked of about 1,000 individuals, in each of those nations. It's this: 'Please imagine a ladder with steps numbered from zero at the bottom to ten at the top. The top of the ladder represents the best possible life for you and the bottom of the ladder represents the worst possible life for you. On which step of the ladder would you say you personally feel you stand at this time?'

This scale was developed more than sixty years ago and is called the Cantril Ladder.[10] Have a go at picking a rung by asking yourself where you stand on living 'your best possible life'. What will you base it on? Work or relationships? Health or finances? Might you be on a different rung today to where you were yesterday, or last week, or last month?

If you're a Finn, your countryfolk say they are almost on rung eight. It's averaged over three years and they are currently at 7.7. If you're in the UK or North America, it's the sixth rung. That's worse than previous years, meaning both have dropped out of the top twenty. Australia and New Zealand are still in there though, within touching distance of rung seven.

The happiness ladder tends to skew towards greater wealth, both on an individual and societal level,[11] and most of those near the top of the ladder are people from Western industrialized nations, with Afghanistan, Sierra Leone and Lebanon at the bottom.

Happiness, or 'your best possible life', seems such an elusive and hard-to-define concept that, if I were asked, I'm not sure I'd know what I was reaching for. Being 'happy' can seem so fleeting, fluid, hard to snatch and harder to hold. Here's writer Helen Garner on her search for it: 'It's taken me 80 years to figure out that it's not a tranquil, sunlit realm at the top of the ladder you've spent your whole life hauling up, rung by rung... It's something you glimpse in the corner of your eye until one day you're up to your neck in it. And before you've had time to take a big gasp and name it, it's gone.'[12] I wonder whether striving towards an ever-higher rung might make some more anxious. Everyone in Finland is on the eighth rung and I'm still on a four. What am I doing wrong? What should I be aiming towards?

The authors of the World Happiness Report acknowledge that happiness is based on more than one question and is about how we feel as a society, not just as an individual. That wallet test was included in their report along with lots of other research, to see whether people had trust in their communities and institutions. They suggest 'prosocial behaviour' like donating, volunteering and helping strangers makes for a happier nation; and loneliness and distrust make for an unhappier one. Kindness and benevolence increase wellbeing, they say, and those who have 'caring motivations' have higher self-esteem and fewer symptoms of anxiety, depression and isolation.[13]

It's not just about you

In *America the Anxious: How Our Pursuit of Happiness Is Creating a Nation of Nervous Wrecks*, British author Ruth Whippman explores the US obsession with happiness and discovers that those who rate it as a strong personal ambition are usually *less* happy.[14] She suggests that the endless and demanding focus on happiness as an individual goal makes us more isolated and anxious. Whippman argues that social connections are more important for our wellbeing, but the time we give to them is lessening as the time spent on self-improvement seems to grow.

About fifteen years ago, I hosted the launch of a new movement called Action for Happiness.[15] Just to give you an anchor in time, it was 2011 and shoppers around the world were queuing up to buy Apple's latest smartphone, the iPhone 4. Takes you back, doesn't it? The founders of the movement were motivated by the fact that, despite increased consumerism and productivity, life satisfaction had not increased. We need, they said, a shift in priorities.

At the launch, there were about a hundred journalists in a room listening to one of the founders, Lord Richard Layard, an economist from the London School of Economics and one of the authors of the Happiness Report, field a question about what we should be aiming to do in our lives. His answer? Aiming to create as much happiness as we can in the world around us. Pursuing a happier society with a focus on improving wellbeing and reducing misery. Lord Layard has always argued it makes sense to do this – and he continues to do so, recently sending me a study suggesting that NHS talking therapies pay for themselves because they get people back to work, where they are not just happier but also pay taxes.[16] It's ethical *and* economical to help those who are struggling.

But back to the day of the launch. The reaction was huge. It featured on BBC TV news that night, and the movement's website went down with the weight of interest. Yet scepticism emerged in the following day's newspaper headlines. 'This pursuit of happiness makes me queasy,' said one columnist. 'Is there any more to this than hello clouds, hello sky?' asked another. But Action for Happiness, which started with just a few thousand members, quickly saw its numbers surge. It now has millions of followers on social media, reaches countries around the world, and its daily action calendar has been downloaded more than 50 million times and translated into more than thirty languages. It has regular events with experts, and volunteers run courses based on changing behaviours – which, research suggests, improves wellbeing, encourages people to help others in their community and reduces mental ill health.[17]

The movement says there are a few key factors that make for happier living, including; good relationships, exercising, becoming more aware of oneself, being kind, trying out new things, learning acceptance and finding meaning. It's sensible stuff, and many people have found value in it. And Action for Happiness has a big backer too, because its patron is His Holiness the 14th Dalai Lama, Tenzin Gyatso, the spiritual leader of Tibet, winner of the Nobel Peace Prize and someone who describes himself as a simple Buddhist monk.[18]

It's a decade after that launch, and I'm back to host the tenth anniversary with one of the co-founders of Action for Happiness, Dr Mark Williamson. It's an online event in front of a live audience of thousands of people from across the world, and will include an interview with the Dalai Lama himself. I ask Mark first – about that word 'happy'. Does he think it can be problematic? He says yes. 'Modern materialistic culture has convinced us that "we'll be happy when…" Instead, we're talking about a deeper authentic happiness which includes resilience, thriving and doing good for others, regardless of what life throws at us.' Happiness as an individual *and* collective aim – self-care with culture change.

Mark thinks that if the movement had been called Action for Wellbeing, it wouldn't have had quite the same impact. 'When parents are asked what they want for their children, they just say, "we want them to be happy".' True. I wonder if we're confused about what that means, though. Perhaps we've let others set the definition for us, painted a landscape of colour and light where everyone else is joyous and we sit outside, stewing in our own anxieties.

We want our children to be happy, and because we've been through life, we know they'll experience pain. Contentedness and suffering coexist. That's why we can get anxious when happiness comes along. We suspect that something or someone will snatch it away from us or those we love. Are you truly present in happiness? Or a bit suspicious about how long you'll feel it? That worry about losing it means you can hold on too tightly and it dies, or slips through your fingers.

In 2011, when the movement started, few people were asking questions about the mind. Now, it's accepted that all of us who are vulnerable and struggle can also live a happier, healthier life. And that often comes if we focus beyond our own happiness goal. As Richard Layard told me after the launch: 'The biggest single source of misery is absorption with yourself. We need our children to be much more focused on wanting to get pleasure from helping other people, engaging with other people, having fun with other people, rather than worrying about their image, which is almost guaranteed to be a source of anxiety.' He once worked in the UK's Department of Education, where two huge banners declared the government's target of 'Staying Ahead'. 'A frightful, competitive ideal,' he recalled. What do you replace it with, I asked. 'Build a happier society. Do more good in the world. Make a difference,' he replied.

Ten years later, the Dalai Lama echoes that thought. When asked for the single-most important secret of happiness, he says, simply, 'Warm heart.' Looking after each other, not searching for your own happiness or cleaving to a particular identity. 'Warm-heartedness is very practical,' he tells us, in his halting English. 'If we create happy humanity, that is the only way.' A woman from Birmingham who lost her father in the Covid pandemic asks for advice on managing her grief. He tells her, 'There's no use to worry and make effort, so be realistic. Your father passed away, very sad, but you still have a lot of brothers and sisters there.' She's wiping away tears as she hears this. 'When my mother passed away,' he says, 'I feel very sad, but that's nature. No use too much worry.'

How can he have such a calm hold on suffering? Because Buddhists believe suffering is inevitable, and the way to relieve it is by showing compassion to yourself, to others, and to the world. It's called 'loving-kindness',[19] and this might feel difficult now. It may seem counter-intuitive to step away from the vortex of worry to be 'kind' to yourself. You might not even know what that means or looks like. We'll give it a go later. It might not make you happy in your current understanding of the word. But curiosity and compassion are good places to start.

Happiness is a well-risen cake

I'm back with the psychotherapist and author Philippa Perry, discussing how 'the demand to be happy' makes us believe something is wrong with us if we don't feel we have it. 'Happiness is a peak experience when you bring your cake out of the oven, and it's risen and you go – yes! But you can't have that feeling all the time. What you want to develop is the capacity for happiness, so you know HOW to be happy. You need those neural pathways of how to be happy nicely oiled and well maintained. A lot of the time, you're absorbed and that feels great. You might be absorbed in a knotty problem, but "happy" wouldn't be the right word for how you're feeling.'

I suggest 'flow' is a better term for that feeling, rather than 'happy', and she agrees. Or it could be a burst of joy. 'I always think of a football game. It's ninety minutes of boredom and thirty seconds of happiness when the goal comes. It's mostly boredom but you need to be happy when the goal does come. You need to go – yay! Sometimes when you're in an unselfconscious flow, you look back on it and realize you were happy. But you don't think "I'm happy! I'm happy!" Noticing when you're happy? When you're happy you don't really have time for that, do you?'

We can be so busy trying to follow someone else's definition of what happiness is, or proving that we are having an amazing experience, that we fail to understand what is unique to us and whether it is actually making us feel good. 'Selfies erode happiness,' Philippa says. 'Well, not all of them, but people who live for online likes outsource their happiness for external approval.'

She gives an example of going on a speedboat – external referencing is when you think 'other people will think I look great in this speedboat'. Internal is when you're absorbed in the ride and the smell of the sea. She prefers the latter.

Philippa gives another example, of someone she knew who had a 'dream job'. At least that's what everyone told him, and they were very happy for him. Except he was utterly miserable. When he came to see her, he spent a lot of time with her cat who he clearly adored. It got them talking about when he was last really happy. On his uncle's farm, looking after animals, he said, but that didn't impress anybody. 'What are you feeling?' she asked. 'From that, work out what you want and whether you want more of it in your life. And then, go for it'. He left his 'dream job', started working with animals, and was 'so grateful to me and the cat'. He sent her and the cat Christmas cards for fifteen years. Then, she laughs, 'he must have lost my address or something'.

Exercise: Getting out of our thoughts and into our feelings

Locating how we feel, and from there working out what we want, sounds simple but is so difficult to do – because, as Philippa Perry says 'we are always "should"-ing ourselves. I should be this, I should be that, I should be happy because... Should-ing means we are suppressing something because we think we should be happy with what we have, but we're not.'

Those of us who spend a lot of time in our heads can overthink and go round in circles, making ourselves more anxious. What would happen if you did it like this instead?

- Go to what you feel, not what you think.
- Work out what it is that you feel.
- From that, work out what you want.
- From that, go for it, or ask for it.
- It may help to locate the feelings by asking questions like: Where do you feel most content?

Try not to intellectualize the experience, otherwise you'll lose the feeling. Ask yourself: What am I feeling? When and where do I get that feeling of contentment, or being at peace? From that, work out what you want, whether you want more of it in your life, and how you might get it.

It's not about following the right rules or sticking to someone else's description and prescription. If we try but don't get to the place that feels meaningful to us, if we are told we should be happy or grateful but don't feel it, if we can't scale that ladder after following the self-care tips we've read about, it can feel like failure.

Look at how happy other people are! They've done it right and we're still struggling with our anxiety, worrying about things that may never happen. We can be in a tough place, feel our anxiety and *still* experience pockets of joy. Real change, real happiness, comes from understanding that life is messy and complicated and that we exist within systems and structures that sometimes don't work.

It comes from accepting things aren't always easy, yet asking questions about what might be getting in the way of us feeling a little bit happier, a little less anxious. Looking at the hooks we get caught on, the thoughts and feelings that nag and judge, the habits and behaviours that trap us.

A potted history of happiness

Think of all the ancient thinkers who have been searching for happiness long before us and where they thought it came from. At least 2,500 years ago, the Greeks thought it could only be bestowed by the Gods. Their word for happiness was *eudaemonia* – 'blessed by good spirits'.

For the Stoic philosophers, like the Roman emperor Marcus Aurelius, happiness was more than a feeling, it was an attitude to life earned through virtue, effort and reason – something that came from 'power over your mind, not outside events'. While we cannot control what happens to us, he wrote, we can control our reactions. 'The happiness of your life depends upon the quality of your thoughts.'[20]

To Buddha, happiness was compassion in the face of suffering: to yourself and to others. America's founding father Thomas Jefferson, who wrote the US Declaration of Independence, believed 'life, liberty, and the pursuit of happiness' was central to the rights of all citizens. Although you wonder how he dealt with that 'pursuit of happiness' himself, given that he was a striving perfectionist who experienced insomnia, depression and anxiety.[21]

The Auschwitz survivor and psychiatrist Viktor Frankl, whose freedom was denied, believed happiness wasn't something to pursue, but came instead from our search for meaning.[22]

We are told so many myths and fairy tales about happiness, including those which say it's our natural state – it's not. That we're defective if we don't feel it – not true. That it's a finite endpoint – nope. That to get there, we must control all our difficult thoughts and feelings – well, that just makes it harder to find.

Little pockets of happiness

I had a client who did experience moments of happiness, but while she was in them, fear crept in that they would be taken away because she didn't deserve them, and she would then be punished by something terrible and sad. Even as she recognized she was feeling a moment of happiness, the anxiety started up about it being snatched away because she was 'worthless and lazy'. Eventually, she learned not to hold on to those moments so tightly that she strangled the joy out of them. She called them 'little pockets of happiness', which she could enjoy without the need to grip on to them.

Life is mad and precious, and if we can act with a kindness borne out of the recognition of the struggle, we can move towards our own definition of what happiness is. It'll be incremental, it'll ebb and flow, and most importantly it won't look like other people's.

Listen to the words of the Dutch woman Etty Hillesum, a Jewish diarist during the Second World War, who wrote that she had already 'died a thousand deaths in a thousand concentration camps' by 1942. But she believed 'when you have an interior life, it certainly doesn't matter what side of the prison fence you're on'. Etty witnessed terrible misery but insisted life was 'glorious and magnificent'. 'Turn inward', she ordered, and sweep away the 'inner litter, the bits and pieces' and apply love to 'small everyday things'.[23] Optimistic, inspiring and with an unbroken spirit, Etty died in Auschwitz aged just twenty-nine.

Before we put new ideas in place, we must sweep away our 'inner litter' and the 'bits and pieces' that might be hijacking any sense of happiness. Gritty happiness comes with courage, compassion, and a committed action to observe with curiosity. It's like the Buddhist idea of being with our 'inner weather' rather than trying to change it.

The former Buddhist monk Matthieu Ricard says happiness is not governed by the fleeting, circumstantial elements of our day like 'a child's smile or a nice cup of tea after a walk in the woods', as lovely as those things are. Happiness is also 'a way of interpreting the world, since while it may be difficult to change the world, it is always possible to change the way we look at it'.[24]

This book is not about forcing yourself to have more positive thoughts, in the same way that it is not asking you to control negative ones, but it is asking you to begin reacting to them differently.

THE HAPPY TRAP

Exercise: Don't think those thoughts

Just to deviate for a while and plunge into a lovely thought. I want to tell you about a bakery, not far from us, where I buy jam doughnuts. They are huge, with just the right amount of sugar. I get them when they're warm and fresh out of the oven, and when I bite into one, the jam is sweet and hot and goes everywhere, and the sugar is on my lips and the jam is dribbling down my chin and the dough is sticking to my teeth and it's glorious. Yum. Doughnuts. Warm, sweet doughnuts.

Right, deviation over. I'm going to ask you not to think about doughnuts for the next few minutes. Don't think about them at all. No doughnuts. Especially not the jam ones. Not those ones. The big, doughy, sweet ones. Not those. If a thought or an image or smell or memory of a doughnut comes up, push it away as fast and as hard as possible. Great. Let's think about something else. Anything else. What are you up to today? What's for supper? How's work going? How's the not thinking about doughnuts going?

It's hard, isn't it? I bet you hadn't given a doughnut a second's thought before I started banging on about them. I gave you an image and then told you not to think about it, to deliberately push it away, ignore it, focus on something else, and yet there it is. Big and bold and warm and sweet and still there. Sorry. A silly exercise, but it gives you an idea of how hard it is to tell ourselves we can't or shouldn't think about a thought.

Some do this 'don't think about' experiment with a shape like a star, or a pink elephant. Why the elephant?

I asked a colleague. 'Because I tell my clients they can't ignore something that's in their head. They must notice and name the elephant in the room, otherwise they'll trip over it on the way out.'

You can't push away thoughts; they just come back stronger, grow larger, assume a greater prominence and importance. Somehow, just saying 'ah, there it is again' – the doughnut, star or pink elephant – minimizes its hold on us. If images can be that powerful, what about your thoughts? The ones that tell you you're worthless, or unlovable, or weak, or not good enough? How's it going banning those thoughts from your head? Impossible, right? Don't give them the power. See them, name them, let them go, move on. Describing your anxiety is the first step in changing it.

A pessimist is never disappointed

Let's look at optimists and pessimists. We know that optimists are healthier and live longer than pessimists. A meta-analysis – a study of studies – suggests the life of a pessimist is typically around eight to ten years shorter than those who believe in good outcomes.[25] That's partly because pessimists are often in fight-flight mode, which tests their blood pressure and heart rate and affects their immune system. Optimists are also more likely to invest in health-promoting habits.

Pessimists are likely to give up more easily, because they tend to overestimate the risks and underestimate their ability to cope.[26] Optimists are more than a third less likely to experience a cardiovascular or heart-related event than pessimists.[27] They also have a more flexible mindset, are resilient, and persist when pessimists may give up.[28] They engage more easily with others, have a stronger support system, and reframe difficult situations as challenging rather than threatening.[29]

Optimism is thought to have a genetic component for a quarter of the population.[30] Well, good for them, I say. They may live longer and be happier, fitter, more resilient and cope with challenges more easily than, say, me. Or maybe you. Are there costs to optimism though? Perhaps. Optimists may not be as prepared as pessimists when the worst *does* happen. And in a study of students waiting for feedback from exam scores, the optimists were more disappointed than the pessimists if their results were not what they expected.[31]

Pessimism can prepare or console us, but when it tips into rumination, that's when problems start. Balance is key. And you can be both optimistic and pessimistic at the same time, because optimism and pessimism are associated with different areas of the brain.[32] You don't have to be either/or, you can be both/and. Hold the definitions lightly and be willing to develop more psychological flexibility towards your thoughts, whether positive or negative.

Find your sisu

But back to Finland. Another measure of their wellbeing is research conducted by the Finnish Happiness Institute.

Nature might be up there at the top of the reasons why Finns are content, but cooperation with others and mutual trust are important too.[33] It's the forests, the community, the faith in one another and their institutions, the saunas. And one last thing: Finns have something called *sisu*.

Untranslatable, it's a unique concept going back at least 500 years which combines resilience, determination and sustained courage. Sisu is said to have helped define the nation when Finland declared independence from Russia in 1917, and again when they resisted the Soviet invasion during the Second World War. As Joanna Nylund writes in *Sisu: The Finnish Act of Courage*: 'Sisu is a verb. It invites you to act, to do, to grab hold of something. It comes into play as you take on a challenge seemingly beyond your capacity. In the midst of a dark moment [it was] a surge of courage that helped you carry on. Sisu begins where our perceived strength ends.'[34]

In other words, it's not the stamina to complete the race, it's not the endpoint, it's the grit and perseverance to keep going, one step at a time. Nylund suggests we go back to a time when we found sisu without even knowing it was there, when we faced a challenge and got through it.

Exercise: Find your sisu[35]

Take a moment to think of a time in the middle of a struggle when you kept your head up until you got through it.

When you had to take a different path from the one you thought you were heading down. A new, scarier, unfamiliar route, but one which shifted your perspective and perhaps your view of yourself and the world. Maybe you've forgotten it, or moved on, or it's got lost in the noise of anxiety. But that surprising burst of life force at a time of adversity will be there.

Search your memory and see if you can find it. Was it a race you thought you couldn't complete and did? Or one where you fell, yet still got up? Was it a time when you spoke your mind, or challenged someone's opinion at work? Whatever it is, hang on to it, because we need to remind ourselves of our power to wade through what is known in Finland as *paska* (crap). That traditional Finnish quote at the start of the chapter states that 'some have happiness, but everyone has summer'. In other words, whatever you're dealing with, better days will come for you.

When I interview guests on my BBC Radio 4 show *Life Changing*, we talk about the event, or the moment, that transformed things for them. I've chatted to people who were caught up in an attack which left them for dead, or discovered they were the product of an incestuous relationship, or believed they were the only survivor of a zombie apocalypse. I kid you not. I've also heard from a woman who pulled her twin sister from the jaws of a crocodile. Twice.

Although these guests are at the 'better now' end of the crisis, I try to take them to the 'stuck in the middle' part – because that's where the understanding and the learning come from. That mucky, vulnerable, frightening place where you thought you might not get to the end of it, or through it, or be done with it.

For a recent episode, I interviewed a young woman who had an online gambling addiction that was so consuming, she gambled her partner's mortgage deposit away. We went to the deepest part of that shame, disgust and incomprehension. What did she think about herself? How did she pull herself out? The show was broadcast to millions, a public exploration of how she thought, felt and acted. Here, you can share that darkness on your own, so try to be honest with yourself.

Think from the middle of the dark place. What were your thoughts at the time? What did you do in the immediate aftermath? What or who helped? What or who didn't? When you look back on it now, what are your thoughts towards yourself? Can you thank yourself for holding on and putting one foot in front of the other?

Have a few of these 'survivor' stories in your back pocket for when you feel things are spiralling away from you. You have done this before. You have, I am sure, got through something difficult and felt a small shot of triumph. It might have been when you were asked to do a presentation and you managed it. Perhaps you are living with pain, or an illness. Or dealing with grief, or a relationship breakdown, or redundancy, or financial difficulties.

Sisu may not be 'happiness' in our understanding of the word, but it is achievement and determination and bravery and that stands for something. Happiness is not eliminating all the negativity in life, or side-stepping the triggers; it's learning how to react to them, so they don't destroy us. It's turning to face difficult things rather than fleeing from them, and remembering to thank and praise ourselves afterwards for doing so.

Don't compare your insides to other people's outsides

There's a huge amount of toxicity and self-punishment that comes with comparison. If we contrast other people's colourful, exciting lives with our humdrum, duller one – if we try to follow their example rather than listening to our own heart – it feels rubbish. Like they are living the premium version of life and ours is bargain bucket.

Humans have always had this insider-outsider comparison. Our primal brain tells us it's not safe to be on the outside of this sparkly, happy group of perfect folks, because then we're at risk from the predators. Safer to make ourselves seem like other people, to be part of the herd. Dr Russ Harris, acceptance and commitment therapy clinician and trainer, says that 200,000 years ago, that might have worked, because we lived among a small group of cave people. The problem now, he tells me, is that 'instantly you can be in contact with all these people all around the world and the problem is you're not comparing yourself to reality, you're comparing yourself to this kind of fake reality that's created through photoshopping and highlighting and people trying to show their life in the best possible light. These things have been there in human culture throughout history, but never to this extent, never so exaggerated.'

Be careful who and what you invite into your home and into your soul. In a world full of uncertainty, where we feel we may lack control, it can be tempting to follow those who seem to have life sorted. Or to go down an information rabbit hole, searching for answers to complex questions which can take us to places which are not good for us. There's too much conflicting opinion out there already, and if we were to live several lifetimes, we would never absorb it all. No one can be better at living your life than you are. Leave them to live theirs. Find your own messy, unpredictable, imperfect way through.

But forgive yourself for *trying* to find the perfect way, or person, or formula. Our mind seeks patterns and order in an unpredictable world. It's just sometimes this ever-louder information isn't useful. Rather than helping us develop psychological flexibility, it keeps us fixed, rigid and anxious. Making us feel like we're lacking and failing. It becomes yet another punishing strategy to quieten a noisy brain and avoid the uncomfortable feelings that come with stillness.

Garbage in, garbage out

We can't out-think our anxiety no matter how much new information we allow into our heads. And a lot of the information we let in is rubbish.

I've hosted a few conferences for Google on misinformation. That's false facts which are not designed to cause harm. Disinformation is false facts which are meant to cause harm. Mal-information is truthful content spread maliciously. Makes your head spin, doesn't it? All this damaging information that deliberately, or unintentionally, deceives. Here we are, trying to pick our way through our bewilderment, not knowing what's true and what's not, and distrusting those who are leading us or telling us.

At one of the conferences, as we navigated the minefield of fake news, we heard about the trust report from global communications company Edelman. Their first report came out in 2000, a year of optimism and hope as we entered a new millennium, when the clock struck midnight on 31 December 1999 and we said goodbye to the twentieth century and welcomed the twenty-first.

I was a presenter on the BBC's Millennium TV extravaganza *2000 Today* at the time. It was a twenty-eight-hour show, and almost 13 million viewers tuned in to see fireworks, celebrations and joy as midnight happened around the world. I was the news anchor, there in case YK2, the so-called millennium bug, brought down planes, business and banks. It didn't. Nothing to see but people enjoying themselves, and a few national treasures reflecting on what the future held.

One of those national treasures was Sir David Attenborough, the great conservationist, who, while sensibly recognizing the date had little significance to many across the world, said the last time he had felt such a sense of perspective was when he first saw *Earthrise*, the photo of our planet beamed back from the Apollo 8 spacecraft. Entering a new millennium brought a similar feeling of awe and unity. Everyone agreed, he said, that it was time for a party; it was time to look back but to look forward too. We are all together on one planet and we have a responsibility to do something about it, Sir David said.

Here we are, twenty-five years later, and I think he would agree that we haven't done a very good job of looking after ourselves, each other, or our planet. The idea of being 'all together' seems to have vanished too.

Globally, we've lost trust in our institutions and feel more isolated and anxious, and the fear of conflict, insecurity and recession has never been higher, according to the twenty-fifth-anniversary Edelman trust report. Government leaders and the media are seen as incompetent and unethical, constantly spinning lies and falsehoods.[36]

People feel as though they are living in an unfair system, and there are high levels of grievance towards business, government and the rich – with some young adults saying they are not afraid to engage in hostile activism, like attacking people online, or spreading disinformation to try to drive change.[37]

This distrust and anxiety mean the number of those avoiding the news altogether is increasing, year on year. Many now get their information away from traditional media, turning instead to YouTube, WhatsApp and TikTok. Social media and search engines, content creators and influencers, are the ones they go to for information, even while they acknowledge concerns about algorithms and artificial intelligence.[38]

Analysis paralysis

We are overwhelmed, confused and distrustful. Perhaps it's not surprising our anxiety levels have peaked. What do we do about it? Finland – again – leads the way, because it teaches its population how language can be used to confuse, mislead and deceive. It's learned that critical thinking, taught early, makes its citizens more able to withstand mis- and disinformation and take pride in their communities, their institutions and their country.[39]

While we wait for our politicians to do the right thing globally that might ease our existential anxiety, we can take advice from the Dalai Lama and Sir David Attenborough. Take notice, they say. And then do what you can, where you can. Work within your community. Be careful about who you choose to listen to. All this information can make us paralysed, frightened and drive us to switch it all off, but there are folks you can rely on. Teachers, doctors, scientists and neighbours are *highly* trusted.[40]

Trust can be local. Don't shut down because it's all too much or you think you have no impact. Seek out and support those you believe in. If you're anxious about the environment, yet trying to stop the world burning seems too huge and anxiety-inducing, do something small to start with. A litter pick, a beach clear-up, backing an environmental charity. Big changes can start from tiny ones. And the impetus for change often comes from those who are most sensitive to the need for it, as we'll see in Chapter 10.

The quest for happiness as an endpoint, the toxicity of social comparison, the information overload, can all lead to higher levels of anxiety. It's the goal you haven't reached, the people with better lives, the choices you feel you're faced with.

Curiosity, connection, compassion. Happiness is found in these things. One step at a time.

Chapter 3: A quick refresher

- Happiness isn't a goal, it's a direction of travel. It's found in the flow, not at the top of a ladder.
- It's destroyed by social comparison and renewed by social engagement.
- It comes in pockets and moments in a messy and mucky world.
- Realistic optimists invest in good habits. But you can be a curious pessimist too.
- Turn inwards to understand what *feels* good, and turn outwards to begin to *do* good.

Ten Top Takeaways from Part One

1. Anxiety is a necessary early-warning signal, but sometimes the alarm keeps being triggered – we can overestimate the danger and underestimate our ability to cope.

2. Patterns of thinking and behaviour in the face of threat are a learned survival strategy and not our fault. Recognize, name and forgive them. They're just trying to help.

3. Fighting, struggling with or avoiding anxiety only makes it bigger. Being willing to accept, commit and change the relationship with it will lessen its power.

4. Worry is a habit formed by trying to control the uncontrollable, but it may not prevent a bad thing happening. Begin to identify when it's productive and when it's pointless.

5. Highly sensitive people are more likely to be anxious and react negatively to the bad stuff around them – but given the right environment, they will thrive and be magnificent.

6. Real happiness is not measured on a ladder of worth, status or achievement. It's found in curiosity, connection, community and compassion.

7. Our minds judge, but try not to compare yourself to others. Live your own messy, unpredictable, glorious life. And be mindful about who you choose to invite into it.

8. Hold your labels lightly. You are not disordered, or defective, or broken. You're human and you suffer. That doesn't mean there is something wrong with you.

9. Start to think about what really matters to you and how you want to behave in the world. Identifying your values will help you move towards a life with clearer focus.

10. And finally... hang in there. Learning new skills to take the power out of difficult thoughts and feelings takes time. Your mind may be telling you it won't work. That's natural. Be proud of yourself for getting here and committing to change. You're off to a great start.

Part Two

4

Understanding the Inner Voice

'What a liberation to realize that the
"voice in my head" is not who I am. Who am I
then? The one who sees that.'

Eckhart Tolle[1]

The voice in my head

There was someone else I met on my *Life Changing* radio programme, whose interview sparked one of the biggest audience reactions we'd had in ten series. Her name is Hazel.

Hazel thought she was stupid. Because, at the age of eight, she was told so. Brought up in a busy and loving home with four siblings, she struggled with school and often stayed inside to finish her lessons while her classmates were out playing. On one of those days, she overheard two teachers talking. 'Who is Hazel?' one asked. 'And why hasn't she done the work?' Hazel was quiet; the teachers didn't know she could hear. 'Because,' the other teacher said, 'she is mentally retarded.'

This was the early 1970s, when such language was bandied about freely. Labels slapped on children like those on a jam jar. 'Who's Hazel?' *The mentally retarded one.* Unarguable, immutable, fixed. 'I accepted it as gospel truth because she was my teacher and I did have great difficulties,' Hazel says. 'And in one sense it was a relief, but I felt so sorry for my parents, and I had let them down. I could see that my life would be very narrow.' Hazel told no one about that overheard conversation, but those words dominated her brain and behaviour for decades.

This part of the book is dedicated to our inner voice, like Hazel's – the internal judge who tells us where we're going right and wrong. The voice of anxiety is often critical, and the next few chapters will help to identify where it comes from and how it can drive perfectionism, procrastination, imposter syndrome, performance and social anxiety. And how we learn to become, as the German spiritual teacher Eckhart Tolle says, not the voice itself, but the one who sees it. Or, as we heard earlier from US author Michael Singer, the one who hears it. Observing it, listening to it, is the first step towards healing it.

But that takes time, and Hazel was just a child. One who learned to be quiet, keep her head down and 'not allow anyone to have any expectations of you, because if you do, you'll fail and they'll become cross with you. Just live life at the lowest possible level and try not to get into any trouble.' Her self-critical inner voice warned her that she needed to be uncomplaining and unchallenging. She left school at sixteen to become a typist, met a man and married him, had two children, her husband left her, she moved homes and countries, worked for a charity and, throughout, believed she was 'not right' in the head.

In her late forties, Hazel decided to complete an access course in what she calls 'very, very basic education'. She did well and the course leaders persuaded her to study for exams in psychology, sociology and English. Hazel got two As and a B and was encouraged to apply to university. Initially reluctant, with that inner voice still nagging, she was accepted at three, one of which was St Andrews on the east coast of Scotland. 'Prince William was studying at St Andrews then,' she says, 'and it's ridiculous but I just thought, "I cannot be what they said, if I'm studying at a university that's good enough for Prince William. I cannot be mentally retarded".'

In the end, she chose not to go there because the study hours didn't work for a single mum with two children, and went to Dundee instead, to do a social work course. Yet she still believed she was 'fooling a lot of people'. At the age of fifty, the chance came up to do a master's in the theory and practice of writing, and Hazel thought, 'If I do a master's, I cannot possibly be mentally retarded.'

On and on it went, with Hazel setting herself challenges to prove she was not something she'd overheard at the age of eight. 'The words I heard were so defining. My master's was the most exciting time in my life and I got a distinction. And I looked at it and I thought, "Well, that's amazing." And after a few minutes I thought, "Well, anyone can write. It's not rocket science, it isn't difficult.

Now, if I can do a PhD, I'm not mentally retarded." And I thought, "No, stop. Stop it. You have to stop saying that. Because I cannot be retarded, if I've got a master's, I can't be, so now I have to stop letting that term define me and ride me and squash me. I am not that."'

I am not my inner voice

Hazel had experienced the pain of humiliation and rejection very early on, and her critical inner voice developed to protect her from experiencing it again. It had learned something as a child that it thought was a fact – that she was stupid – and it kept reminding her of it to stop her from trying things which might confirm or reveal it to other people. Her inner voice became a way of shielding her from guilt and shame, failure and embarrassment. Yet it was so punishing, she felt all those things anyway. The eight-year-old had taken a thoughtless, inaccurate remark and turned it into a core belief which stayed with her for more than four decades. But it was not who she was.

Late in life, Hazel was diagnosed with ADHD. She's in her sixties now and I ask what she'd say to that eight-year-old, if she could go back in time. 'I'd say, "It's all right, you'll be fine. Mum and Dad love you and you'll be absolutely fine."' She's happy with her second husband and two grown-up children, so why did she want to talk publicly about what she overheard all those years ago?

UNDERSTANDING THE INNER VOICE

'This incident hugely changed the arc of my life, and that's why,' she says. 'A lot of people are held back by things that are said knowingly or unknowingly. They've slapped a label on someone and it's held them back and it's so good to get out of it.' Hazel was not stupid. But she had overheard that she was, and her inner voice believed it and set it up as a mantra for life. How sad she should have held on to that for so long. How liberating to finally let it go.

Our stupid friend

Dr Gabor Maté, the renowned speaker, author and expert on trauma, calls this judgemental voice our 'stupid friend' and says its roots are often found in childhood.[2] He points to studies suggesting that brain development starts even before birth, with the most important influence being the emotional relationship between parent and child in the very early years.[3]

Most mums and dads do their best in often difficult circumstances, and it can be isolating and stressful bringing up children, but if the child picks up on that loneliness and stress, they can absorb and internalize it. If there's anger and criticism, if they're told that showing emotion is wrong, or are shouted at, then they grow up believing they are the ones at fault. These children can become anxious adults with a harsh self-critical voice, who believe emotional vulnerability is weak or dangerous, who fear making mistakes, and who can find it difficult to trust others.[4]

Think about a child growing up with a bullying, neglectful or abusive parent. Their brain will be constantly scanning the environment for threat – and if it detects it, will try to work out how to stay safe. That might mean being overly compliant or submissive; the child may shut down or numb emotion, and turn it in on themselves rather than risk showing it. If they don't know what they're doing wrong, their mind will come up with their own explanation for being rejected or diminished: 'I must be worthless', 'I don't deserve love', 'I can't do anything right'.

This reasoning, however false, stays into adulthood, resurfacing with any new danger that presents itself. A compliant child can become an adult who never wants to say or do anything to rock the boat in case they feel that rejection again. People-pleasing feels safer, and it can be hard to voice opinions or show intense emotions.

Maté says although this 'stupid friend' helped you survive in childhood, 'it's stupid because it can't learn. It doesn't know that you're no longer two years old, or four years old. It just keeps pestering you with the same information. It can't help it. It's a brain circuit programmed with a certain message.'[5]

I wonder what your inner voice says to you, when you first heard it, and in what situations it becomes louder and more critical? One way of identifying whether it is a fair and compassionate judge or a belittling and bullying one is to look at the questions below. Over the next few days, try to take a helicopter view of your self-critical voice. Notice how you talk to yourself, and what daily

UNDERSTANDING THE INNER VOICE

decisions you make after listening to it that might hijack your wellbeing.

Exercise: Noticing self-criticism

Ask yourself the following questions:

- What is your internal voice saying?
- Is it your voice or someone else's?
- If someone else's – did those individuals criticize you out of genuine care?
- How did it make you feel?
- When you use, or hear, this voice, what emotions is it directing back at you?
- How does it help you?
- How do you treat yourself on those days?

Perhaps answering these questions reminds you of how hard it can be to show yourself self-compassion. There are several reasons for this. The first is that, as we've heard, if the brain detects threat or danger, it goes to 'safety first'. It reminds you of a previous time when you were hurt, or shamed, or rejected, and will replay it to prevent it happening again. It's doing its best to protect you, but not in the kindest of ways.

The second reason is that, for many of those with anxiety and a critical inner voice, compassion has not been modelled for them. Those who faced harsh, critical, dismissive parents or carers, for whom compassion and kindness meant weakness and selfishness, will have grown up not knowing how to soothe themselves in a crisis. Instead of accepting difficult emotions, their mind is set to critical – telling them they can't cope, because they're not strong enough, or good enough, to manage.

The 'not good enough' voice

I've worked in both a large London NHS teaching hospital and a charity setting, helping people with cancer. For many, self-criticism was easy to access, self-compassion much harder. And that 'not good enough' script came up again and again, especially with women. Whether you've had a cancer experience or not, I'm sure you've gone through something in life which has tested you, and I wonder how your voice talked to you at the time. Here's how these women initially responded. I've changed their names.

When I first meet Sally, she is recovering from surgery, radiotherapy and chemotherapy after cancer. Sally has a mind that 'spins out of control' with catastrophic and punishing thoughts. She beats herself up for being anxious and failing to cope, but says being judgemental is a fundamental part of her. Like Hazel, it comes down to what she heard as a child, she says, and some of the things her mum would tell her: 'She said, "Well, you might be top of the class now in the junior school. But just get to that grammar school!" And then, "Well, you might be top of the class at the grammar school but just wait until you get your first job! Then you'll find out!"'

Sally recognizes the self-critical voice in others too, who are 'waiting for the point at which they're not good at something. But you could have become, I don't know, a prima ballerina or something. But Mum would have said, "Just wait until you fall off that stage!"'

This deeply ingrained and long-standing fear of not being good enough affects how many individuals I counsel respond to challenges like cancer. Barbara, living with acute side effects of the disease, also puts her anxiety down to 'very harsh mums who bring their children up to get on with life and just had no compassion at all. Don't even want to talk about it. Don't ask you how you are. Whatever you've got wrong with you, it's worse for them, even though it's cancer.'

Lucy, recovering from surgery, says: 'I realized that the negativity wasn't necessarily my voice, it was someone else's voice, like your parents and your teachers. It was just like "You're not good enough. You're not good enough. You're not good enough."'

These women did not know what compassion felt like because no one had shown it to them. They understood criticism though, and that was the voice that stuck.

Should-ing, ought-ing and must-ing

The angry, punishing self-critic is linked to our core beliefs – the things we think about ourselves, others and the wider world. Core beliefs are deeply held convictions based on past experiences. If we were judged as not working hard enough, then, like Hazel, a core belief might be that we are stupid. If we have not been shown love, it might be that we are worthless or undeserving.

These beliefs – which we can mistakenly see as unassailable truths – can dictate our thoughts and rub up against our values. Here's how. If one of our values is to strive towards success at work but we have a core belief that we are not clever enough, then any failure confirms what we already believe about ourselves. If a value is to develop more loving relationships but we have a core belief of worthlessness, then any rejection or difficulty will 'prove' that we are not deserving of affection. Our values work for us, motivating us and aligning us with a life of purpose and meaning, but our core beliefs can often work against us, presenting false truths and rigid thinking.

These core beliefs can also drive rules for living – the self-protection strategies to help us get by in daily life. As we heard from psychotherapist Philippa Perry earlier, these rules often have 'shoulds' attached to them. But there are also the 'oughts' and the 'musts': 'I should keep pleasing this person otherwise they'll leave me', 'I ought to be more successful because I had a decent education', 'I must work harder to prove my worth'.

When we don't feel we are living up to these life rules, the alarm bells go off and the inner voice reminds us of previous experiences or worst-case scenarios which fill our heads with worrying thoughts and images. We can feel angry or frightened and take precautions like withdrawing, hiding or people-pleasing to get back to safety. Our self-critical voice then bullies us for doing this, confirming the core beliefs. 'That's it, I knew it, I'm useless' – further damaging our self-esteem. This age-old, familiar, 'not good enough' script can dominate our life and profoundly impact our mental wellbeing. But it's also utterly exhausting, as this next exercise from acceptance and commitment therapy shows.

Exercise: The piece of paper experiment

Think of one of the negative things you often believe about yourself. In fact, let's go further. If you can, get a big piece of paper and write it down. It can be one word, or many. Here's a prompt: complete the sentence 'I am...'

Once you've done that, hold the paper up, so it's clear what you've written. Hold it for a couple of minutes in front of your face.

After you've held it there for a while and your arms start tiring, put the piece of paper on your lap and come back to me. It's still there, the paper. With the thought on it. But when it was in front of your face, what could you see, apart from the worst thing you think about yourself? Probably not much. You can't see the bigger picture because the paper with the critical thought on it is right there, blocking everything, preventing you from moving forward and getting on with your life. It's tiring as well, holding that thought front and centre.

Once you lay it down on your lap, you can still see it, but the rest of life is there too. It's just one part of a much bigger whole.

If you can't write the thought down, do the same experiment with a voice note using that same sentiment. If it's at a high volume, it blocks everything else out. If it's lower, you still hear it, but you're allowing other things in too.

I am not asking you to get rid of your self-critical voice. I'm asking you to be more sympathetic to the struggles, thoughts and feelings that come with it. This is about changing your relationship with your thoughts, not eliminating them. That also means making room for emotions that you may be blocking or frightened of, like anger.

The anxious, angry imploders

Here's a hypothetical mother-and-daughter situation. Perhaps the mother is frustrated or angry, she may want a job but is busy looking after the kids, or she may work but not be rewarded for it. Maybe she's balancing a budget with little cash. She might have experienced heartache, grief and trauma that she doesn't feel she can show. Whatever it is, she rarely gets the credit for what she does, and often feels subsumed by everyone else's wants and demands. The daughter is young and doesn't understand why her mum can be emotional or snappy, or why she must be quiet or 'stop showing off'. But she wants to make her happy and she becomes someone who works hard and demands little. She can't be angry because there isn't the tolerance or space for it, so she keeps it inside, turning it on herself, judging her every move to correct her behaviour in case she's criticized or rejected. The girl grows up knowing that if emotions are held inside, rather than shown outside, there's less risk. The negative self-talk, the held anger and the self-silencing take her into adulthood, with the risk of becoming corrosive and implosive. A lot of us have lived this experience.

Self-silencing makes us sick

Many cultures value women being pleasant, self-sacrificing, and negating their own needs for the sake of others, but this has damaging consequences across generations. Women who self-sacrifice are at higher risk than men of experiencing auto-immune diseases, chronic pain, insomnia, migraines, irritable bowel syndrome and poor heart health.[6] They may self-sacrifice because they believe it's the best option in a bad relationship, to keep quiet and protect themselves. Or they may feel worthless and work hard for others to prove their validity. Externally, they are sacrificing and caring; internally they are angry and frustrated, with repressed emotions and unmet needs.[7] Being good and doing everything for everyone else is making them ill.[8]

These are the women that 'should' themselves. They fill their lives with tasks to achieve and demands to fulfil, to show they are strong and worthwhile, and then become worn out trying to complete them all.

Emma, living with uterine cancer, says she would start a million jobs to show she was capable, but didn't have the energy to complete them: 'I always felt a failure because I hadn't met all the demands that I put on myself, thinking I had to do everything and be everything to try and make people understand that I was okay.'

The busy bully

Emma and the other women in this chapter were taking part in a research study that I'd set up, to see whether an eight-week group mindfulness course shifted their ruminating, self-critical, negative thinking. It did.[9] Part of it was about noticing the inner voice and what it was doing to them. Another part was developing the skills of self-compassion and not feeling like a fraud, or selfish, or weak, or self-indulgent when using them. Emma now identifies when she is 'harsh on myself, and I do really like myself. I'm much calmer. I don't panic as much. I don't go to a million miles an hour. I also identify that I don't have to keep filling my life with jobs to get through the day. I'm much nicer to be around now. I didn't think I was being horrible or mean. I was just frantic and impatient.'

Being frantic, impatient and busy doesn't make the inner voice quieter. We know from our doughnut experiment earlier that blocking and ignoring thoughts doesn't either. Neither does letting them dominate and exclude, as we saw in our piece of paper exercise. It takes enormous amounts of emotional resources and cognitive energy to block, avoid or try to get rid of our self-critic. Whatever yours is saying and whenever it chooses to make itself heard, know that the stupid friend, the inner voice, is just throwing thoughts, ideas, memories and judgements at you. Don't argue with the rights and wrongs, don't try to answer its demands. Don't let it make you feel like a worm wriggling on a hook. Noticing it and naming it – 'ah, here's that familiar voice again' – helps us unhook, as does understanding where it might have come from.

We also know self-compassion works, and we'll develop that in Part Three, but first it's important to recognize another important thing about the inner voice.

Sometimes, the inner voice is right

The inner voice can be huge, nasty and quick to point out faults, whether it's a sharp whisper in the ear or a jeering heckle from afar. But sometimes, it can help encourage and motivate. It can anticipate your challenges and triggers, so you can put your coping mechanisms in place ahead of time, to react well.

We can work on making the voice calmer, more assured, less judgemental. Or, at least, a more helpful, balanced, caring judge – one who's genuinely decent and works in your best interests. Acting more like a good friend would – how I'm sure *you* would react if someone you loved was in a spiral of self-doubt and anxiety. Helping you to see your positives and your strengths, and guiding you towards an action plan while keeping alert to the self-defeating thoughts that try to hijack it all.

When you're overwhelmed, you can lose your flex and perspective. The inner voice can prevent rather than encourage, punish rather than praise, and be critical rather than caring. But with enough distance to disentangle from the negative thoughts and with enough compassion to bring in a different tone, the questions it poses can also be prompts to look at life and see what's missing, or what needs attention.

In the next chapter, we'll hear more from Daisy Goodwin, a TV producer and playwright, who has an inner voice that drives her to achieve but can just as quickly undermine her. 'I have the energy and the optimism to do lots of new ventures. I think, "Oh, it's all going to be brilliant." And my head goes to my Oscar acceptance speech. But then quite often I'm sitting there going, "Oh my God. I'm going to be broke. I've got no money." There's no rationale.'

Daisy has so-called high-functioning anxiety or HFA, a non-diagnosable, whirring sense that something awful is about to happen, even among those who seem supremely organized and efficient. More on high-functioning anxiety, perfectionism and procrastination shortly.

We'll also hear more from Philip Selway, the drummer from one of the most brilliant and influential bands of the past thirty years, Radiohead. He told me that his inner voice almost stopped his career at the height of the band's fame by telling him: 'You're not the genuine article. You've messed up before. You're going to mess up again. You're going to look an absolute fool in front of all these people.' If he was to continue doing what he loved, he needed to hear his inner critic differently. He'll tell us how he did that in Chapter 5. But in short, both Philip and Daisy learned when their inner voice was helpful, and when it was harmful. Here's a way of working out which it is for you.

The self-critical payoffs

Self-criticism has many different forms and functions. A couple of different measures were used to explore depression in female psychology students, including this next exercise, which looks at the function of self-criticism – is it about improvement and correcting mistakes, or about attacking and punishment?

Exercise: What function does self-criticism play for you?[10]

Mark the box for the number that best describes how much each statement is true for you: 0 = Not at all like me, 1 = A little bit like me, 2 = Moderately like me, 3 = Quite a bit like me, 4 = Extremely like me.

I get critical and angry with myself:	0	1	2	3	4
1. To make sure I keep up my standards					
2. To stop myself being happy					
3. To show I care about my mistakes					
4. Because, if I punish myself, I feel better					
5. To stop me being lazy					
6. To harm part of myself					
7. To keep myself in check					
8. To punish myself for my mistakes					
9. To cope with feelings of disgust with myself					
10. To take revenge on part of myself					
11. To stop me getting overconfident					
12. To stop me being angry with others					
13. To destroy a part of me					
14. To make me concentrate					
15. To gain reassurance from others					
16. To stop me becoming arrogant					
17. To prevent future embarrassments					
18. To remind me of my past failures					
19. To keep me from making minor mistakes					
20. To remind me of my responsibilities					
21. To get at the things I hate in myself					

UNDERSTANDING THE INNER VOICE

Self-criticism has different functions: one is to try to improve yourself and stop yourself making mistakes, another is about being angry and wanting to punish yourself. Statements 1, 3, 5, 7, 11, 12, 14, 15, 16, 17, 18, 19, 20 refer to self-correction; statements 2, 4, 6, 8, 9, 10, 13, 21 refer to self-persecution.[11]

Exploring whether you use self-criticism as a way of correcting or persecuting yourself might help with understanding the reasons behind why you do it. Some of the functions of self-criticism are negative, some are positive. Here are a couple of examples that show the difference:

Situation: That work project has a deadline and it's coming up.
Negative: I'll never finish it, it's not worth starting.
Positive: I'll set aside time this afternoon to tackle it.

Situation: There's a party tonight and I haven't washed my hair.
Negative: Don't go, you look dreadful, you'll embarrass yourself.
Positive: I'll go for a bit, there's bound to be someone interesting to chat to.

We may self-attack as a panic or defence response to fears of mistakes or loss. It might be our way of trying to get rid of the stuff we don't like or to criticize ourselves before others do. It may be a habit, something we use often in a push to achieve.[12] The reasons why our self-critic is loud are complex and individual, but there is a big difference between motivation and bullying, between problem-solving and ruminating, between trying to make sense of something and jumping to conclusions that confirm a negative belief. Perhaps it's time to ask whether your internal judge is genuinely fair, accurate and helpful. And if it's not, how to change it.

Where kindness comes in

If we haven't heard enough constructive, kind voices in our lives, learning how to speak to ourselves in a compassionate way can feel weird and even wrong, because it's so unfamiliar. But if we do it often enough, it can become as natural as the critical voice. There are exercises to help strengthen that kinder voice in Part Three, and they are informed by something called compassion-focused therapy (CFT), which was developed by Professor Paul Gilbert and colleagues, who came up with the exercise above. This way of thinking was developed for those who are high in shame and self-criticism, who typically come from backgrounds with a history of neglect, abuse, bullying or lack of affection.[13] I've used it with many people who have a punishing inner critic and who find it hard to accept or show themselves kindness.

Some of these clients had tried cognitive behavioural therapy (CBT), which challenges negative thinking by offering alternative thoughts and behaviours.[14] Although they could see and understand the logic behind that, they couldn't feel it emotionally. It didn't shift their negative critic. This book – and my approach – uses compassion-focused therapy and acceptance and commitment therapy, both of which encourage a willingness to recognize, accept and allow the inner voice while also encouraging a move towards a more compassionate, values-led way of living your life. I've found them to be more helpful in understanding the power of anxiety – and this simple CFT idea, which comes from Paul Gilbert, explains it beautifully.

Threat-Drive-Soothe (or the Three Circles)

It's helpful for us to understand when our threat brain dominates and how to flip the switch from critical to compassionate. One way is by recognizing the Threat-Drive-Soothe systems, or the Three Circles approach.[15]

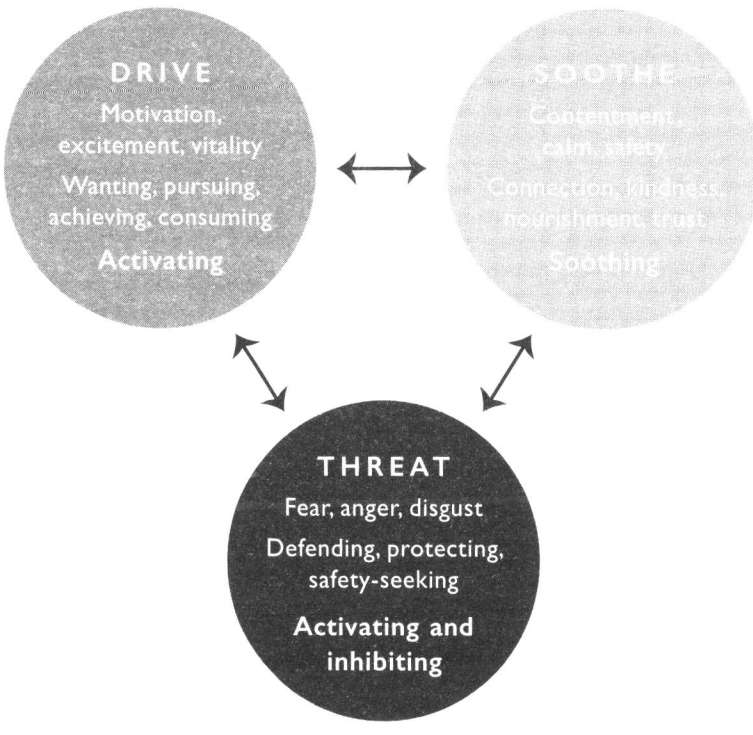

Imagine the brain has three systems, or circles. The first one is Threat. That's the one that triggers the fight-flight-freeze reaction. It scans for physical dangers, like being followed, and is also activated by thoughts, such as worrying about something bad happening. Threat takes a 'better safe than sorry' or 'worst-case scenario' approach. When we are in Threat, the body produces stress hormones like adrenaline and cortisol, our heart rate and blood pressure change, and we can get feelings of anxiety, anger and fear.

The next circle or system is Drive, which is sometimes triggered by Threat but is also linked to motivation and excitement. This is the one that tells us to pay attention to what we want and to change our behaviour to get it. It can feed into Threat by reminding us of what we're doing wrong and what we might lose unless we pull our finger out – for example, 'work harder or you'll be sacked'. It can also move us towards reward and pleasure, such as getting a hit of dopamine by playing video games or binge-watching TV. Threat and Drive both stimulate our sympathetic nervous system and get us ready to act.

The third system or circle is Soothe, or rest and digest. This is the one that calms us down by stimulating the parasympathetic system, releasing hormones like endorphins and oxytocin that give us a feeling of contentment, safety and trust to help dial down stress. It also deactivates the Threat system.[16] With anxiety, Soothe tends to be the least dominant one, but we can strengthen it by noticing when we have excessive levels

UNDERSTANDING THE INNER VOICE

of anxiety and negative thoughts which are controlling our feelings and behaviours. Then, rather than identifying with them, we observe them, creating a distance and defusing them. In other words, if our self-critical voice is keeping us in Threat and Drive, self-compassion gets us back to Soothe.[17]

We need all three systems working together – to recognize and respond to threats and dangers, to feel motivated to provide and achieve for ourselves and others, and to calm and soothe us to give us time to recharge. Sometimes though, one system is overactive and affects the way we think, feel and behave. Have a look at which of your systems is triggered more powerfully or frequently, and which isn't experienced as often.

Exercise: How balanced are you?[18]

We need all three systems – Threat, Drive and Soothe – working together in order to recognize and respond to threats and dangers, feel motivated to provide and achieve for ourselves and others, and calm and soothe ourselves to give us time to recharge. Sometimes though, one system is activated more often than the others and this can affect the way we think, feel and behave.

Have a look at this exercise and answer the questions honestly.

Then, when you're done, ask whether one system is triggered more powerfully or frequently, and which isn't experienced as often. Are there any which seem hard to access?

	THREAT	DRIVE	SOOTHE
How often is this system triggered? (daily? weekly? monthly?)			
What triggers it? (situations? people? places? thoughts? memories?)			
How powerful is it? (from 1–10: 1 being weak, 10 being strong)			
What thoughts come up when it's activated?			
Where do you feel it most in your body?			
What do you do when this system is triggered?			

If you feel a bit out of kilter, Part Three will give you some ideas about how to strengthen your Soothe system and start being a kinder friend to yourself. Before that, here's one more way of dealing with our 'stupid friend'.

UNDERSTANDING THE INNER VOICE

A Glaswegian approach to the 'stupid friend'

The brilliant Glaswegian comic Billy Connolly experienced abuse in his early years, and struggled with depression and alcohol problems. In a newspaper interview, he spoke about his negative self-talk and how he once heard it when he was in a flotation tank. Remember those? Lukewarm water in a pod, which you lie in, trying to relax. As he lay there, he became aware of what happened whenever he tried to make plans. That's when his inner voice would pipe up saying, 'No, you'll never do that. No, you're not good enough, not clever enough, you'll never go there.' He believes the voice relates to his past, to those who beat or shamed him, and he doesn't think he'll ever lose it. But he's learned to live with it. And in the tank, he raged at it. 'Away with you!' he yelled. 'Fuck off!'

I had a psychotherapist and mindfulness teacher called Lorraine who had a similar strategy. 'I have a psychological phrase that I'd like you to use for your self-critical voice,' she once said to me. 'I want you to tell it to fuck right off.' We laughed. She and I both knew that telling the negative inner voice to go away, shouting and yelling at it, feels good in the short term. But it always comes back.

I'll give you a glimpse into my self-critic in a bit. But first, here's psychotherapist and author Philippa Perry: 'I don't like "fuck off" because it fights right back and a bit of you still believes it. What you say is "this is familiar and just because it's familiar, it doesn't mean it's true". Or you say, "Thank you very much, I know you're trying to help, but if you wouldn't mind taking a back seat? I think I'm going to go into this one positively." I find if you talk respectfully to it rather than fighting it, it's fine.'

There's a technique called Passengers on the Bus that works for many of my clients, and it's explained in Chapter 8. But I also like this analogy of Philippa's: 'I think of those Japanese soldiers that were isolated in the South Pacific and they never realized that the war had ended in 1945. They kept finding them, wandering around, living off pigeons and still on high alert, ready to shoot the enemy. And what the Japanese government did when they found one, was say, "It's OK, you can stop fighting now. You've done a brilliant job." And I think that's a good way of talking to your critical voice. Retire it with full honours. Otherwise, it's going to get upset.'

Your punishing inner voice is not intentionally malicious or wrong; it's just based on an old script which may not serve you well now. You don't have to believe it, just acknowledge it, allow it to be there and bring a more compassionate view to it. You'll need to work a bit harder at developing those kinder neural pathways, because the brain's default is towards the negative. That's why to start with, it may feel counterintuitive, or wrong, or stupid. But developing compassion is just another habit – and the more we do it, the easier it becomes. Your brain is a muscle like any other. Exercise it, feed it with the right stuff and it gets stronger.

Billy Connolly laughs about how he used to respond to his inner critic and says he's still a work in progress.

UNDERSTANDING THE INNER VOICE

But what he now realizes is that 'you must never make decisions in your life based on that negative voice in your head… so many people do just that. You must always instead go with your primary thought, your hopeful thought. And that's what I try to do.'[19]

Chapter 4: A quick refresher

- Don't let the stupid, false voice make you feel a failure. You are not. You have strength and grace.
- Our self-critic often grew in childhood. It tries to help and motivate but can be harsh and judgemental.
- 'Should', 'ought' and 'must' punish and restrict. 'Might', 'like to' and 'willing to' open and expand.
- Self-silencing is rage turned inwards. Make peace with anger. Speak up. Say no. Find your voice.
- Busyness is the brain's way of avoiding the uncomfortable. Soften, soothe and allow for it.

5

High-Functioning Anxiety, Perfectionism and... Procrastination

'I've been absolutely terrified every moment of my life – and I've never let it keep me from doing a single thing I wanted to do.'

Georgia O'Keeffe[1]

The anxious creative

Georgia O'Keeffe knew what it was like to live under the weight of expectation, both hers and other people's. And yes, to forge on, even when terrified or criticized. She produced powerful paintings – often strong, sensual yet delicate flowers like lilies and orchids, which, as we know, are sensitive to their environment, just as she was to hers. The freedom to create was both exhilarating and exhausting, and you may understand that terrifying feeling of wanting to do something yet constantly questioning yourself whenever you try. Each time you allow yourself that opportunity to go with your instinct, your inner voice comes in, doubting you.

Another brilliant artist who experiences fear when she puts her life and emotions out there is the British singer and actor Self Esteem, or Rebecca Lucy Taylor. There's a track on her album *A Complicated Woman* called 'I Do and I Don't Care', with a line that goes, 'If I'm so empowered, why am I such a coward?'[2] In a newspaper interview she said that line sums up one of the album's big themes: 'I am political and I am outspoken and I really mean what I say. At the same time I'm shitting my pants that I get it wrong.' She says that since she became more visible as a performer, 'I'm terrified all the time. People are foaming at the mouth for women to make a mistake, especially confident women... walking on eggshells makes me overthink and gets me depressed.'[3]

Wanting to succeed, being terrified of getting it wrong, doing it anyway – the fear that comes with achievement is something I'm sure many of you can relate to. Competent, successful and accomplished on the outside. But inside, it's probably a very different picture.

High-functioning anxiety

I'm in the BBC's New Broadcasting House in central London and about to meet a screenwriter, TV producer and novelist. Daisy Goodwin is behind the hugely successful television show based on Queen Victoria's life, *Victoria*, which sold to nearly 150 countries. She also helped create series like *Grand Designs* and *Escape to the Country*, which have been running for more than twenty years on UK television. She's curated poetry anthologies and written bestselling novels. By anyone's reckoning that's a stunning CV. Oh, and when we get together, she's about to go into rehearsals for a stage play that she's written.

I got in touch with Daisy after she wrote a newspaper article on high-functioning anxiety.[4] She had described herself as calm and collected on the outside, but like custard on the inside, her mind 'fermenting' with anxiety. High-functioning anxiety (HFA) is not an official diagnosis, because those who experience it are usually efficient, disciplined and organized and their lives don't appear to be falling apart. Anxiety motivates them to achieve but it can also feel, as Daisy says, 'like a fire alarm that keeps going off in your head. Sometimes it goes off for a reason, sometimes it's just the batteries running down – but you can't be quite sure which it is.'

To see whether she still hears alarms going off, I read out some of the questions from her article. 'Is the book/script/play I'm writing any good? Are my children happy? Do I have any friends? Do they really like me? Am I a good person? Do I spend enough time talking to my family? Are all my thoughts inherently racist?' The list goes on and gets to existential questions about whether she's done anything worthwhile in life and if she's been a good mother. 'Do you still think those things?' I ask her. 'Yes,' she says, definitively. 'All those things. I mean, doesn't everybody feel like that?' 'Not everybody,' I say.

Daisy looks like she has it all under control. Colleagues call her powerful, brave, sometimes terrifying, which she describes as a weird disconnect to all this noise inside her head. How long has she felt like this? 'I've always had it,' she replies, simply. 'I've had two bouts of fully fledged depression which is different. But I'd say my default mode is anxious. And it's not anxiety like "have I turned the taps off or is the plane going to crash?" It's just always feeling the worst is going to happen. There are anxious people who are hypervigilant, and there are people like me who are constantly worried. Constantly, constantly worried.'

She worries about whether her two adult children will lead happy, successful lives, but mainly, it's about work. 'In the past that's been pathological to the extent where I get really upset and worried – times when I think, "Oh my God, I'll never work again. I'm going to be bankrupt and I'm going to live on the street." I mean, I know it sounds ridiculous but that's where I go to in my head. Lots of catastrophizing.'

When I speak to her, her current source of anxiety is around her play *By Royal Appointment*, and she talks through the new internal alarms going off now tickets have gone on sale. 'It hasn't sold out immediately and it wouldn't because it's not on until June, but you know, all the reviews will be shit. Will my leading actress, who is ninety, remember her lines? They are things that make me anxious.'

Think back to the Threat-Drive-Soothe systems. Daisy says she is on Threat and Drive all the time, and mostly it works for her and she gets some pretty amazing stuff done. Until she's so anxious, she can't do anything. 'It's about feeling that I'm not enough,' she says, 'so I'm constantly having to do more and more and more and more to prove that I have value.'

The fear of not being enough, which we heard about in the last chapter, is rooted in fear which makes those with HFA work harder and harder to prove their worth. They can overachieve, find it difficult to say no, and will spend their life people-pleasing and overthinking. They may discount compliments but soak up and believe perceived criticism or negative feedback. Many of those with HFA will also be perfectionists. Conscientiousness and diligence are fine, but if they come with a critical inner voice and unrealistically high standards, if you feel every bump in the road as a sign of failure, you're destined for guilt, shame and burnout.

Perfectionists, aka the maximizers

Many years ago, when you went for a job interview and sat in front of real people, they would ask you a question along these lines: 'What would you say is your greatest fault?' And you would reply, with a self-deprecating smile: 'Perfectionism.' Because who doesn't want a perfectionist on their team? They check the details, they stay late, they get stuff done. With high standards and even higher expectations, perfectionists are the anxious overachievers, the maximizers who squeeze every drop out of their social, home and work lives. They drive hard, are relentlessly busy, and make each moment count in their pursuit of excellence – but they are also likely to experience higher rates of anxiety, depression and eating disorders.[5] These perfectionist maximizers appear to make great clients, because they want to 'do therapy' perfectly, they'll take the advice and do all the homework, but they also need to see results, quickly. If they don't, they tend to drop out and blame themselves or the therapist, for failing to make it work.[6]

I know all this, because I have been both a perfectionist client and a perfectionist psychologist. And neither turned out well. During a particularly difficult time in my early adult life, when I was struggling with headaches, stomach pains, insomnia and fatigue, and thought I must have some crippling ailment, I took myself to the doctor. He said everything was fine physically, but when he asked me how I felt, I started crying. He sent me to a therapist with a note saying I had anxiety and depression. I'd never seen a psychologist before, nor did I think I needed one, although I knew I was tired and wired and if I wanted to keep my job and look after two small children, I had to pull myself together.

I entered the therapist's office to see a middle-aged woman with untidy grey hair in a bun and an unreadable expression on her face, sitting in a leather chair with a box of tissues on the table next to her. The clock on the wall ticked loudly, reminding me of every second that I was paying for her time. I sat down, opened my notebook and said, 'I'm here because the doctor thinks I'm anxious and sad. How do I feel better?'

She had that psychologist's sympathetic head-tilt. I've done this, we all have. I know, it's infuriating. 'Why don't we start at the beginning?' she said. 'Tell me about what life was like as a child.'

Tick, tick went the clock. 'Not sure that's relevant,' I said, with no psychological knowledge whatsoever. 'Can we just jump to the bit where you tell me how to stop feeling sad and anxious?'

Her heart must have sunk. Because it takes time, looking into the crevices of the mind, and I didn't seem willing to give it or go there. I wanted a quick, results-driven way of getting from A to B, from anxious to balanced. Preferably a plan which didn't involve the mucky stuff. Let's maximize the therapy. Get in, get out and get on with my life. Please.

If she *had* gone back to childhood, she would have found parents who weren't university-educated but knew the value of education. My father understood poverty and wanted none of us to go there. Do well at school, get decent jobs, save for a pension. Give more than anyone asks of you, don't cause a fuss, be kind, keep learning and pushing forward. He was a fiercely intelligent and curious man, completing A levels during the Covid lockdown in March 2020, starting a degree in his seventies and completing a novel in his eighties. He set the bar high and I was always trying to reach it. Mum used to say he was proud of me, although he didn't tell me explicitly. I was with him when he was dying in the hospice, and when a doctor came and stood by his bed, she introduced herself to him. 'I'm Dr Wilson,' she said. My dad pointed towards me. 'My daughter,' he said, barely able to speak. 'Also, a doctor.' Now, I thought. Now he's proud.

Perfectionism – good, bad, or both?

Those values of hard work and constant improvement have served me well, as they probably have you. When things are in balance, the inner voice can make you conscientious and help you better yourself. It can be encouraging and motivating, reminding you that the exam is not going to pass itself, or that it might be fun to try something new, like learning a new language or dance step or changing career. Sometimes though, as we know, it can become punishing. Researchers call this 'good' and 'bad' perfectionism.[7] The good seems to help you strive and thrive; the bad can lead to stress, anxiety and burnout. The good appears to have a dose of kindness to it, reminding you to stop and recharge. The bad is hectoring and, as well as anxiety, forms the root of many other mental health issues like obsessive compulsive disorder, social phobia, insomnia and disordered eating, including orthorexia or obsessively healthy eating.[8] If you're interested in whether that voice pushes you or punishes you, this short exercise, developed by US psychologist Alexandra Burgess and colleagues, might be for you.

Exercise: What kind of perfectionist are you?[9]

Look at the statements below – how closely do you agree? 1 = Strongly disagree, 2 = Disagree, 3 = Neither agree nor disagree, 4 = Agree, 5 = Strongly agree.

1. If I fail at work/school, I am a failure as a person.
2. I set higher goals than most people.
3. If someone does a task at work/school better than me, then I feel like I failed the whole task.
4. I have extremely high goals.
5. Other people seem to accept lower standards for themselves than I do.
6. If I do not do well all the time, people will not respect me.
7. I expect higher performance in my daily tasks than most people.
8. The fewer mistakes I make, the more people will like me.

You'll see that one set of statements (2, 4, 5, 7) are about having high goals and expecting the same from others – *striving*. The second set of statements (1, 3, 6, 8) are about the fear of failure or mistakes and what that means for your self-worth and perceived likability – *evaluative concerns*. With both, the higher the score, the more perfectionistic you are, but it's the second set, the evaluative concerns, that generally links to more distress. In one large study of hundreds of students, those with higher perfectionistic scores on evaluative concerns were the ones who were more anxious and depressed.[10] That's understandable.

You're more likely to experience anxiety and depression if you think your failures and mistakes are attributed to self-worth and being liked and valued. Striving *can* be adaptive – but pushing too hard, for too long, with unrealistically high standards, can also lead to burnout.

I ask Daisy Goodwin whether she considers herself to be a perfectionist and she replies that she doesn't know, so I read out some of the common perfectionist traits to see if she recognizes herself. These Five Processes of Unhelpful Perfectionism come from clinical psychologist Jennifer Kemp.[11] See how many ring true for you.

The Five Processes of Unhelpful Perfectionism

1. Setting very high, inflexible and ambitious standards, which are repeatedly raised and which you think say something about who you are.

2. An intense fear of failure, with little or no celebration when you meet a goal or standard, just relief that you haven't failed.

3. Relentless self-criticism and shame, which leave you thinking you are never good enough.

4. Persistent attempts to avoid failure and self-criticism by avoiding people, places and situations, or using busyness, overwork or obsessiveness.

5. Long-term problems in life, such as procrastination or burnout, because of avoidance and an unwillingness to experience failure.

Daisy answers a definitive 'yes' to all of them. 'They all make total sense,' she says. The high standards, self-criticism and shame really resonate. 'I mean, if I lie in bed in the morning, I feel guilty that I'm not doing something.' Daisy's go-to self-soothe is a second-hand clothes site. 'When I'm feeling anxious, that's what I do to calm myself down. I look at all the second-hand clothes and I look up an hour later.' Does it stop negative thinking? 'Quite often, yeah, it's displacement activity. An hour on the site and I'm no longer ricocheting in my head. The bump, the ache has gone.'

Temporary relief and soothing for a while. There's a fine line though, between an engaging distraction that allows you to rest and recharge and something you use to block or avoid difficult emotions. Noticing why you're doing it gives you a pause to step back and see if that line's being crossed.

For Daisy, guilt propels her back to work and she works phenomenally hard. When the compliments come in, they are harder to believe than her own self-critical voice. She says she may feel 'burnished' for a while, but it doesn't last because 'self-criticism kicks in and no one wants to be the person who believes their own publicity'. Her fear of failure drives her hard, forcing her to do 'more and more and more' to prove she has value. Yet working harder and doing more is risky because 'with that, of course, is the threat of rejection and all those things. It's a horrible spiral to be in. I am doing more, but in doing more, I risk failure.'

'Is it being seen to fail, or the failing itself?' I ask.

'Both,' she says.

The rise of perfectionism

There are lots of high-functioning, anxious perfectionists like Daisy out there. Perfectionism has become more common in the past three decades with a rise in competitiveness and individualism, increasing the pressure to succeed and excel.[12] Dr Thomas Curran, a researcher in perfectionism and associate professor at the London School of Economics, says overly focusing on achievement means even those who accomplish a lot and are seen to be doing so, may not feel good enough. They reach the goal, they feel like they have more to prove, they set another, even higher goal.[13]

Perfectionism is experienced differently by all of us, and it exists on a spectrum with different dimensions to it too.[14] The first dimension, 'self-orientated perfectionism', is when you have extremely high standards and a strong self-critical voice. This can drive you to succeed and be healthy if you enjoy what you're doing, can occasionally be less precise and know when you need to take a breath and a break. 'Neurotic' – or highly anxious – perfectionists don't.[15] They strive for excellence to an unhealthy extreme and will self-attack if they don't think they're getting there, either working to burnout, constantly re-adjusting the goal or persistently procrastinating. More on how to deal with procrastination later in the chapter.

The next perfectionist dimension is called 'other-orientated', which means expecting others to match your own high standards and feeling angry or let down if they don't meet them. Someone who jumps out of bed in the morning because they feel like they're wasting the day and they need to be maximizing their waking hours may become frustrated, and show it, if their partner doesn't do the same. Colleagues who put everything and more into their job, setting goals and targets for themselves and perhaps working more hours than they're paid, might get tetchy when others don't appear to put in the same effort. It can feel as though you're constantly being let down and disappointed.

Finally, the biggest and most destructive dimension, 'socially prescribed perfectionism'.[16] That's when you think other people expect very high standards from you and you must meet them to be accepted. For those with low self-esteem and a strong self-critical voice, making mistakes or showing imperfection may reveal what you truly believe about yourself – that you are worthless and unlovable. Far safer to keep striving, keep achieving, keep reaching towards that perfect person, who will be so much better than the self you are now. There you will be energized, successful and confident, and then, finally, you can afford to loosen up a bit and show your authentic self. The problem is, you may never reach that goal and you may not know what an authentic self feels like anyway, because you have spent so long second-guessing what you think other people expect of you. When praise, love and recognition come through achievement, continuing to succeed might be the only way of understanding how worthwhile you are as a person.

This is the difference between the internal and external referencing we heard about in Chapter 3. External referencing is when our identity is set by how we see ourselves in the world. Internal referencing is when we are guided by our own values – our North Star, if you like. An externally referencing perfectionist will think that if they are good, hard-working, compliant and as near to their ideal self as possible, then they'll be accepted and loved. If they show frailty or failure, they won't be. In a study of studies looking at more than 40,000 students across the UK, Canada and the United States over the course of nearly three decades, all forms of perfectionism had risen but this socially prescribed perfectionism saw the biggest spike.[17] That's damaging, because it's the one linked most closely to depression, anxiety and suicidal thoughts.[18]

I saw a lot of this kind of perfectionism when I worked as a counsellor for a top London university. Many of the students who came for therapy were international. Their parents or grandparents helped them financially and they needed to get the results to prove they were worth it. The pressure often led to a common perfectionist avoidance tactic – procrastination. One student told me her self-doubt about what was expected of her had stopped her attending lectures and workshops, which was a 'waste of money, as I'm not learning'. This led to her falling behind, which created shame and stress, intensifying the anxiety and leading to more avoidance.

A medical student who came from a family of doctors told me: 'My siblings are more focused, reliable and will achieve much more than me.' I asked her what her positive qualities were. She said it felt arrogant to talk about them but freely gave me the negative ones, including being childish, undisciplined, unfocused and apathetic. 'I NEED to succeed,' she stressed. Another said she thought she was always being judged and had become obsessed with an 'ideal' body shape. She would go for long periods without eating, then binge and purge, resulting in deep feelings of shame, disgust and the belief that she was 'out of control, stupid, ugly and undesirable'.

These students were at a university that was incredibly hard to get into. Some were master's students. Most had parents who were critical or had high expectations of them. All were perfectionists, struggling with self-esteem, who felt incredibly lonely.

Why lonely? Because this high-achieving, performative way of being and the hyper-competitiveness that comes with it can lead to isolation and disconnection. Wanting to be perfect so others will like and value you, may be the very thing that turns them away. It's also exhausting. In a study of UK schoolteachers and healthcare workers, those with higher levels of socially prescribed perfectionism were more likely to suffer from workplace stress, inefficiency, burn-out, exhaustion and cynicism.[19] I bet none of their co-workers knew they were struggling, instead praising their efficiency and giving them more work. As the phrase goes, 'If you want something done, give it to a busy person' – the one who seems to be plate-spinning, effortlessly. Until they tire and grind to a halt and the whole lot comes crashing to the ground. In their heads at least. On the outside, you may not see it at all, so effectively have they masked their own distress.

Embracing failure

Perfectionists often see failure as dangerous. But it's worth asking yourself what failure you fear most. Perhaps it's academic failure, or parental rejection. It may be that you fear your workmates will realize you don't fit in, because you're not clever enough. If your internal self-worth is based on external praise or feedback and you don't get it, that's a crushing blow to your confidence. It might lead to deep feelings of inadequacy, with heightened levels of overthinking and overworking. In this threat state, we can discount our strengths and key supports. We can't hear the good, we can only hear the alarm bells of the bad.

Are there positives to failure? Well, if you have been brought up thinking that failure gives you a chance to learn, you are more likely to have a growth mindset, rather than a fixed one. Parents with a negative approach to failure might comfort a child by telling them that it's OK because they don't have the ability or intelligence for the task anyway. That child then believes those qualities are fixed and can't be developed. But the parents who see failure as a chance to learn have children who tend to have a more flexible, growth-based approach to making mistakes.[20]

Daisy's mum wasn't around to teach her how to manage failure. She left her when she was five years old. Disinherited her, too. Daisy puts her anxiety down to that early trauma of suddenly feeling rejected and unsafe. Now, she won't allow herself to feel safe very often, because, 'it could be taken away, which means I'm powerless'. Hence the need to keep working, striving and driving, to prove she's good enough and has value. Together with a need to make sure no one gets cross with her.

People-pleasing perfectionism

Daisy tells me she was once in therapy and wanted to finish it but was too anxious to do so, because she thought the therapist would become upset. Instead, she waited until the therapist retired. She says yes to things she doesn't want to do. She buys things because she 'can't bear the idea of disappointing the shop assistant'.

Also, she cannot show anger, and we've already seen how damaging this self-silencing can be for mind and body. Anyone with a strong inner voice who has been rejected or dismissed, or grown up in an unpredictable, chaotic environment, may feel anger – but it might be too risky to show it. Instead, like the anxious imploders we heard about in the previous chapter, perfectionists learn to be conflict-avoidant and turn the anger on themselves, which heightens the self-criticism and affects their body's stress response.[21] Perfectionists also learn that achievement, pleasing people and ensuring they are 'good' feel safer than expressing what's really going on. Daisy and I joke about creating a 'rage room' for high-functioning, perfectionist, anger-avoiding people-pleasers. Until then, she's learning how to box, because she thinks 'hitting things is quite helpful'. For me, I take my rage outside and occasionally have a scream, deep in the fields where no one can hear. It's a great stress release and there's a proper psychological term for it, too. It's called 'somatic release', and we'll explore it in Part Three.

Until then, here are some other ways of managing it...

Tips to manage perfectionism – and procrastination

Know when it's useful

In sport, psychologists think perfectionistic striving can be useful in pursuing excellence and pushing athletes to do their best, potentially leading to better results and greater progress.[22] These sportsmen and sportswomen place a high value on perfectionism and may not want to give it up, believing it drives them towards the goal they train for hours, days and months to reach. And they can be right about that. The precise, exacting rules for life and the dedication and discipline that come with them can lead to great success. But when perfectionists worry that they'll be judged harshly, if they are terrified of not meeting their own standards, or if fear and doubt sneak in and affect their performance, that's when the trouble starts.[23]

Know when it's not

American gymnastic legend Simone Biles pulled out of the team competition at the 2020 Olympics in Tokyo after experiencing something called 'the twisties'. The twisties is a mental block when the body and brain stop talking to one another while the gymnast is airborne, causing them to lose their sense of where they are as they are in the air. Biles told US podcast host Alex Cooper that it's like driving, except one day you wake up and 'have no idea how to drive a car, your legs are going crazy, you have no control of your body. You've been doing something for so long, and you now no longer have control. It's terrifying.'[24]

Simone was experiencing anxiety and panic before the Olympics, and said she was already fighting demons and having twisties in training but wanted to compete for her team and country. At the beginning of the team final, she was chalking up her hands, looking at the vault, when she suddenly realized she didn't know what she was going to do. She ran, she jumped, she completed one and a half twists, but she was a twist short and her body and brain didn't know where she was. When she landed on her feet, Simone's first thought was not 'thank goodness I'm alive' but 'America hates me, the world is going to hate me'.

She has won eleven Olympic medals and thirty World Championship medals, is the most decorated US gymnast in history, and what was expected of her was gold. If she didn't get it, she said, it wasn't worth going back home. Simone knew she needed to stop and prioritize her mental wellbeing. To learn to live with less-than-perfect. 'Put your mental health first,' she said afterwards. 'It doesn't matter if you're on the biggest stage, that's more important than any medal you could win.'[25] Back in competition in the 2024 Olympics in Paris, Simone made mistakes in a floor exercise which cost her the gold. She won silver instead and she beamed with pride as she collected her medal, commenting afterwards that 'you win with grace and you lose with grace'.[26] Win or lose, gold, silver or walking away with nothing, give yourself the grace to fail.

Dump the self-blame

Think about what you were told about mistakes and failure when you were growing up. The fixed or growth mindset on failure I talked about earlier was also shown in a study in the US and China looking at how parental responses to failure affected a child's functioning. If that child came home with a lower-than-expected test score but the parents focused on what they got right rather than wrong, the child showed greater wellbeing. It's called a 'success-orientated response'. A 'failure-orientated response', concentrating on what they got wrong, led to worse wellbeing, including higher levels of depression and anxiety.'[27]

Embrace imperfection

This is a hard one, especially when we are bombarded with pro-perfectionist messaging on social media, such as images of the perfect life, career, skin, body, relationship, meal, outfit. I suggest you seek out more supportive online areas, with less perfectionist tendencies. There's evidence among perfectionists with disordered eating patterns that seeing contrasting pro- and anti-perfectionist messages, some in favour, some against, can help tackle perfectionism and provide a more balanced approach.[28] Be an imperfectionist for a while and see how you respond to it. Start very small, like wearing mismatched socks or going without make-up. In the next chapter I'll tell you about a fascinating experiment which suggests that while your mistakes and imperfections seem huge, hardly anyone notices but you.

Spot when you're trapped in perfectionist thinking.

Common perfectionist thinking includes thoughts like 'I must make the most of every minute', 'I must always be working towards something', 'I find it hard to do nothing', 'I never feel at ease', 'I get frustrated, irritable or angry when things don't work out', 'I always push myself to do my best', 'I must please someone', 'I am always under pressure'.

If you find yourself saying some of these things to yourself, recognize them as coming from a place of perfectionism. It's only your brain trying to protect you from failure, perceived criticism and rejection. Perhaps ask yourself what striving for perfect achieves, and whether you can make room for feelings and thoughts that come with uncertainty and making mistakes. What can you move towards without believing that you're compromising? And ask yourself too: Whose praise are you still seeking? Whose love are you hoping to earn? How much do you need to succeed before you feel you have worth?

Be kinder to yourself

Perfectionists who have unrealistically high expectations and are overly critical of themselves are also less likely to show self-compassion,[29] the very thing that can help them. As we know from the previous chapter, self-criticism comes so much more easily than self-compassion, because our old, primal brain needs us to keep watch for threats and dangers even when they don't exist. Compassion brings self-forgiveness to our ordinary human frailties, and if we weren't taught it or shown it, it can be hard to find. Part Three has exercises designed to help develop it, for those who didn't learn how to soothe themselves, or who can't find a kind voice in their head. The brain is plastic. Well, not literally, but it does respond to a change in habits, even if it feels weird and wrong at first.

See if you can set lower standards

Psychotherapist Philippa Perry believes 'perfectionism is the enemy to getting anything done, because you can't perfect anything'. She tells me perfectionists need a 'that'll do' attitude. 'If you're a perfectionist, you can get frozen. You can't make a choice, whereas if you're a that'll-doer, you have a much better life. I think you're only allowed to be a perfectionist when you're decorating a cake, that's it.'

Recognize when you're procrastinating

If you feel overwhelmed by the things that need doing and panicked by failing at them, there can be a tendency to just... stop. Everyone procrastinates, and the worse we feel, the easier it is to avoid the task. Whatever we choose to put in its place – watching videos on the internet, getting another snack, tackling smaller non-urgent tasks – we are avoiding uncomfortable feelings and replacing them with a short-term, feel-good hit of something else. Later, with the big task still not done, we may beat ourselves up for it.

Boston-based psychologist Dr Ellen Hendriksen says that 'for those of us who are hard on ourselves, procrastination is stickiest around tasks that involve some kind of judgment: we'll get graded, reviewed, reacted to, or open ourselves and our work to the opinions of others'. This, she says 'takes the task to a kryptonite level of aversion'.[30] How to get out of procrastination? Start, even if you feel crappy, accept the negative emotions and break down the task into tiny micro-steps. Understand, be patient and forgive yourself your procrastination.[31] And then jump towards your future self and try to vividly imagine what you might look and feel like from there.

Dr Eve-Marie Blouin-Hudon did this with nearly 200 Canadian students. She tested their levels of procrastination and visualization and then divided them into two groups. One group did a present-moment awareness meditation for four weeks; the other was asked to visualize themselves at the end of the semester, through their own and other people's eyes. After a month, those able to vividly – and empathically – imagine their future self, procrastinated less. She suggests that procrastinators tend to be impulsive, focusing on how they felt in the moment, rather than seeing the effort they'd put in from an imagined, future point. Looking back from a future self helped them to feel more empathic and connected to their goals.³²

Find your flow

Several perfectionists find being in a flow state gets them out of their thinking brain and into a more meditative, less self-conscious mood, where they are not overanalysing every move. Have a think about how it feels when you are in a place where you find your focus and can be swept along, conscious and content but without the soundtrack that's alerting you that someone's watching, or you're doing it wrongly. When you're in a flow state, that's when you are authentically responding to the things you love doing and being.

Here's a personal example. I loved presenting *BBC Breakfast*. Loved it. Eleven years, working with a great team, reacting to news as it's thrown at you. Three and a half hours of live TV with no time to overthink. Stuff went wrong, constantly. You'd muck up an interview, or the technology would go down, or you'd suddenly have to fill because the next guest hadn't shown up. It was a high-wire act and one where I felt mostly in control, but if the wobble came, I knew I could steady the pole, find my footing and right myself. Occasionally though, when I presented the flagship *BBC News at Ten*, my inner critic would go into overdrive. I'd spend all day preparing, then chatting with correspondents, writing, and then waiting to get on air. And in the waiting space came the self-doubt and, with that, questions that weren't helpful – like whether I deserved to be there in the first place. When you are in your body but also looking back at yourself with a harsh self-critical voice, you can't be in the present. You're already trying to second-guess how others are reacting to you. In the next chapter, Radiohead's drummer Philip Selway chats about how he managed when his inner critic got the better of him.

Flow is a way out. When Daisy Goodwin is 'mega-anxious', flow takes her out of it. 'The only thing that combats anxiety in my experience is actual work or the pleasure of creating something, when I get really lost in a project. When I know that I'm going to get up and write 1,000 words and if I can get lost in the creative process, then that's when the anxiety goes away.' It comes back when she allows her self-critical voice to intervene. 'It only takes one email or whatever and you're suddenly like "wahhhh!" And then you're in a vortex of horrible and you can't even remember what triggered it.' That email or comment fires up the anxious inner voice and fears of judgement and failure, but Daisy tries to put it to one side. 'Yes, it will be judged,' she says, 'but people are more compassionate than we think.'

Remind yourself that you matter

Healthy strivers may get knocked back, fail and experience rejection, but inside they know they still matter. Feeling like you don't matter to others, or that you need to achieve or succeed to matter, can lead to self-promotional perfectionism, isolation and depression.[33] Perfectionists who don't feel they matter, especially those with a tendency for socially prescribed perfectionism, may engage in endless self-publicity or avoid revealing failings and mistakes.[34]

It can be hard to feel that you matter if you've spent a lifetime trying to please those who can never be pleased. We know that feeling valued by others, irrespective of expectations or success, leads to lower rates of anxiety and depression and higher levels of motivation.[35] If you haven't had that, you'll need to nurture it in yourself. You *do* matter. You have always mattered. Don't let other people's expectations, judgments and opinions convince you that you don't.

People don't care about you as much as you think they do

We are not the focus of attention for most people, even if we might think we are constantly being noticed and evaluated. This feeling of being under scrutiny goes back to our hardwired brain and needing to defend ourselves from the threat of being excluded, and it's called 'the spotlight effect'. In the next chapter, we'll look at how this heightened sensitivity can lead to performance anxiety, imposter syndrome and social anxiety, and what to do about it.

Chapter 5: A quick refresher

- Maximizers live on the Threat and Drive systems until the body burns out – learn to pause and bring in the Soothe.

- Perfectionism and procrastination are ways of trying to avoid criticism and failure. Try being imperfect.

- There is no finish line when you finally become perfect. Enjoy the relief in letting go of the goal.

- Striving can be useful but always ask yourself: who am I doing this for and when can I stop?

- You matter. With your flaws and failures and frailties. You have always mattered.

6

Imposter Syndrome, Performance and Social Anxiety

'I'm a creep, I'm a weirdo. What the hell am I doing here? I don't belong here'

Radiohead, 'Creep'[1]

What am I doing here?

It's 1993 and the band Radiohead are on their first world tour, following the release of their debut album, *Pablo Honey*, and the phenomenal success of their first single, 'Creep', with its angsty themes of alienation and shame. Banned by the BBC for being 'too depressing',[2] the song became a UK Top Ten chart hit and helped launch the band's career on both sides of the Atlantic. A year before, the group of student friends were playing in pubs in Oxford; now they were on a 350-date tour across Europe and North America.

For Philip Selway, Radiohead's drummer, that year of touring was one of the most uncomfortable of his life. 'There were expectations of what you should be, what you *feel* you should be as a musician. Trying to navigate all these new experiences and all this feedback – positive, negative – everything became very intense,' he tells me. 'And that really fed into imposter syndrome for me and I had very intense performance anxiety for a lot of that year. I can think of one tour, which happened in the autumn in the States, and I just couldn't really play. It became quite noticeable.' Noticeable to him, or to others, I ask. 'Very strongly to me,' he says, 'but to other people as well. To the point where it was mentioned. And there wasn't a magic solution to that.'

Imposter syndrome is where you doubt your skills, intellect or achievements. It was first identified as 'imposter phenomenon' back in the 1970s by two American doctors, Pauline Rose Clance and Suzanne Imes, who initially noticed it among high-achieving women – but it can affect all ages and genders.[3] Clance later said that they should have called it the 'imposter experience', because 'it's not a syndrome or a complex or a mental illness, it's something almost everyone experiences'.[4]

There is no official diagnosis of the imposter phenomenon or experience, but it's linked to what we've already talked about: perfectionism, impossible-to-reach standards, overestimating mistakes, excessive comparison with others, and a fear of failure.[5] Those with imposter syndrome can also fear success, as doing well means you just set yourself a higher target.[6] Because they think their achievements are down to luck, that they're not good enough to be where they are, that they'll be found out, they keep working and working, driven by the self-critical voice – often experiencing anxiety, depression, low self-esteem and burnout.[7]

Philip Selway had experienced this kind of anxiety before, at school. 'That kind of anxiety that you get from impostor syndrome, feeling less than. I think how I navigated that was I'd be fired up about music and I would just jump in with both feet and think, "ohh, God, did I do that? No, that's not like me."' But on the band's debut tour in front of thousands of people, instead of immersing himself in music, all he could think about was not being able to perform. Night after night, for a whole year, all over the world. 'When what you're doing and what you're recognized for doing isn't working for you, then you can't mask it at that point,' he says. As he struggled, his inner voice was telling him he wasn't the genuine article – that he was going to mess up and 'look an absolute fool in front of all these people'.

Before we hear what happened to him, let's clarify a few things. Anxiety about being in front of others is normal. Few of us will get to perform to an arena full of expectant fans, but most of us will get nervous if we're suddenly asked to present in front of colleagues, or we're invited to a party where we don't know anyone. We fear we'll embarrass ourselves or we won't fit in, and that's understandable. If this anxiety becomes persistent, though, if we overestimate the threat and underestimate our ability to cope, if we start worrying about worry and avoiding people or situations, that's when it gets in the way of life. These feelings can go under different names, but they share similar characteristics.

Performance anxiety is related to the imposter phenomenon, but different. To feel like an imposter, you are usually in a job where you appear successful but believe you don't deserve it or will be found out as a fake. Performance anxiety can happen to anyone. Its main characteristic is a fear of speaking or performing in public before the judgemental gaze of others. The effects are like the other anxiety fight-flight-freeze symptoms: you might experience a rapid heartbeat and breathlessness, you may sweat or shake, have a dry mouth and difficulty swallowing, your stomach may clench, you might blush or find your mind has gone blank. This typically comes with thoughts about failure, embarrassment or humiliation, which only make the anxiety worse.

Social anxiety is also a real fear of people thinking badly of you. But while performance anxiety occurs when you're performing or public speaking, social anxiety can happen in everyday situations like being in a queue, or eating with others,[8] or chatting in the workplace. The hallmark of social anxiety is a fear of *any* social situation which might provoke ridicule, criticism or rejection. Social anxiety is not shyness or introversion. An introvert can enjoy social situations but will probably need to recharge afterwards. Someone who is shy may feel socially reserved or uncomfortable but will not feel the same level of fear as those with social anxiety.[9]

Although this book isn't about specific anxiety disorders, it might give you an idea of how common social anxiety is if I tell you that, in the US, more than one in ten people will experience it in such a persistent and distressing way at some point in their lives that it qualifies as social anxiety disorder – appropriately called SAD – or social phobia.[10] To be officially diagnosed with it, you need to meet several conditions – to have intense fear and anxiety provoked by social situations, causing feelings of humiliation, embarrassment or rejection out of proportion to the actual threat, which you endure or avoid and which has been persistent for at least six months.[11]

If the figure of around one in ten people experiencing SAD sounds high, it's much, much higher in those with autism. Around half of those with autism are thought to experience social anxiety, and it looks and feels different to those with autism too.[12] Later in this chapter, one of my clients explains why her autism means she would 'rather stick pins in my eyes' than go to some social events.

I don't belong here

But back to drummer Philip Selway, on a stage in 1993, struggling to find the beat and knowing his bandmates could hear that struggle too. 'That was probably the strongest kind of anxiety, because they're dependent on you performing, so you don't want to let them down. And we've always been very cohesive as a band, but there was a slightly competitive element to what we were doing and you just think, "Oh my God, I'm writing myself out of this particular story at the moment." And you're trying to process all of that in the midst of a show.'

Among what he called all these 'bizarre events', he was just starting a relationship with his future wife, Cait, 'and it was like going through a period of rewriting yourself quickly but trying to hold on to the essence of yourself as well.' Cait was incredibly supportive during this time, when not being able to play felt dangerous. 'I was carrying a lot of tension in my body and there was this lag between the limbs, which isn't great as a drummer, and I really felt it in my bass drum. And that just all went to pot. I had no control over it, so it would just throw all the play. And you're there, with so much of the spotlight on you.'

The spotlight effect

Philip's experience was an extreme example of the spotlight effect.[13] That's when you think everyone's attention is focused on you and they're judging you, harshly. Most of us don't get to perform on world stages, but we all overestimate how much people notice our flaws and mistakes. The only person really paying that much attention to you is you. The thoughts of how you look, or sound, or behave are just that – your private thoughts. No one else can hear them, but it feels like they're on loudspeaker. It's called 'the illusion of transparency'.[14] We assume that all our thoughts and feelings, all our shame, embarrassment and terror, are leaking out for everyone to see, making us even more anxious.

Here's an example of the spotlight effect from a study where American students at Cornell University were given a T-shirt with the face of the singer Barry Manilow on it. The students felt embarrassed wearing it. I wouldn't have been. I've seen Manilow in concert. He was great. In this experiment though, the T-shirt was considered uncool, and the students believed the social spotlight was suddenly shining on them. But they significantly overestimated how many people clocked the T-shirt. They thought around half would see it, and only a quarter did. When students were given a cooler T-shirt with Bob Marley on it, again they thought lots of people would be paying attention to them, but few noticed. Researchers then looked at positive comments and minor gaffes made by individuals in a group setting and, once again, the contributors thought they'd stand out far more than they did.[15]

Whether it's an embarrassing T-shirt, a gaffe, a poor public performance or even just a bad hair day, the research suggests people are much less aware of our feelings, failings and faults than we fear. And if we just kept doing the thing we think is humiliating, it would start to feel a lot less painful too. When students started wearing the Barry Manilow T-shirt more frequently, they became less embarrassed and thought fewer people would notice them. In other words, repeated exposure and becoming used to something reduces the spotlight effect. The trouble is, we often don't allow ourselves to sit with the discomfort and get to that stage.

The avoidance trap

Escape seems to be the best option in a profoundly uncomfortable social situation where you think you'll be criticized, rejected, humiliated or judged. But the more you fear and the more you avoid, the less opportunity there is to see how you'll manage, and whether you can develop and test your coping strategies. The more you avoid, the more intimidating those situations become, the more you fear them, the more you avoid them, and so on.

Anxiety, shame and embarrassment are common, but those with social anxiety are more likely to experience envy too, comparing themselves to others and finding themselves lacking.[16] Typically, they are also prone to distraction, can find it hard to judge reactions, have difficulty remembering positive experiences, are intolerant of uncertainty,[17] and can't shift their attention away from the social threat. Envy, fear, misjudgement and threat – throw in negative thinking and a feared lack of control, and it's not surprising they just want to high-tail it from the threatening social environment and get to safety.

Professor Oliver Robinson at the Anxiety Lab in London is currently using a social anxiety stress test, 'where you tell someone out of the blue that you've got to prepare for a speech to give to twenty people. It makes people feel anxious because they've got to do something. But it's *social* anxiety because you're worried about embarrassing yourself.' That anxiety is often rooted in a previous experience. Say you remember delivering a presentation which you felt you bombed at. When you're asked to do another, you're reminded of it. That activates thoughts of feeling worthless or stupid, which makes your mind run through all the worst-case scenarios and prompts your body to react to this latest request with a hot flush of fear. To avoid all this, you either work insanely hard, or procrastinate, or try to duck out of it altogether. Which means when you *do* come to present, you may be tired and perform badly, confirming your original belief that you must be rubbish.

Flexing our social muscle

A lot of us lost the habit of social behaviour during the pandemic. Even psychotherapist Philippa Perry, who loves meeting new people, felt her social muscle atrophy. 'I was so looking forward to my first social thing after lockdown,' she says, describing a friend's book launch. 'I strode in confidently and I just didn't know what to say to people. I've never felt so socially awkward in my life. I lasted forty-five minutes before I thought "I can't stand it anymore" and left. I just couldn't cope with it. I just couldn't do it.' She kept thinking, 'I don't know what to say, I'm making a fool of myself. Everyone else seems so competent.'

It took a long time to return to her pre-pandemic sociable self. 'And I forced myself through, because I knew from the past that, yeah, I enjoy this sort of thing. I like parties, I like book launches and private views and dinner parties. But it took me months, if not a year, to get fully back into the swing of it. Now I'm looking forward to every party on the calendar, looking forward to you coming round this afternoon, really looking forward to things.' I ask her what helped. 'Nothing really helped, except for exposure and doing it again. I just had to flex my muscle,' she answers. 'I just had to flex the social muscle.'

The only way out is through

Learning to live with your anxiety means seeing the difficult moments through to the other side – step by step.

Step One: Do the thing you fear

Avoiding social situations makes life smaller and reinforces the anxiety. And as Philippa Perry says, the most effective way to deal with it is to push on through. It can be frightening and uncomfortable, but doing the thing you fear is the top intervention for social anxiety, because you build up a tolerance for uncertainty by experimenting and testing your assumptions. This does not mean staying in a frightening situation if you are panicking, but predicting what you think will happen, then going into the situation – and afterwards, judging whether it accurately matched your fears. You test your prediction with the outcome, and you do it across lots of different social situations. Let's find out first what situations make you anxious and why.

Exercise: My feared situations[18]

Write down all the social situations which make you anxious, rank them, then rate how distressed each one makes you feel, from 0 (no distress) to 10 (maximum distress) and finally, what strategies or safety behaviours you use to deal with the feelings.

Rank	Situation	How distressing?	Strategy/safety behaviour

Next, take one of those situations and really imagine what it would be like to be in it. What are your first automatic *feelings*?

Now fill in the table below.

Thoughts about what others will think/feel about you and how they will behave	My own thoughts and feelings about myself
They will think/feel... 1. 2. 3. My key fear is that they will:	I think I am... 1. 2. 3. My key fear is that I will:

Given these key fears, what are your main coping behaviours and what might you do to stop any possible feared outcome? What have you learned from this exercise?

Ranking your hierarchy of feared situations is a common CBT technique which can help you understand what is driving your anxious behaviour and what you try to do to escape, avoid or withdraw from it. In exposure therapy,[19] you would normally test them out, taking one of the situations, predicting what you think will happen, engaging in the social activity and then measuring predictions against what *actually* happens. This can help rebuild self-confidence one small step at a time, but do not rush this. If the situation that you're testing feels overwhelming, then go to a less feared one. You can also practise one step many times.

Step Two: Notice your safety behaviours

You will have noticed the exercise asked you about strategies to manage your feared situations. Not going into *any* fearful situation is one. Another is the use of props, or safety behaviours. That might mean wearing headphones on a bus not because the journey is boring and you want to listen to music, but because you're frightened of someone talking to you. If they try to chat and you don't know what to say, you might worry that they will think you're weird. Having headphones is a way to reduce the chance of those social fears becoming true. And it works in the short term, so you rely on it.

The problem is, if you forget those headphones, you may panic because you think you can't manage without them. That puts you in a threat state and makes it almost impossible to engage in conversation, even if someone were to try. You are not testing your fears; you are simply confirming them. The same is true of using alcohol or drugs to get through a situation and not having access to either. In other situations, you may avoid eye contact because you fear interaction, or you over-rehearse a conversational script because you're frightened of stumbling, or try to blend into the background, or always have someone with you.

You might need safety strategies to start with, but in most cases the aim is to pay attention to them and then drop them, because they are another form of avoidance. They can stop you testing and using your social skills, which lowers your confidence and means you may miss out on something worthwhile. Some of these feared situations will be fun and interesting, even if you must really psych yourself up beforehand.

Step Three: Label it and accept it

Notice, without judgement, what's happening in your body, brain and behaviour. Are you breathing faster? Are your hands sweaty? Is your mind swimming with negative, catastrophic thoughts? Just labelling the fear, emotions and thoughts reduces activity in the amygdala, the part of the brain associated with anxious responses. Stating your feelings during the exposure, such as 'I'm having the thought that… I'm boring/worthless/stupid', rather than being hooked up and believing those thoughts, helps you become an interested observer of them – helps you unhook. If you're not ready to do the unhooking yet, remember the work you've done so far and wait to complete Part Three to build up your curiosity and self-compassion bit by bit. Then try it.

Dr Russ Harris says he used to deal with social anxiety in his teens and twenties 'either by drinking a lot or just by avoiding socializing'. He still has high levels of social anxiety, but now says 'I can let the anxiety flow through me. I don't fight it. I don't struggle with it. Instead of focusing on my feelings, I focus on the conversation and the social interaction. And now I can socialize without alcohol, I can still go along and enjoy it, even with my anxieties.'

Russ and I are chatting online – he's in Melbourne, Australia, and I'm in Kent, England, and although the time zones are all wrong, we find common ground when we start talking about how we have learned to live with anxiety. He says he was anxious about talking to me, because 'I've got to come up with something that sounds reasonably intelligent and so, my anxiety levels go up, but I don't really see that as a problem. It's like, "Oh, this is just part of the experience."' He mentions a physical symptom of his social anxiety. 'You probably can't see on the camera, but my hands are quite sweaty right now. That's the most common thing that happens for me. My hands get really sweaty.' He starts shaking them, vigorously. 'Shake it out!' he laughs.

We talk about one of his workshops that I'm attending in London and he says, 'You'll see people come up and shake my hand at the end of the workshop. And at least half of the time, there's this flash of horror on their face as they grip this sweaty, clammy hand, and they try to hide it.' He pauses. 'But in that split second, I can see the shock!'

Even when you understand what your reactions might be, you need to accept there's a risk with any social interaction, he says. 'I mean, you might screw it up. You might do it wrong. People might not like you.' Russ has stopped seeing anxiety as a problem and now sees it as part of the experience – something that comes along with him. 'That was just such a huge shift,' he says. 'I guess I take it for granted now, but it was massive at the time.' Another tip he has is to get out of your head and back into the room.

Step Four: Turn the spotlight on to someone else.

Most people with social anxiety find that the more they try to control or suppress their anxiety, the less effective they are socially. 'You can't stay in the conversation,' Russ says. 'You can't keep track of what's happening because you're in this struggle with your feelings.' If you concentrate on the other person, or you tell yourself before you leave that you'll discover interesting people who you want to learn from, then you find yourself being curious and asking questions, rather than being self-conscious about how you are coming across.

A while ago, I spoke to comedian and mental health advocate Ruby Wax about having proper, meaningful conversations with people. When asked how we are, we apparently say we're 'fine' around four times a day. Ruby wants to ban 'fine' altogether – because, she says, 'it's lost its oomph. Maybe it meant something 200 years ago but it's beige. Who's fine?' I ask what she would prefer to ask, to get a thoughtful reply. 'I always say, "Tell me the weather condition that's going on in your mind?" and they know exactly what I mean,' she says. 'Be honest with them, too, because if you're honest, people are honest right back. Look them in the eye and stick around for the answer. Because people really like to feel that you care.'

Philippa Perry also knows how to get people talking. She grew up with an outgoing, sociable father, and at dinner parties, if there was a conversational lull, he would walk past her and say 'Talk!' She learned to, fast. 'I'd say something like, "Oh, what interesting weather we're having." And I learned that small talk is actually big talk. "What gorgeous weather, how nice it is to be out." That way of talking is the gateway into more interesting talk. Just like "what do you do?" or "where do you live?" It's a ritualized dance just to find out what the atmosphere of somebody is. What their vibe is.'

And if she's tired, or stuck, or hasn't got much patience? 'I go, "What's foreground for you at the moment? What's on your mind?" Because I'm interested in what's on their mind. And if they say, "Oh, it's these lovely Rembrandts," then if I think I can get away with it, I'll say, "I'll give you one more chance. What's *really* on your mind?"' I laugh and tell her that feels quite 'out there'. But she says it works. 'I've had some really good conversations with people, like "well, my daughter doesn't talk to me" and I'm like, "OK, now we're cooking with gas. Let's get into this."'

When you've had an interesting interaction, however brief, store it up. Then keep hold of them all and squirrel them away so you can remind yourself of enjoyable social experiences when you next feel frightened of one.

Step Five: Zoom out and see the bigger picture

Don't let one or two situations, or even a year of anxiety, shape your view of who you are. Philip Selway taught himself to build up a backlog of good experiences, rather than focus on what he thought he couldn't do. 'It might not be that every single show there's going to be no anxiety at all and you're spot on, but it's a cumulative thing. You think, "OK. On the whole, my experience of playing has been good and my body has done what I want it to." It is gradually rebuilding that belief in your ability to do it and acknowledging that anxiety isn't who you are as a musician. Those moments where it falls into place for you – *those* are the moments that actually define who you are as a performer, as a creative.'

He says he had to go back to childhood and remember his unselfconscious playing, before the expectations went 'through the ceiling'. He learned to enjoy it and hang on to the moments when it went well because 'having those moments is a contrast between the light and the dark. The dark are the gremlin moments, but they really show up the lighter moments of when you feel connected to yourself, connected to your creativity and able then to connect with an audience.'

Will he ever be comfortable living alongside the gremlin of anxiety, I ask? 'I don't think you ever tame it or change the nature of it, but you can make it a bit more of a manageable housemate,' he says. Some days it shouts louder than others. He's confident drumming when he's playing live, but when he steps away from his kit and moves to the front of the stage to sing or play guitar, the self-critical voice can make itself heard again. 'You just have those moments of where that voice goes, "You're shit, you're shit."' He loves performing, he says. He doesn't enjoy the anxiety and self-doubt that go with it.

But even the gremlins can be useful as a 'very good

signpost to showing who you genuinely are as a musician, who you are as a person,' says Philip. They can be useful pointers to what he needs to work on. 'If you think of yourself as a work in progress, it kind of diffuses some of that performance anxiety. People are coming to see you, there is something that people connect with. And so, it may not completely look like you'd like it to look in your head. But you're always moving towards that point and what happens in the meantime is still valid creatively and performance-wise'.

He says in those moments when anxiety is loud, mistakes seem bigger but 'nobody notices if my bass drum is just slightly off. Generally, nobody notices. It's just all part of the bigger experience for somebody listening to it, that's what you focus on. There's a lot of music going on.'

Step Six: Use anxiety's energy to fuel you

Philip Selway manages his performance anxiety by seeing it as 'fuel to the fire'. He says the gremlin of anxiety 'doesn't feel as though it particularly likes or respects you. But if you try and fight it, you just get anxiety from fighting it and end up in these ever-decreasing circles.' He reached a point where he couldn't side-step anxiety's power any longer, so he chose to accept it and use its energy differently.

Anxiety, he says, is 'part of the process, uncomfortable though that might be. It is something that takes you to a heightened state, which you need for performance.' You can let anxious feelings overwhelm you, or you can see them as excitement. 'They could be interpreted as you're just about to have this very good experience. Your body is getting you to that point that you're ready to engage.'

I get what he's saying. When I've anchored live, seemingly high-stakes programmes such as the Olympics, general elections and royal weddings and funerals, this reframing really helps. Noticing the anxiety build as the clock counts down to transmission, then breathing into it, understanding it's just what the body and brain are doing to get you ready – that thinking can steady and strengthen.

Russ Harris agrees. 'There's a purpose to anxiety. It revs you up to deal with a challenging situation. Your body knows there's something coming up. Your muscles are getting ready, your heart rate's getting faster, your adrenaline levels are preparing you for action. And if you go, "This is my body getting prepared to deal with something that's challenging," that's very different than – "Oh my God! This is anxiety. Anxiety is terrible. What's wrong with me? I shouldn't be feeling this way!" The problem is because anxiety gets such a bad press, most people struggle with it. And then struggling with it makes it bigger.'

Rethinking the power of anxiety as a fuel, not a fear, isn't something that happened overnight for either of them. It took time to shift perspective, and when Philip is vulnerable, 'those voices start to take over a little bit'. But when anxiety is around, he interprets it differently. 'It's not going to hold you back. It's not going to trip you up. It's something that you can channel into your life. I think that's a wonderful thing, isn't it?'

Step Seven: Connect to something bigger

At the height of Radiohead's fame, when they were touring, selling millions of albums and making some of the best, most creative music around, Philip would step away to be at the end of the phone for people who were in crisis, and in some cases suicidal. He was a listener for the Samaritans charity for twenty years. 'It was just such a contrast to what I was doing in this music world where there's so much facade, self-aggrandizement and these intense experiences. I guess it's like social media, isn't it? It can become a bit too much like looking in the mirror and it just hinders you, it becomes an obstacle. It's just not a healthy place to be, and then to actually step out of that to be in a very definite space where you leave yourself at the door and then using that to tune into somebody else, that was such a good counterweight to whatever else was going on in my life.'

When you feel too wrapped up in yourself or overly focused on expectations of what you should and shouldn't be doing, or achieving, or saying or being, take Philip's advice and step away to engage with others who may need your help. Get out of your head and into someone else's for a while.

Step Eight: Be on your own side

Those with social anxiety can often be curious, having the competing feelings of wanting to avoid a situation and yet knowing they may get some reward from it if they go.

Threat can often outweigh potential benefits – but if they miss the experience, regret sets in.[20] Recognizing these competing emotions means you may see yourself engaging in a more curious, perhaps more realistic, way. And remember to tell yourself that you are wonderful, even if you struggle to believe it. That's what Philippa did when she was socially anxious. She would say, 'I'm interesting and attractive, and so are all these people, and they think I'm interesting and attractive. I just sort of drowned the bad voice out with another voice. Of course it's not true, but neither was the other voice. So, if I'm going to have a fantasy about what other people are thinking, I might as well make it a good one.'

Autism and social anxiety

The ITV newsreader Nina Hossain is friendly, engaging and outgoing. She loves travelling, live music and her work. And she is just the person you want in the chair when a big news story breaks. Calm and professional, unflappable even when the autocue or teleprompter goes down, or the guest isn't there, or it's a few minutes to air and the running order's changing. But she can also experience social anxiety so crippling that it feels 'like a lorry sitting on my chest'.

Nina and I have been working together to manage her anxiety for a couple of years. She describes it as a pervasive, overwhelming and frightening physical sensation which can come out of nowhere and which she can't control.

'At its worth it could be a whole week of just feeling like that,' she tells me. Nina is OK in many social situations, but there are times, especially at a work event, when 'it is so uncomfortable, I'd rather stick pins in my eyes. And if I can avoid it at all costs and not feel guilty, I will.'

Not knowing the rules

When Nina first came to me for therapy, there were signs and symptoms of undiagnosed autism. I'd seen it before with clients who have anxiety, depression and trauma and have grown up in a world where they don't feel like they fit. 'It's like feeling like everyone else has got these rules and I've just never been given them,' she says. 'When you interrupt, when you don't interrupt, how you introduce yourself, how you get into a group of people, the eye contact thing. I'm really conscious of whether I'm looking at somebody's eyes too much or not enough. I just don't have the rule for it.'

She doesn't feel she can look in their eyes all the time because that's too much, but she's also thinking, 'Right. I should look away in a minute. I should look away now. But where do I look? Because if I look to the sky, it's like I'm looking at something. If I look at my phone, that's rude.'

The thought of walking into a room and approaching someone to strike up a conversation is 'hideous', she says, because 'I really, really, *really* can't abide small talk. And I get very nervous about the extraction from a conversation. How people "work a room" – well, I find that impossible.'

How social anxiety looks different if you're autistic

Someone who has social anxiety and is neurotypical, for want of a better word, might be worried about what others are thinking and whether they'll embarrass or humiliate themselves. They may fear people will react badly to them or reject them. And they'll probably be told that their fears are usually unfounded.

But if you're autistic, that social rejection may feel very real and something you've experienced forever. If you don't know 'the rules' of conversation, or how to pick up on social cues, then you might worry that people will see you as awkward or difficult, and you may feel lonely and isolated and experience bullying and stigma. That increases the risk of depression and anxiety and can make you more sensitive to rejection. Much of the research on social anxiety is not done with the autistic person in mind, and if they do manage to get an appointment with a therapist, they may be told their concerns are disproportionate – meaning they feel invalidated. Their symptoms can become chronic and entrenched, and their anxiety just gets worse.

When I was a trainee counselling psychologist, I worked with an autistic student who was in their first year at university. Bright and hard-working, they were also keen to engage with college life and make new friends, but no matter how hard they tried – and boy, did they work hard at it – they just couldn't seem to connect. They felt profoundly self-conscious, they didn't know how to break into conversations or read people's faces, and it was incredibly frustrating and exhausting because the sense of difference and the not-knowing was something they'd always experienced.

The social anxiety protocol I was using had not been designed for autism. It suggested that feelings of not fitting in can be challenged and that there may be alternative explanations for feeling out-of-place. My autistic student thought, quite rightly, that this was wrong. They *were* out of place, they *didn't* fit in, they *had* been rejected. There was no quick fix to help them engage in a society that didn't understand them, but we worked on strategies to manage the anxiety – like finding out what to expect in a social situation, having an ally alongside them, knowing when to take time out, and connecting with others with similar interests.

The 'lost girls' of autism

The British neurobiologist and psychologist Gina Rippon has done a lot of work with what she calls the 'lost girls' of autism.[21] She says that being social is a universal characteristic; it's how our brains evolved, to help us engage with other people and stay in the tribe. But if you're autistic, it's not automatic. Look at popular girls in the playground, she says. Young autistic girls are always on the outside. Their social instinct is different, and the motivation and drive to be social may be different too. They know it's important to belong, but they often don't know how. And if you can't socially integrate, rejection can be swift, painful and incomprehensible. For all of us, social rejection is powerful and horrible, but for autistic females it's more likely to happen, and they can't easily find a way to get back in. People who are autistic might experience this throughout life, so perhaps it's not surprising that autism often comes with anxiety, depression or trauma. If you're autistic, you can live in a world that doesn't make the effort to understand you – or worse, to accept you. The effort of trying to fit in, of 'masking' the autism or camouflaging it, is utterly exhausting.

Being social when autistic

That's certainly what Nina Hossain found, and it's been a relief for her to finally understand that many of the issues she was experiencing were tied to her undiagnosed autism. 'At least now I know what it is, what I'm dealing with and what steps I can do to try and alleviate those very real physical feelings,' she says. She gives me an example, describing going to the theatre with a group of friends.

The sun was shining and they were chatting excitedly about being together again. Nina was walking with someone who she'd known for years but then, she says, 'I just froze. I suddenly thought, "God, I'm exhausted and I've got nothing." I had nothing to give. I couldn't say to him, "What do you think of the weather?" I couldn't even generate a question. This is a no-brainer in terms of a good weekend and yet here I am feeling frozen. I'm just thinking, "How is this so hard for me? Why am I finding this so hard? Why can't I just think of anything to say to him?"'

Nina and her friend talked about it later and it turned out he couldn't do small talk either. But the self-awareness allowed her to reflect on it, talk about it, and think about how best to manage it. Here are a few things that work for her, that she wanted to share, in case they help.

Know when your tank is depleted

Even with good friends, Nina knows that if she is tired, the thought of engaging becomes utterly overwhelming and she doesn't have the resources to 'dig deep' to do it. 'I've cancelled a dinner with a friend for tomorrow night, in the same way that I cancelled you last week because of being exhausted, and I'm still exhausted,' she says. 'If you have a feeling of dread about something because you just haven't got the resources, or enough energy left in the tank, and it's not vital, just don't do it. It's better to do that and do it properly the next time than force yourself to do it.'

Be open

If Nina has dried up in conversation, or is finding something hard, she is honest about it. She describes being with a close friend and suddenly becoming overwhelmed. She later told her, 'You're going to think I'm mad. I find your company so rewarding, it's always been easy meeting you and I don't know why, but today I just found that hard. I felt really self-conscious.'

She uses that approach with those she doesn't know, too. 'There isn't a magic pill that's going to stop people being autistic, but I can explain it. I think people who are open to learning about anxiety and autism are interested in how it impacts you. There's a kind of safe space with most people. Also, I've got nothing to lose. It's not going to change the way I am, and it might help people who are neurotypical and other people who are autistic.'

Be aware of what you can change, and what you can't

'Sometimes noises that wouldn't irritate somebody who's neurotypical can just drive me mad,' Nina says. Like the sound of people eating on the early morning train. 'There are days when the sound of somebody's cutlery scraping and tapping... I have a physical reaction to that noise. I'm just completely overstimulated and all people are doing is eating normally. But my brain is exploding, listening to it.'

Remember those safety strategies we talked about earlier? This is why it's different for those with autism, because Nina needs her headphones. 'I can try and make things better by putting my headphones on. Because you just can't change it. It's going to take more out of you to be cross with yourself about something that you can't change.'

'Jazz hands' your way through it

This is like the feared social situation experiment above. It's not for everyone with autism, but for Nina, most of the time 'it's better to push myself out of the comfort zone'. Her daughter is autistic too, and when I ask what advice she'd give someone who struggles socially, she tells me the advice that she gave her: 'She doesn't want to miss out on things by feeling too overwhelmed about what might lie ahead, so my advice to her is always – just "jazz hands" your way through it. Just get into your head that this takes more of an effort for us than my husband or my son or my next-door neighbour. Accept that and then say, but I want to do it. I want to see that person, I want to go to this place, I want to socialize with that group of people.' Avoiding is not the answer, she says, because 'if I avoid it, then the danger is I'd never go out. And then I've missed stuff that was enjoyable.'

Advice for the neurotypical? Be kind – we're working from a different rule book

In social situations, Nina thinks she is often misinterpreted. 'Yeah, definitely the resting bitch-face and the perception that I'm a pessimist or that I'm gobby or opinionated. That has been thrown at my daughter as well. You put up with that. But it's just because we're not using the same rule book as everybody else.'

It is not the job of those who are autistic to educate those who are not, but they can enlighten them to the fact that they're working from a different set of rules.

And if there is little energy or enthusiasm to have to explain or inform, then one failsafe that Nina uses when anxiety feels overwhelming is one that Ruby and Philippa also recommend and one we can all turn to. She pays attention and shows a deep curiosity in the person in front of her. 'If I just fire a series of questions, it helps me get through that bit of thinking. People like talking about themselves. They often don't get the opportunity to be listened to. And if I can just listen, people will fill the gap because they actually like talking about themselves.'

It has taken time for Nina to understand herself and her anxiety, but it's been transformative. 'Discovering it was anxiety and being able to, for example, do breathing exercises to cope with that, has been just overwhelming in another way – to feel as if there's a solution to dealing with this. At least now I know what it is, what I'm dealing with and what steps I can do to try and alleviate these very real physical feelings.'

Seek help

Nina says she was 'really lucky to have had some therapy and had the right therapist for me, not only with the diagnosis, but also with the job. It's important to be completely open and honest about these things.'

She recognizes that her thoughts about what helped her through her anxiety are her individual perspective. There is no universally accepted terminology or treatment for autism. But the number of those diagnosed and needing help is growing. Over the course of twenty years in the UK alone, autism diagnoses went up by nearly 800 per cent.[22] According to NHS England, as of 2018 it was thought that up to three-quarters of autistic adults remained undiagnosed.[23] Autistic adults are more likely to experience physical and mental ill health than those who are not, many will also experience ADHD or other psychological conditions, and they are more likely to face issues with housing, finance, employment and social isolation.[24] There is a pressing need for more efficient, early, targeted community support, and for all clinicians to make sure they have the proper training to recognize and support those they see and care for.

If you have autism and social anxiety, try to get specialist help. Make sure your therapist understands your neurodivergence and how it has impacted your life. Know that not all ways of treating anxiety will be right for you, and find your own ways of coping. Be compassionate and seek out others who understand and get who you are.

Research in young autistic people suggests CBT can work, but can be better if it's adapted to neurodiversity.[25] Group settings help develop knowledge and understanding of autism and might improve social skills too, but clear introductory sessions, consistent facilitators and smaller group sizes may be key to preventing overwhelm.[26] There's also evidence about the potential of emerging computer-based systems like virtual reality headsets, allowing autistic people to engage in social situations and scenarios virtually, before trying them out in real life.[27]

Social anxiety looks and feels different if you are autistic, and 'traditional' therapies may not be appropriate.

Research suggests doing behavioural experiments can work, but there may be specific factors which mean you need to amend or adapt them.[28]

Take your time, because whether you are autistic or not, social anxiety is depleting. Imposter syndrome and performance anxiety are debilitating. They can choke all the joy out of human experiences that might be rewarding and invigorating. In Part Three we'll look at how to manage and calm the anxious body, brain and behaviour, so you can finally learn to stop struggling and start living.

Chapter 6: A quick refresher

- Fear of rejection keeps us anxious – but people pay much less attention than we think.
- If you feel the spotlight is on you – turn it on to someone else – curiosity is a great connector.
- When your social fuel tank is low, stop to fill it up – it'll burn out if it's running on empty.
- Test your fears one small step at a time. See it, name it, feel it, accept it and do it anyway.
- Social anxiety is different in autism – if you're at higher risk, go slowly and seek specialist help.

Ten Top Takeaways from Part Two

1. Your inner voice, or stupid friend, criticizes you because it thinks it keeps you safe. It may have had a function once. Now you can thank it and let it go.

2. People-pleasing perfectionists and procrastinators often have a hurt, rejected child inside – show them the love and acceptance they didn't get growing up.

3. Reducing the power of anxiety and perfectionism is not laziness or failure. It's self-preservation. It's taking the power back.

4. If success comes and you rush to set a higher goal, ask yourself: Whose validation are you seeking? Whose race are you running? What do you still need to prove?

5. Threat and Drive can push and motivate you for a while, but without Soothe, your engine will soon burn out.

6. Anxiety is energy. Notice when it's around and then direct its power to propel you rather than punish you.

7. No one notices you as much as you think. They're too busy worrying about their own hair, clothes, opinions. If you're socially anxious, ask more questions. People will love it.

8. Anxiety looks different in autism. If you're autistic, know when you're depleted, find safe people and spaces. If you're not, then be an autism ally.

9. Embrace the imperfections. Accept the failures. Find peace in the flow. And know that kindness is always the best way in and the only way out.

10. You matter. You have worth. You have value. You always have. Don't let anyone, ever, make you feel otherwise.

Part Three

7

How to Soothe our Anxious Body

'The body's wisdom is better than any philosophy'

Friedrich Nietzsche[1]

Panic stations

I'm on the eighth floor, in a radio studio in the BBC's Broadcasting House, and my guest is telling *Life Changing* listeners when she first felt panic. 'I had this overwhelming bodily feeling of being trapped. Once it happened, it started happening regularly. I didn't know they were panic attacks, I thought I was going mad.' It's taken months and a lot of planning to get Angela Tilley into this studio. She's walked up sixteen flights of stairs because she can't get into a lift. The room we are broadcasting from is the only one with windows, because she needs to see air, light and the possibility, however improbable at this height, of escape. Now in her sixties, Angela describes the panic and agoraphobia which started when she was seventeen. 'It's like hot and cold liquid nitrogen going from my head to my toes,' she says. 'Physically my heart's beating, my stomach's churning. Am I going to be sick? Am I going to have a heart attack? Am I going to make a complete fool of myself in front of all these people?'

The panic attacks were happening daily. She couldn't go to a supermarket or get on a train; she stopped driving because she feared she'd be trapped if a motorist broke down in front of her. 'Panic follows you and I was running away from wherever I was having a panic attack. My world was shrinking,' she says. Angela believes the anxiety and hypervigilance began when she was harassed for a year by a work colleague. The anxiety created panic and fear of collapse, which caused embarrassment and shame, which kept her inside and fuelled her fear. I'll explain the rather unusual way Angela started to recover later, but her experience demonstrates the connectedness of mind and body.

The path through panic starts with the body

This next part is divided into chapters about how we calm and soothe our anxious body, brain and behaviour, but they are all interlinked, as you'll know if you've felt a cold rush of dread or a hot flash of panic which has you thinking the worst and looking for the exit. There is no divide between body and mind. Both influence how we interact with life. The brain predicts a threat, the body reacts, the behaviour determines how we deal with it. When I saw Dr

Bessel van der Kolk, author of *The Body Keeps the Score*,[2] speak in London, he told the audience, 'We are our bodies, we are our brains and we are our reactions, we cannot separate them.' We can listen to what each is telling us though, because it is only by paying attention that we can start to change our relationship with anxiety. And really listening to what our body is telling us is a good place to start.

Dr van der Kolk is an expert on trauma, and that's often where anxiety has its roots. Trauma is less about the event or experience that happened to us and more about what it does to us inside. The word 'trauma' comes from the Greek for 'wound' – and that is what it is, a wound to our soul. The pain of that wound can keep us stuck in the past, rerunning events, making us live *back there* rather than *here*. Anxiety looks to an imagined future. Our minds and bodies are inflamed by that scar of the past, so we try to protect ourselves from further damage by scanning for other potential dangers, keeping us alert, rigid, nervous, closed, brittle. Primed for panic.

But while anxiety often stems from trauma, they are different. And anxiety doesn't always follow a traumatic experience because different people respond differently, according to their genetics, background, early attachment relationships and anxiety sensitivity. The risk factors for anxiety and depression are complex and, in the UK, there's a huge clinical trial underway called the Genetic Links to Anxiety and Depression (GLAD) Study, which hopes to shed light on why some of us experience them while others don't. At the time of writing, tens of thousands of volunteers have already submitted surveys and saliva samples, and we'll know more about the role of genes and our environment in anxiety and depression after all that data has been analysed.[3]

But we do know there's a two-way link between trauma and anxiety – anxiety sensitivity can make you more prone to trauma symptoms, and the trauma makes you more sensitive to anxiety.[4] The orchids among us are more likely to interpret trauma signals, such as a pounding heart or racing thoughts, in catastrophic ways, believing they are having a heart attack or going mad.[5] They are also more likely to experience panic attacks and be avoidant or use safety behaviours to try to control them. As van der Kolk says, 'When you have a persistent state of heartbreak and gut-wrench, the physical sensations become intolerable and we will do anything to make those feelings disappear.'

Always running from the fire

Here's another example of trying to escape the intolerable. I'm a broadcaster, but as I mentioned earlier, I've spent several years as an NHS psychologist, helping those affected by London's Grenfell Tower fire disaster. The following is an example of many people I've spent time with who were unable to work or sleep or live a normal life because they'd been so profoundly affected by the events of that night.

HOW TO SOOTHE OUR ANXIOUS BODY

Let's call my client Ali. Ali is a firefighter experiencing severe anxiety, but they are reluctant to seek help because, as many first responders say, it's the job they're paid for. They got out, many didn't. But they can't run away from the memories – even now, eight years on. Ali describes being sent into the burning building to rescue those who were told to stay put:

> The ceiling and floors are cracking with the heat. The smoke makes it difficult to see or breathe. The stairwells are full of people trying to get out, or those attempting to, but they are beaten back by the flames. People see, hear and smell things no one should ever experience. Whole families die. The youngest victim is a six-month-old baby, the oldest is an eighty-four-year-old woman who'd lived in the tower for decades.

Ali says that life has changed since they charged into that twenty-four-storey tower block in June 2017, to put out a blaze which burned for sixty hours, fighting through dense, toxic smoke to try to rescue those trapped.[6] It suddenly becomes impossible to walk down a staircase, stay in a small room or travel by public transport. Walking to the clinic from home takes hours, but travelling on the Underground is unthinkable because the screech of the wheels, the smell of the brakes and the risk of a sudden slowing to a halt in the tunnel provokes a reaction so strong it feels like suffocation.

Ali starts experiencing panic attacks, with high, fast breathing and hands so sweaty that they can't open a door handle – and even if they could, they fear what might be behind it, the images of the past feeling real, happening now. Working, travelling, socializing, exercising – panic has changed everything. Even watching the TV is out, because there's an advert for a mobile phone network where a man is buried beneath the ground. The risk of seeing it sets off a new wave of fear. As life becomes smaller, the shame about not being able to deal with it becomes larger.

Choking with panic

The Greeks understood trauma, anxiety and panic. I mentioned that trauma derives from their word for 'wound'. Well, anxiety comes from the Greek word *ánkhō*, 'to choke', and the root word for 'panic' is the adjective *panikós*, which refers to the Greek god Pan who caused humans to flee in terror. Raw, choking, fearful, wanting to escape. That's exactly how panic feels. The intensity is physical, the breathing accelerates, the heart races, the mouth dries, swallowing becomes difficult, digestion shuts down, you can feel dizzy or nauseous.

A panic attack can have an obvious trigger, but it can also seem as if it comes out of nowhere. If there's a shortness of breath or an increase in heart rate, the mind can leap to catastrophic endings, like a heart attack, or throwing up or collapsing in public, activating all our survival reflexes and provoking more fear and panic. Attacks usually last about ten minutes, but they can go on for longer. And if it's particularly horrible, you may

HOW TO SOOTHE OUR ANXIOUS BODY

worry about them happening again, which sets off a new panic cycle.

Panic attacks are common though. In a huge worldwide survey, more than one in ten reported experiencing at least one attack, with the highest rates in the United States and New Zealand, where it was more than a quarter of all those questioned. More women than men say they're affected, with the onset in their mid-thirties – and those who had regular panic attacks were more likely to experience other anxiety and depression issues too.[7]

Because panic symptoms mimic some serious health issues, those who experience them want to avoid any situations where they think they might reoccur. Worrying about the next attack and the possible, mortifying consequences – *I'll lose control, or faint, or vomit, or wet myself* – means that they change their behaviour, their life, to cope.

These physiological or bodily changes are driven by the autonomic nervous system (ANS). The ANS has two parts: a sympathetic nervous system and a *para*sympathetic nervous system. Think of the sympathetic as the fast 'low road', getting the survival instinct to kick in, activating all those stress hormones like adrenaline and cortisol, and pumping more blood and oxygen to the muscles to fight or flee. The slower, 'high road' is the *para*sympathetic system, which calms you down and keeps you steady. Interpreting the signals from the body, and being a curious observer of them rather than caught up in them, can restore balance to the ANS and help you understand that what you are feeling is part of an alarm reaction and will not kill you.

Learning different ways of thinking and reacting to panic is crucial, but without steadying the body in panic, you cannot work on the anxious thoughts or avoidant behaviours. Anxiety is as interwoven through the body as it is in the mind, but we often try to out-think it or outrun it, instead of turning inward to notice what's going on with us, physically. Some of my clients with anxiety are so 'in their heads' that if you ask them where they are feeling their anxiety in their body, they can't locate it. Because they have used their thinking brain for so long and their body seems to have turned against them, they try to rationalize the panic away. The problem is, in a state of panic, the part of your brain in charge of regulating the emotional state – the prefrontal cortex – isn't working effectively. We can't rationalize or think clearly because, when we are panicking, the body and brain are telling us to get out. We need to ground ourselves in the present first, breathe, and then the thinking brain will start working again.

You can't out-think panic

I was at work as a newsreader when panic hit me. I'd just come off air and received a phone call from a very senior person on a national newspaper who was furious about one of the stories in that night's bulletin. They had been part of the story but thought they hadn't been given sufficient credit. I put the phone down, got up from my desk, and as I was walking out of the office to get some air, my legs gave way and I slumped against the photocopier. My heart was beating hard, I had a feeling of intense heat and a sense of unreality and nausea. I didn't link it to the call; it seemed to appear out of the blue. A colleague spotted me, hauled me on to a chair and calmed me down before anyone else saw. I told no one else. I felt shame, shock and anger at not being able to deal with it quickly. Those feelings and the fear that it might happen again – or worse, while I was on air – dominated my thinking when I went back into the studio the following day. Thankfully it only happened the once. And let's face it, I'd fallen off air in a spectacular fashion in the past anyway. Knowing what panic was, and how to manage it if it showed up again, helped. I wasn't dying. It was just telly.

I also knew what it felt like because, ten years earlier, I'd been given a panic attack, deliberately, at the University of Cambridge, in the name of science. Dr Annette Brühl was the scientist and I was making a BBC Radio 4 programme called *How to Have a Better Brain*. We wanted to see what the body and mind do when we panic, so Brühl strapped a mask on to my face, through which was pumped a mixture of oxygen and elevated carbon dioxide, designed to provoke anxiety and distress. It did. It also took over my body and completely affected my ability to think. I wrote about it in my first book, *Rise: Surviving and Thriving after Trauma*, because, not to be overly dramatic, but that panic reminded me of all the times I had lost physical control after a traumatic experience.[8] Collapsing into unconsciousness after experiencing hyponatremia – low salt – during the New

York Marathon. Losing more than four pints of blood after the birth of my third son. Being told that my heart stopped on the operating table during post-cancer reconstructive surgery.

Dr Brühl tells me I am in no danger as she starts cranking up the carbon dioxide. 'What's the worst that can happen?' I ask. 'Suffocation,' she replies, with a straight face. But that's unlikely, she adds. I start to breathe but struggle to take in enough air, so breathe faster and faster, up to three times more than normal. My blood pressure soars from 92/60 to 144/83 and my heart races. I feel numb, dizzy and sweaty. And throughout all this, Dr Brühl is asking me to do some memory and decision-making tests, such as matching pairs, remembering numbers, putting objects in the right boxes. It's like doing an exam when you think you're going to die. I am frightened and confused and try to tear the mask off but it's solidly attached. 'How much longer?' I squeak. 'Six minutes,' says Dr Brühl. 'Why can't I breathe?' I gasp. 'It's the brain under stress,' she says. Too right. When I yank off the mask at the end, I shoot angry daggers at my producer, Dixi, who is taping it all. 'I hated that,' I say. 'Yeah,' she answers. 'Makes good radio though.'

Here's how panic affects our thinking. I completed a test before the gas experiment, but during it, I was making many more mistakes and my error rate went up by 30 per cent. When we are in a real state of threat and survival, we don't need to perform complex tasks, we just need to escape. Putting me in an artificially induced panic attack meant my brain stopped doing the non-essential stuff like

HOW TO SOOTHE OUR ANXIOUS BODY

remembering numbers, because it had recognized physical changes in my body which signalled danger. I reacted to them by thinking I couldn't breathe and needed to escape, which escalated the panic.

When I speak to Professor Oliver Robinson at London's Anxiety Lab about the experiment, he tells me he also performs these tests because it's a good way of measuring what happens to the body during anxiety. I tell him I felt panic consume body and mind and he replies that, yes, people feel it everywhere. 'The heart, the lungs, the brain are all communicating with each other in a positive feedback loop. And it's why, if someone has panic disorder, you might tell them to stop and take some deep breaths, because that gets more oxygen into the body, slows the heart rate down. Then those peripheral symptoms of panic can subside, because you're not pant-pant-pant-panting.'

Coping with panic and soothing the anxious body

Step One: Ground first

Yes, we need to slow our breath, but sometimes if you are in panic, you need to ground yourself first. Grounding in the present brings us back from the terrifying future where we are imagining having a heart attack or suffering the shame and embarrassment of collapsing or vomiting. Living in fear of that fear – however improbable – just adds to the sense of panic. While panic attacks are often frightening, they're not dangerous. Grounding brings us away from the memories of the past and the future fears, and roots us into the here and now.

Try the 5-4-3-2-1 method whenever you feel you're becoming distressed. Take a moment to focus on each sense and notice:

- FIVE things you can see around you – e.g. a tree, a picture, the clouds...
- FOUR things you can feel or touch – e.g. your hair, your fingers, a chair...
- THREE things you can hear – e.g. a bird, the wind...
- TWO things you can smell – e.g. the air, perfume...
- ONE thing you can taste – e.g. coffee, chewing gum...

If one of these senses is inaccessible to you, just do four of them, or three. The important thing is to pay close attention to the things around you.

Step Two: Breathe better

Few of us learn to breathe well. In anxiety, we tend to over-breathe, just like I did during that panic attack that Dr Brühl induced. The body thinks it needs more oxygen to prime the muscles to run. This is what causes

HOW TO SOOTHE OUR ANXIOUS BODY

hyperventilation, dizziness and feeling light-headed. If I had tried to breathe more slowly and less often, the panic symptoms would not have been so severe. Journalist James Nestor, who has studied the importance of breathing, underwent the same panic experiment as me and here's what was going through his mind: 'I can't breathe. Every sense feels like it's being torn from my control. Vacuumed out.'[9]

He describes how his self-talk – trying to tell himself that the feeling of choking was an illusion – did work. Rationally, the reaction is just a mechanical process, his sensory receptors detecting chemical changes in his body and provoking a response. But knowing that didn't help. What *did* work for him was doing it more often. Yes, he deliberately went through more panic attacks so he could learn to manage and breathe through them when they struck again.

In his book, *Breath: The New Science of a Lost Art*, Nestor says the one major, life-changing lesson he learned in all his experiments and research boils down to this: there is a perfect breath, and it is 5.5 seconds.[10] In for 5.5, out for 5.5. Practice for a few minutes or a few hours. Measuring exactly 5.5 seconds is a big ask. But breathing more slowly, less often and through the nose rather than mouth is a free, easy, natural and ancient response to panic and anxiety. An efficient and accessible way of calming our anxiety and preventing panic from spiralling. Try these techniques, find one you like and then practise so that when you need them, they're already in your toolbox and easily accessible.

The US Navy Seals do tactical breathing, sometimes called box breathing.[11] It's 4-4-4-4, like a box. In for

4, hold for 4, out for 4, hold for 4. This is a good one if you're in a passive but anxious state, like trying to sleep.

A popular one among psychologists and some yoga practitioners is 4-7-8 breathing: in for 4, hold for 7, out for 8. That's a better one when you are struggling and need some active coping right now. The reason the exhale is longer is because, when we inhale, we stimulate the sympathetic nervous system, which sets off chemicals to fuel the body – and when we exhale, we trigger the parasympathetic (rest and digest) system. The two should work together, keeping us in balance and regulating our body's response. The breathing helps get us there.

Step Three: Nurture your vagus nerve

Slower breathing also affects something called the vagus nerve, which connects our brain to the internal organs like the heart, lungs, stomach and intestines. It's often called the 'wandering' nerve because its reach is so extensive. It helps slow the heart rate, reduce inflammation, calm the digestive system and steady our breathing. Dr Stephen Porges noticed that when we are stressed, the vagus nerve can slow the heart rate and circulation so dramatically that we get into a state of hypo- rather than hyper-arousal.[12] Helpful if we are under attack and can't fight or run, because everything slows down and we can 'play dead'. You see it in animals like rabbits or mice, who freeze and faint when they're taunted by a cat and then leap up and scarper when the cat stops toying with them.

HOW TO SOOTHE OUR ANXIOUS BODY

As I've mentioned, I'm a fainter. I must look after my vagus nerve and try to support a healthy and balanced vagal tone – so that I don't faint at an inconvenient moment, like reporting on the opening of the Diana Memorial Fountain. Here are a few tips to steady your vagus:

- Recognize how your body responds to stress – fight, flight, freeze, faint or fawn (appease).
- Use the 4-7-8 technique and breath from the belly, not the chest, to activate the parasympathetic nervous system.
- Do regular physical activity like a brisk walk, along with strength training, to regulate the autonomic nervous system.
- Make meaningful social connections where you engage with others, to promote a sense of trust and safety.
- Take five minutes to be mindful and present, slowing down and unwinding, inducing calm.
- Try certain yoga poses, like downward dog, to stimulate the vagus nerve and encourage relaxation.

Dr Porges has been studying the vagus nerve for decades and developed the polyvagal theory – 'poly' because there are many ways this nerve acts. Look it up if you want to develop a healthy level of activity in the vagus nerve – or vagal tone – to help get you quickly back to safety.[13]

Step Four: Soothe the anxious part of you

If you haven't been shown how to stimulate that Soothe part of you and have spent a lot of time in high Threat or Drive, this is for you. Some of my clients with anxiety are thinkers, not feelers, and, as I've mentioned, when I ask them to locate anxiety in their body, they can't find it. That's why panic seems to come out of the blue. They haven't noticed that their breathing is high and fast, or that their digestion has switched off, causing butterflies or a tight gut. Our muscles contract when we're tense and anxious, but often we are barely aware of what our bodies are doing in a state of anxiety and where we are holding it.

Soften-soothe-allow was developed by mindful self-compassion experts Christopher Germer and Kristin Neff. It's designed to reverse the body's tendency to resist and react to the impending anxiety – and instead, direct a softness and kindness to the parts that are putting up a fight. Paying mindful attention to the parts of the body that hold tension, and then softening and allowing that tension to be there, is very effective. When you scan your body, you might notice your shoulders are rigid, or there's a compression in your chest or a heaviness in your stomach. I've adapted Germer and Neff's exercise here, and your best bet is to read it a few times, then give it a go so you feel more at ease with your anxious body and know how to look after it, when you need to.

HOW TO SOOTHE OUR ANXIOUS BODY

Exercise: Soften-soothe-allow[14]

- First, scan the body and see if you can notice where you are holding tension.

- *Soften* into that part of the body. Direct attention there. If it's a tightness in the stomach, for example, focus on smoothing the edges of that tightness and allowing the muscles to soften. You're not trying to make it go away, or go right into it; you're just softening it, easing it. It may help to say to yourself 'soft' a few times. It might feel weird, but no one is listening.

- *Soothe* yourself for having to struggle with your anxiety like this. Maybe place a hand on your heart, another on your stomach, and feel your body breathing. You're trying to bring a kindness and compassion to this emotion. You know it's doing its best to keep you safe and protected, but it's also painful to have this experience of anxiety. Talk to yourself as you would a child who's hurting, or a friend who is in pain, or just say, 'Soothe… soothe… soothe.'

- *Allow* discomfort to be there. You're not trying to ignore or banish it, just allow it to come and go. You can repeat, 'Allow… allow… allow.'

- Finally, repeat the words 'Soften, soothe, allow… Soften, soothe, allow', reminding you to be kind to yourself in this moment, rather than harsh, or criticizing.

There are lots of ways of strengthening and developing the compassionate self. This exercise is just one. If you are interested in doing more visualization and self-practice to move away from self-attacking and towards a kinder way of being with yourself, then Germer and Neff's Center for Mindful Self-Compassion has a free resource hub,[15] as does the Compassionate Mind Foundation, set up by Paul Gilbert.[16]

It may feel odd doing these practices at first, especially if no one has taught you how to look after yourself when you are stressed or upset. More on the importance of attachment and touch in compassionate-based work coming up in Chapter 9, when we look into how our behaviours can shift the power of anxiety.

Step Five: Dare to rethink cortisol

Cortisol, the so-called stress hormone, gets a bad rap. It's essential, regulating our digestive, reproductive and immune systems. If we sense a stress, our cortisol rises and stays high for a few hours to regulate our blood sugar and give us energy to cope. It falls when the threat is over, staying lower in the evening to help with a good night's sleep. But if we are in acute stress – catastrophizing, ruminating, thinking of worst-case scenarios, or social embarrassment, or failure, or dwelling on pain – then our cortisol levels can go awry, causing inflammation, intensifying the pain, increasing the risk of disease and making our system super-sensitized to further stress.[17] More on the link between anxiety and pain in Chapter 10. But cortisol needs to be variable – high when we need it, lower when we don't. Not too much, not too little, just right.

The buffers to managing chronic stress are things we've talked about – accepting challenge and uncertainty and confronting fears. Having people who love and stand by us is pretty crucial too. And another is reframing, or finding the positive, in what seem like anxiety-inducing events. Remember Philip Selway using anxiety to fuel his performance and change his perception so he saw it as an energy source, rather than something to be afraid of? Well, those who notice and utilize their stress response do just that.

I have spent a long time trying to understand my reaction to new challenges. My children will tell you that I tend to overthink my way out of things that may be fun. Early in my career, when the *Strictly Come Dancing*s and *Celebrity Bake Off*s came calling, the anxiety prompted days of toing and froing before the inevitable, decisive 'no'. But if someone had dared me, that might have been different.

Remember when 'I dare you' was a thing? I'd pretty much do anything if I was dared to, but thankfully, I'm not dared very often. The first time was when my twin brothers, Dave and Pete, dared me to knock on the door of an elderly neighbour and run away in what was called back then, in a very un-PC way, Knock Down Ginger. From our garden, over the wall, across the road, knock, run back, hide. Easy as. I did it, we all sniggered afterwards, and about fifteen minutes later there was a knock at the door. It was our neighbour telling my parents she was reporting me to the police. I got a spanking for that, which in those days seemed to be the only available parental punishment, other than an early bedtime and no telly. Oh, and writing an apology to the neighbour. My brothers escaped most of the punishment as they were younger, cuter, and didn't do the actual knocking. They remember it differently. Of course.

The second dare was walking on hot coals, for a television programme. There were millions watching, so of course I did it. It didn't hurt, the waiting being more nerve-racking than the doing – or the anticipation worse than the bang, as Hitchcock would have it. The third time, again on live TV, I was dared to ride on the back of World Champion James Toseland's superbike at 140 miles an hour. I said yes and got white, skin-tight leathers made, but as the date approached I noticed they were feeling a little snug. Turned out I was pregnant. The BBC wouldn't insure me. I still have the leathers (and the child is now an adult). The fourth time I was in a church, hosting a charity fundraiser, and the vicar asked, in front of hundreds of donors, whether I would jump out of a plane to raise money. I said yes. As soon as I got back to my seat, my husband turned to me and hissed: 'You have five children, raise it some other way.'

I regret not doing the skydive. Now I no longer seem as necessary to the children, perhaps I'll give it a go, partly as a psychological experiment to test what happens when you are put in a potentially life-threatening situation. Although a team from Northumbria University have already done that, with fascinating results.[18] They compared novice skydivers with much more experienced ones – those who'd done more than 1,000 jumps. Before they boarded the plane, each group – new and veteran – had their cortisol levels measured, while also filling out a questionnaire about whether they felt anxious. When they landed, the tests and questionnaires were repeated.

Understandably, those who had never leapt out of a plane before reported feeling much more anxious than those who'd jumped multiple times. But when their cortisol levels were looked at, both the novice and the experienced jumpers showed the same level of stress hormone. Even though there was a marked difference in anxiety, there was no difference in cortisol between those jumping for the first time and those doing it for the thousandth.

Why didn't the novices show a greater stress response? Because we need that cortisol. If you face a bear in the woods you want to run away before it kills you, no matter how many times you come across one. If you jump out of a plane, you're still hurtling towards the ground at 120 miles an hour and need to respond quickly if your parachute fails. Both sets of skydivers needed to be prepared to think and act fast, hence the cortisol; the experienced ones just interpreted the surge differently. As Professor Oliver Robinson says, although everyone's bodies were behaving similarly, the experienced jumpers 'were used to reacting to the condition they found themselves in, in more adaptive ways. And it's not like the experienced skydiver is less worried about their parachute not opening. Both are worried about dying. It's just that one of them has worked out their strategies to deal with it.'

THE POWER OF ANXIETY

Perhaps the experienced skydivers didn't believe they *should* feel worried. Perhaps they dissociated from any nervousness. Maybe they had run through the risk of their chute not opening many times before. We don't really know. But their bodies reacted the same way as the novices'.

As I've said before, a short burst of cortisol is not a bad thing. Neither is 'state anxiety' – that fleeting rush of nerves. Both can prepare us for whatever we're about to face. If a rise in cortisol and stress is temporary, it's not a problem. If it's long-term and chronic, that's an issue.

For nearly forty years working in live TV and radio on the BBC and ITN, there were many occasions when something would happen which could either momentarily inject me with fear or put a fire under my feet and get me moving. Here are a few. The autocue goes down, all your scripts disappear, you don't have hard copies and you have to ad-lib the news. This happened on the BBC's *One O'Clock News* when I was telling the nation about the death of Baroness Thatcher, the former British prime minister, which had happened shortly before we went on air. Another time, there was a power cut across the whole of Television Centre and the only place still broadcasting was the *BBC Breakfast* studio, but there was no autocue – again – and we relied on reading long segments from the newspapers for what seemed like hours. No one noticed or complained. Then, there was the excruciating moment when I was having a joke with my co-presenter during a recorded item but the camera cut back to us early and we were doubled up with our ugly, laughing-crying faces and couldn't pull ourselves together to speak. One more, although I have decades of these: a Very Very Important Person died while we were on air, and all we had was one line from the Press Association. All the BBC networks joined us and we were asked to 'sustain broadcasting'. Thankfully, there are long, pre-prepared obituaries for just these occasions. Except the voice in our ears was shouting, rather hysterically, 'We've lost the key to the obits cupboard! Keep talking!' Protocol probably dictates that I shouldn't tell you who it was. Oh, OK then. It was Princess Margaret. When I left daily news after almost four decades, I had my cortisol levels measured. 'Depleted,' the clinician said, simply.

Step Six: Smell the things you love

I should have had some essential oils under my desk. Smell is a powerful sense that can evoke emotion and influence mood because it goes straight to the limbic system, the bit of the brain associated with memory and emotion, bypassing other brain mechanisms.[19] That's why smells, like the zest of fresh oranges or cooked sardines, cut grass or baking bread, can transport us instantly to holidays, or home. Negative smells can take us to memories but they can also protect us too – a whiff from food that's gone off, or the sudden smell of smoke from a fire, alerts us to danger. Anxiety can affect so much of the way we interpret the world that even neutral smells can seem bad, and those smells get worse the more negatively we feel.[20] But there are positive ways smell can help us too.

Lavender can be relaxing, slow down reaction time and impair memory – useful in reducing pre-treatment anxiety in potentially stressful situations like going to the doctor or dentist.[21] Rosemary can reduce fatigue and enhance memory.[22] If you like the smell of either, it can be helpful to have a little bottle with you. Bizarrely, human sweat may lessen feelings of anxiety, too. Researchers gave a group of socially anxious women some sweat to sniff. Another group had clean air. The sweat-sniffers did better when trying to manage their anxiety.[23] It's early research – if you're anxious, I wouldn't advise going around stuffing your nose in strangers' armpits – but it adds to studies showing the importance of our sense of smell.

Step Seven: Reach out and touch somebody's hand

Touch is crucial, and could have a whole chapter all to itself. Being held is a basic human need. Being soothed when we are babies makes us feel safe. That attachment is a secure base that can stay with us for life, and affects all future relationships.

You may have heard of attachment theory, first proposed by British psychologist John Bowlby and his colleague Mary Ainsworth. They suggested that babies follow, cling, smile and cry to keep their attachment figure close, if they're frightened or insecure. It means they can explore, away from their secure base, as long as they know there's a safe haven to come back to.[24]

The first year of life is a critical period to establish this, but it's still a sensitive time up until we're at least five. An attachment figure can be a parent or a carer – the important factor is that they provide safe, consistent, loving care. If they don't, a child can become insecure, because they think they're unworthy of stability and attention, which results in issues like anxiety. A secure attachment results in better wellbeing and more stable future relationships. Loving ones.

The other types of attachment are anxious or avoidant. Anxious attachers might be overly clingy, making more demands for affection. Avoidant attachers might have grown up being independent because their caregiver wasn't there for them and so they had to be. There's disorganized attachment, too, which is a mixture of both.[25]

American psychologist Harry Harlow discovered something else about attachment: the importance of touch. He did a series of experiments on monkey babies – probably now illegal, certainly unethical – where he took them away from their mothers a few hours after birth and put them in cages with surrogate monkey mothers.[26] Each infant monkey had access to either a mother made of wire or one covered in sponge rubber and soft terry cloth. Both provided milk and they could choose which fake mum they went to. They were so desperate for touch, they went to the cloth mum almost every time, and Harlow suggested the main reason was not for food but for comfort. As they got older, some of the infants were exposed to frightening things, like a toy bear with a drum, and would run to the cloth mum for safety. Heartbreaking.

Researchers who came afterwards found the same key markers of attachment. You need a place of safety and a platform for growth in order to feel secure. Adults high in anxiety who receive touch, feel more cared for and are less distressed. That goes for avoidant attachers too. Although they may indicate they do not want touch, avoiders may benefit from giving and receiving it.[27] Be careful with that one though. Always good to ask first.

Physical contact with other people reduces our body's perception of stress but you can soothe yourself too, if that's not around. Giving yourself a hug,[28] or putting your hand on your heart, or having a weighted blanket,[29] or finding something comforting like a soft toy animal to stroke,[30] is scientifically proven to help stimulate the 'love' hormone oxytocin and the reward and pleasure neurotransmitter dopamine. Touch matters. Do it more.

Step Eight: Resculpt your anxious body.

Earlier, we did an anxiety sculpture, where our internal emotions like fear and panic were demonstrated externally. Now we're going to try it the other way. Allow your body to express the opposite of anxiety. It may be compassion, or joy, or peace – it doesn't really matter. Simply move yourself into a position where your body feels calmer, where your movements are lighter. Your shoulders may drop, your neck may loosen, your hands, face and pace might slow. Stay with that for a while and notice how shifting your body can subtly alter your mood. Learning an anti-anxiety pose can settle you and remind you that, if you are anxious, you have a choice about how your body responds.

HOW TO SOOTHE OUR ANXIOUS BODY

Our body language communicates a lot of things about us. We had to read bodies before complex language developed to know who was friendly and who was not, and that skill has stayed with us. It can also influence how we feel about ourselves. Go online and look at Amy Cuddy's talk on 'power poses' for what she calls a free, low-tech life hack to change body and mind.[31] You may have seen Cuddy already: hers is the second most watched TED Talk of all time – currently around 75 million – and she says it's probably because it offers an insight into the imposter experience and how to take a stance to make us feel less self-conscious.

It's about opening. All primates do it when they feel powerful. They reach, they stretch, their chin lifts, they use their non-verbal language to communicate how they feel. Those who feel less powerful try to make themselves disappear when they feel anxious. Cuddy is a social psychologist and looked at how our body language mirrors to others what we are feeling. But she also examined how it influences our emotions in either a positive or negative way.

She asked people to do high- or low-power poses for two minutes in a lab and measured their hormones. Those who adopted the high-power poses, like a wide stance and hands on their hips – think Wonder Woman – lowered their cortisol and increased their testosterone. The low-power posers – making yourself tiny, crossing your legs and arms, lowering your head – saw stress hormones rise. The way you hold your body can change your mind.[32]

Step Nine: Know your F-word

Fight, flight, freeze, faint, fawn. Our threat reactions are instinctive and automatic. We don't choose which one to do, they just click on to keep us alive when we think we are in danger. Panic about the possibility of panicking can set them off, because of the lack of control and the potential embarrassment and shame of 'falling apart' or collapsing.

Both Angela and Ali discovered that the more they worried about panic, or tried to fix, avoid or prevent it, the worse things got. When they noticed and leaned into the bodily sensations – 'ah, there's my heart beating a bit faster, that's familiar' or 'I notice my hands are beginning to sweat again' – they were able to tolerate it, and the less regular their panic symptoms became.

Recognizing your bodily sensations and allowing them to be there helps create the distance to steady, ground and use the breath, so you can bring compassion to how you're feeling. As US psychiatrist Dr Dan Siegel says, 'That's the strange thing about panic. When we lean into it, it loosens its grip on us. The power of reflection allows us to approach, rather than withdraw, from whatever life brings us.'[33] Dive into the body, stay with the experience, be open, present and curious. It's not easy, but it's better than the alternative.

Step Ten: Safe place, secure base

For those living with panic, it is a work in progress, just like with social anxiety in the previous chapter. With Ali, our firefighter who fears having a panic attack in enclosed spaces, it was a bit-by-bit approach. When they got back on to a train, headphones helped get them to the first stop. Then the second. Then they could do a whole journey and back again, without safety props. The first car journey was meticulously plotted with potential diversions and emergency escape plans in case panic struck again. Now, they can drive without them. They can sit in a cinema without needing to be by the exit. Learning to register and be curious about what is happening in the body has brought an understanding, kindness and acceptance to feelings of panic, rather than fighting or blocking them.

Angela Tilley does the same. 'I just knew I had to challenge it, even though I knew at every point, those challenges were so great and so difficult, that each challenge was like climbing a mountain. I just did it with baby steps.' Angela 'felt ridiculous' about her panic and the way it controlled and limited her life. Those four decades of panic prevented her experiencing adventure and fun. One day, she and her husband made a quick decision to buy a camper van. They made it cosy and started venturing out. Life began opening in concentric circles. They'd explore a few miles from home, then a few more, then further still, taking the camper van to places where she could get out and explore – and get back safely. She is now spending time with her four grandchildren in ways she couldn't with her own kids, and says she is reliving some of her youth, forty years on. I ask what part agoraphobia plays in her life now. 'It's in my life and the scars will be there but I have some control over it,' she answers.

Step Eleven: When the body speaks, learn to listen

I'd advise you – if you are regularly experiencing physical symptoms of anxiety – to take the right precautions before you start experimenting and making changes. Physical health concerns can mimic anxiety and panic. You'll know how, if you've eaten too much sugar, or drunk too much coffee, your nerves can start jangling. Anxiety is the body telling us that something is wrong and we need to listen and pay attention. Think of it as a warning light, an intuitive nudge, letting you know what's askew and encouraging you to get back into balance.

Dr Ellen Vora, who describes herself a 'holistic psychiatrist', says we need to recognize the difference between 'false anxiety' and 'true anxiety'. She says false anxiety is often physical, driven by caffeine, lack of sleep, the after-effects of alcohol or not enough exercise. Perhaps we haven't been exposed to enough naturally occurring light, or we've eaten food that harms our gut microbiome. Our body is out of kilter, so our brain produces a reason, telling us something's wrong. She says false anxiety can be tackled by eating better, sleeping more soundly, doing some activity. Easier said than done, you may say – but again, small steps. True anxiety is 'our emotional compass telling us something is not OK', and these feelings are something to acknowledge and investigate, not get rid of. As Vora says: 'Our uneasy feelings are no longer the enemy or something to vanquish – they become our tools and allies instead.'[34]

HOW TO SOOTHE OUR ANXIOUS BODY

I like Vora's thinking, but if you struggle with the idea of 'false' anxiety – because it always feels so horribly real – try 'tricky' and 'sticky' instead.

Step Twelve: Tricky vs sticky anxiety

I think of 'tricky anxiety' as the things which trick our brain into making our body stressed and panicky – those which have a physical root, like food and sleep (there'll be tips on how to improve both in Chapter 10). 'Sticky anxiety' may have been around a long time and is there even after we've done all the 'right' things. That involves looking at our sensitivity levels, experiences, background, our quest for happiness and perfection and so on. In other words, all the stuff we've been talking about so far.

There's another way our biology can trick our brain. Anxiety is twice as common in women as in men. Hormones, especially oestrogen, can increase the risk of both anxiety and depression,[35] but it's a complex area and we know many factors can play a part in creating and maintaining them. Fluctuating hormones do affect the function of our brain though, and we need to be aware of what role ours are playing. When oestrogen drops, the 'plasticity' – or adaptability – of the brain can fall too, increasing the likelihood of anxiety. Non-binary individuals and transgender men who are menstruating can also experience a drop in hormones, and a study of studies into the quality of life among transgender people overall found decreased levels of anxiety following gender-affirming hormone therapy. The authors of that research acknowledge that the strength of evidence is not robust enough yet.[36] It's the same with a review into menopausal anxiety which looked at fifty years of research and concluded that none of the data was solid enough to confirm that it rises during menopause and falls afterwards.[37]

What does this mean? That as much as I love the research, sometimes the trials aren't 'gold standard' enough to draw definite conclusions. We are individuals and experience life, anxiety and hormonal swings differently. If you believe your anxiety may have a physical cause, please see your doctor. And this is what you might say: 'My anxiety is affecting my quality of life and I'd like to rule out physical causes. Please can I have a full blood test and can you also test my hormone levels, thyroid and anything else you think may be a contributor.'

Step Thirteen: And finally – it's (still) not your fault

Panic – and other bodily reactions to anxiety – are not your fault. They are an instinctive, involuntary, primal reaction. What helps is really noticing and naming what's going on, allowing and accepting it, then letting go and breathing slowly. As does building a self-compassionate, values-based way of looking at life which we'll go into in the next chapters. Focus on what you want in your life that your anxiety stops you from getting. That will provide the impetus and incentive to try something which will inevitably feel tough. And listen to the wisdom of your body. Learn to hear its vibrational frequency. It's usually telling us something we need to hear.

Chapter 7: A quick refresher

- Anxiety is a bodily thing, as well as a thinking, behaving thing. Listen to what your body is telling you.

- The body has learned to scan and react to danger, but it can sometimes misread warning signals.

- In panic, be here, now. Root yourself in the present, not the past or future. Plant your feet on the ground.

- Ask yourself: 'Does anxiety come from neglecting/misusing my body or is it alerting me to something real?'

- Listen to the wisdom of your body when it tells you something. It may be right, it may be a misfire, but you need to pay attention.

8

How to Calm Our Anxious Thoughts

'We do not see things as they are,
we see them as WE are'

Attributed to Anaïs Nin

Back in the spotlight

In early 2025, I went back on BBC TV news for the first time in over a decade. I was asked to be on a panel voicing opinions on a political breakfast show, a bit like the daily one I'd presented for eleven years. Except this time, I was answering the questions, not asking them. Professionally, I've spent many, many years deliberately not having any views – at least not ones I voice in public. As a mother of children who range from their teens to their thirties, I've also spent the past three decades putting other people first. If someone asks me what I want, my answer is invariably: 'I don't know, what do *you* want?'

When the programme editor asked me to be a guest on the show, my first, visceral reaction was avoidance.

My brain took me straight to the after-party in my head when all the naysayers and haters barge in, grab a drink, say horrible things, vomit on the carpet and leave. And worse, by opening myself up to scrutiny, I would have invited them in. It'd be my fault. I'd fail or say something catastrophically career-ending to millions of people or freeze or faint. And then I'd go on social media to punish myself and be reminded that my first instinct not to do it was the right one.

I dither and overthink, with all the 'shoulds' and 'musts'. I've got a week of shows for Mental Health Awareness Week that I should be plugging and it'd be helpful to get my face back on screen. I must stop running away from things that could be fun. That last sentiment is echoed, kindly, by my teenage children, Seth and Eve, who are trying to convince me to say yes, constantly reminding me how gutted they are that I didn't accept all those early reality TV offers, and pleading for me to be more adventurous. And I also have in my mind a quote from my older sons, Joss and Alex, who sent me a little brass plaque when I left *BBC Breakfast*, which read, 'A ship is safest in the harbour, but that's not where it's meant to be.'

I know this. All my kids, including my stepdaughter, Emily, are bold, enthusiastic and courageous. Much more than I was at their age. So, I say yes to the appearance and then, in a pattern that fellow perfectionists and self-critics avoiding failure will recognize, I over-prepare to the point of exhaustion on the likely topics of immigration and a recently signed transatlantic trade deal, then can't sleep the night before. My brothers, who often watch the show, send me reassuring messages along the lines of 'Just be yourself!' 'You've done telly for ever!' 'It's like muscle memory, it'll all come back!'

On the morning itself, I head into the BBC studio and meet the other panellists. One of whom is the Nobel Prize–winning American economist Joseph Stiglitz. Of course it is. And I'm answering questions on a trade deal? Someone who has never passed a maths exam at school? 'Imposter! Imposter!' my brain screams.

The red light goes on and I'm looking at the autocue and preparing for the interview with the British Home Secretary and... oh. That's not your job today, Sian.

The host asks me questions on migrants and the politics of a US-UK trade deal. What are my thoughts? What are my thoughts? And then there's an interview with a woman who was groomed, which is powerful and unsettling and reminds me of those who brought their stories of trauma and pain to me. This, I understand. This feels important. Because it is not the politics, or the Home Secretary, or the Nobel Prize–winning economist, or what anyone says about my appearance or performance afterwards; it's the woman who has taken every ounce of strength and bravery to speak the unspeakable and tell the world that sexual trauma is a life sentence and what needs to happen to make things right for her and other survivors. This, I can talk about. I thank the survivor and speak about the importance of trauma-informed approaches and it reminds me of the lesson I always come back to when anxious and feeling out of my depth. Be authentic, be true to your values, be compassionate to others.

HOW TO CALM OUR ANXIOUS THOUGHTS

Confidence, comfort zones and choice points

As you'll remember from Chapter 1, worry is when we ruminate and catastrophize, paralysing our thinking. It's hard to feel confident with all that going on. 'Confidence' comes from the Latin *con fides*, or 'with faith'. It's not about feeling self-assured and decisive; it is about having faith in ourselves. That immediately feels more forgiving, open and curious than the brio that comes with an image of confidently striding out in the world, full of smiles and self-belief. You will be accompanied by your anxiety, but have faith that you can ride out the waves, even if they come with some doubt, because you can do it. You have done it before, you will do again. I bet that even your most cringe-worthy mistakes and faux pas make good stories, seen from a distance. You're still here, telling them.

Do not wait to live your life until you are assured enough, certain enough, in control enough, because that day will never come. The future you is still going to be living with difficult thoughts, feelings and sensations.

Thinking about whether to do the TV show, I realized there will never be a good time, when I am feeling optimal, intelligent and poised, with great hair and the right outfit and incisive views on all topics. And there will always be reasons to duck out of it. When we are anxious, it feels easier not to take the risk, not to lean into the discomfort and instead to stay in our comfort zone. When Dr Russ Harris asks his workshop attendees what a comfort zone means, we shout out the words 'safe', 'secure', 'familiar'. And what does he call it? 'A dead zone, a half-lived life zone.' A comfort zone might feel safe and familiar, but it is a place where nothing happens and nothing grows. We need to step outside it and allow room for nerves, fear and self-doubt. To experiment, practise and make mistakes. Have faith, even if you fake it at the beginning. Acting confident comes first. Feeling confident comes later.

Developing the skills to handle difficult thoughts and feelings more effectively, and shifting our focus to what we want out of life, takes time and practice. It's like going to the gym – you start with the small weights and build up. You don't run a 5k without first going through the early stages when your lungs burn and you want to throw your trainers in the bin. You will get there, you will learn to live better with your anxiety. It'll still be with you, but it won't have the same negative power, because by reading this book and going through the exercises, you are already:

- Recognizing life is difficult and you are human. Not disordered or defective.

- Understanding your sensitivity makes you feel things more intensely than others.

- Noticing when anxiety is hooking you up and keeping you trapped.

- Knowing that avoiding, blocking or fighting it makes it worse.

And you are beginning to realize that:

- Fusing with a story of past hurts or future fears stops you being present.

HOW TO CALM OUR ANXIOUS THOUGHTS

- Should-ing, ought-ing and must-ing are self-imposed rules and judgements.
- Seeing your mind is looking out for you helps bring a kindness to what it's doing.
- Naming the narrative helps unhook you, creating a space to move.
- Opening and breathing into thoughts, feelings, emotions and memories creates flexibility.
- Staying where you are, or going towards what matters, is always your choice.

If that looks like a lot, boil it down to three things: Be present. Open up. Do what matters.

You can choose not to do this. You can let your brain tell you this is a waste of time, that you've tried everything before, that it's easier to give up. That's valid. Your mind is looking out for you, so it would be surprising if you didn't think like this. The brain is like a problem-solving machine that judges and then tries to exert control over a difficult situation – of course it wants to distract, or disconnect, or disengage. And sometimes it throws a wobbly, metaphorically folding its arms and stamping its feet and shouting, 'This is hopeless! I'll never do it!'

Notice it, name it, know that it's part of being human and that its purpose is to try to protect you from failure and avoid bad things happening. And then, make a choice. Stay hooked up with the difficult thoughts, feelings and sensations if you choose, or unhook from them to move in a different direction – one that takes you towards the life you'd prefer to lead. Where you are acting and behaving like the sort of person you want to be. Where you are living out your values.

Values

As I mentioned earlier, values describe how we want to live and engage with the world. They can inspire, motivate and propel us towards a life where we are acting and behaving like the person we want to be. Remind yourself of the miracle question in Chapter 1, where you woke up tomorrow and were not struggling so hard with difficult thoughts and feelings. Ask yourself again:

- What would you be doing differently?
- What would you be doing less of?
- What would you be doing instead?
- What would other people notice about you?

This is a good way of teasing out what's important to you, deep down, and what you want your life to be about. You might want to strive for more balance, or learning, or embrace more courage and adventure. You may want to focus on family, or self-care, or taking up opportunities you've shied away from. Whatever these things are, they'll give you an idea of what your values are. What has meaning for you, when everything else falls away. It can be helpful, if you're struggling to identify values, to think of someone who you look up to, who you respect and admire. Have a think about what they stand for, how they treat others, what it is about them that you like and what qualities you'd like to bring into play in your own life.

Another way of identifying values is thinking about a landmark birthday, with all your friends, family, even some work colleagues there. I had one of these recently and it was like being at my own funeral, but in a good way, because people were saying lovely things. And already my self-critical voice is saying, 'Show-off! What are they saying behind your back though?' So, I am thanking my inner voice and recognizing that, actually, some of the values they spoke of, like being loyal, caring and tenacious, are those I'm proud to hold.

And here's a great way of clarifying values too. It's called the 'Bull's Eye' exercise, developed by Tobias Lundgren, adapted by Russ Harris,[1] and tweaked by me. I've done this with a room full of sceptical police officers who were leaning back in their chairs, arms folded, giving me hard stares. Ditto exhausted ambulance workers and battle-weary journalists. But it works – each group softened into it and each person got something unique out of it. If you are doubtful too, that's OK. It's just your brain doing that thing again. Give it a go, just for fun.

Exercise: The Bull's Eye

Values are not goals. They are actions and directions. For example, a goal might be to get married; a value would be a fulfilling relationship. A career goal would be promotion;

a value would be to find satisfaction in work. You may reach a goal, you may not, but your values will be there for as long as they're important to you – probably forever – although they may shift in priority.

The Bull's Eye exercise is a values dartboard divided into four: your work and education, your leisure, your relationships and your personal growth and health.

Start by writing down your values in relation to these areas. There's no judgement here, just write what comes to mind, remembering you're not looking at goals, but the direction you'd like your life to take if there were fewer obstacles than now. What's most meaningful to you? What do you want you and your life to stand for? What do you care about and would like to experience more of?

Once you complete this, you'll have a better idea of what is important to you. Somehow, seeing it in black and white makes you think: Ah! My emotional investment has been here, but I'm neglecting this part and that's why something feels off.

Anxiety has more power to make us feel miserable and unbalanced if a part of our life is askew.

1. Work/education: This can be your workplace and career, volunteering or learning. What is it about doing these things that has value to you, beyond salary? Financial security is a goal; values might be professionalism, a can-do attitude, respect towards colleagues, achievement, integrity, innovative thinking and developing skills.

....

....

2. Relationships: Partners, friends, your social circle, parents, colleagues. Think about what has meaning for you in these relationships and how you want to be in them. Perhaps what qualities you'd like to develop. Examples might be: respect, honesty, compassion, communication and transparency.

....

....

3. Personal growth/health: This is about what best supports you in life. It might be exercise, nutrition, being in nature, religion, spirituality, developing mindfulness practice, or addressing health concerns.

....

....

4. Leisure: What's important in your home life? Whether it's hobbies, sports or music, it can be any way you have fun or rest and relax. It might be physical fitness, mental stimulation, creativity, adventure. Don't worry if there's overlap with any of the other areas.

....

....

Once you've got your values, have a think about how close you are in each of the areas and then put an 'X' on the dartboard below. If you hit the Bull's Eye, you're pretty much living by your values in that area. If your X is off the board, you're off the mark.

The Bull's Eye[2]

Since there are four areas of valued living, you should mark four Xs on the dart board.

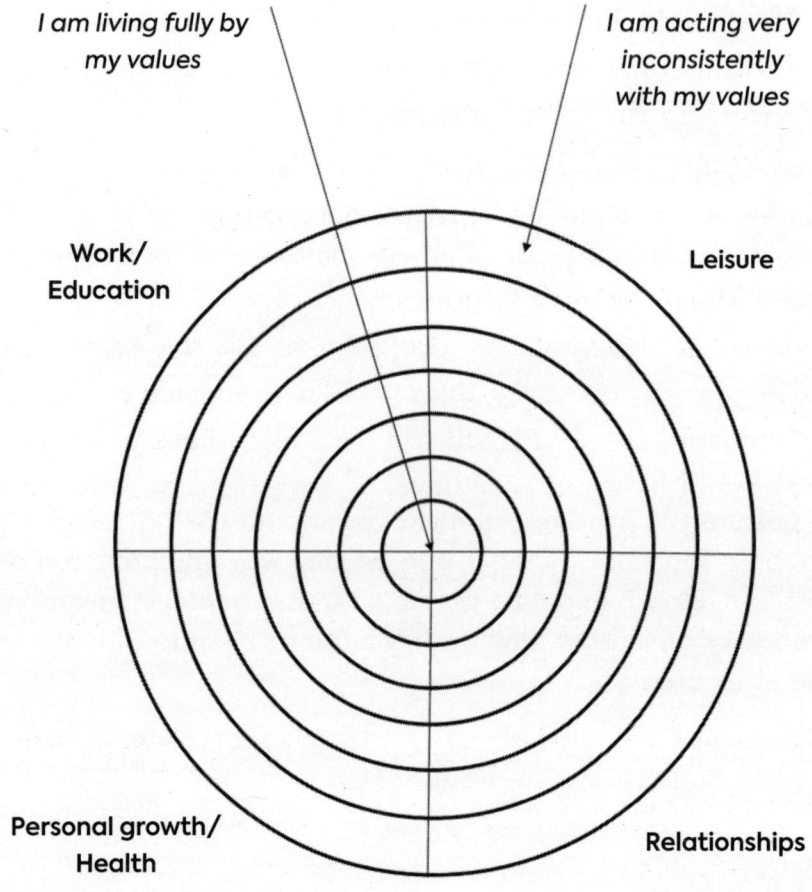

You can usually see what's off-kilter here and start thinking about what you want to do about it. Because you have a choice. You can choose to move towards your values and closer to the Bull's Eye. Or not. Bear in mind that the 'not' might be the thing that keeps us stuck in anxiety. That fearful, doubting, self-blaming stuff, with its avoidance, distraction and inflexible rules. The unhelpful, unproductive thoughts, feelings and behaviours that move us away from a purposeful life.

If, after the Bull's Eye exercise, it's still hard to identify and locate what your values are and how you might live by them, try this next exercise.

Exercise: Living my values

There are 100 common values in this list.[3]

Without thinking too deeply, tick all the ones that resonate with you. The values you'd act on when being the person you believe yourself to be. Not the ones you think you should have, or must have, or need to have. The ones you believe you *do* have. That add purpose and meaning to the way you live and behave.

If your value isn't here, add it at the end.

Acceptance	Dignity	Inclusivity	Professionalism
Accountability	Diversity	Independence	Reliability
Achievement	Empathy	Individuality	Respect
Adventure	Encouragement	Industriousness	Responsibility
Ambition	Equality	Integrity	Resourcefulness
Assertiveness	Ethics	Intelligence	Safety
Authenticity	Excellence	Intimacy	Self-awareness

Autonomy	Excitement	Joy	Self-care
Balance	Fairness	Justice	Self-development
Beauty	Faith	Kindness	Selflessness
Being the best	Family	Knowledge	Service
Boldness	Fitness	Learning	Spirituality
Caring	Flexibility	Love	Stability
Challenge	Forgiveness	Loyalty	Success
Compassion	Freedom	Making a difference	Supportiveness
Connection	Friendliness	Mindfulness	Tenacity
Contribution	Fun	Open-mindedness	Thoughtfulness
Cooperation	Generosity	Order	Trustworthiness
Community	Giving back	Originality	Truthfulness
Courage	Grace	Passion	Understanding
Creativity	Gratitude	Patience	Usefulness
Curiosity	Growth	Perfection	Versatility
Daring	Honesty	Perseverance	Warmth
Dedication	Humility	Pleasure	Wealth
Dependability	Humour	Power	Wisdom

You'll have ticked loads, I'm sure. But you'll notice some values fall together naturally, like caring, kindness, compassion, generosity, fairness, selflessness. Or ambition, power, knowledge, intelligence, professionalism, success, wealth, being the best. Or balance, stability, self-care, growth, mindfulness. Or courage, daring, adventure, boldness, independence, freedom. You get the idea.

Now, of all those values – choose just three and write them here:

1.

2.

3.

Then, with your top three values, create three sentences, with an action attached to each. For example: Act with (insert value) or embrace (insert value), or seek, promote, encourage, strive for (insert value). Write them in the spaces below.

When a situation comes up with difficult thoughts and feelings, I will…

1.

2.

3.

This is how you live your values. They are your go-to phrases when things are tough and they belong uniquely to you. And the beauty is, they are adaptable and changeable. They don't come with 'musts' and 'shoulds' and 'oughts' attached. They're flexible and positive and might move around a bit. Professionalism and success might be more or less important as the years go by. Ditto family, or faith, or giving back.

Here's an example of mine after I completed this exercise with a group a few years ago.

1. Act with kindness

2. Embrace curiosity

3. Seek joy

My husband's top three values were integrity, creativity and fairness. One of my sons picked justice, courage and perseverance. We want all of them, don't we? We believe we can be all these good things. But the Rule of Three is ancient, powerful and memorable for a reason. Three is enough to keep in our minds, or in a book, or on a sticky note by our desk or bed. And those three little phrases can form part of our future story as we learn to live alongside anxiety.

Practising values

These are pointers, not a plan. Anxious people don't want to lose the healthy desire for striving and nor should they, but be willing to be clunky. Be willing to mess up. If you're too rigid, you're at risk of burning out or beating yourself up if it goes awry. It's about workability and flexibility.

The aim is not to get rid of anxiety or even reduce it. It's to have realistic ways of working with it – recognizing when we have a choice over how to respond in a difficult situation and going back to our values, our internal moral compass, to guide us.

Here's an example. I'm off to a work party tomorrow night where I won't know many people and my anxiety began as soon as I accepted the invitation. Thoughts started bouncing around about judgements, expectations, concerns about what I'll wear, what I'll say, how I'll look. Once again, my default action is to avoid. Creating temporary relief, followed by further anxious feelings and more worrying about missing out, or upsetting the host.

Once I've decided to go, there's another choice. How do I manage my nerves between now and then? I might tell myself: 'I will not worry about the event I should go to' or 'I'm going to stop caring what other people think of me'. That's unrealistic. I know that trying *not* to think something will only make the anxiety worse – and I will still care what others think, too. How about: 'When worry comes up, I'll notice, pause and check in with my values of connecting with and being curious about other people' or 'If my "not good enough" voice appears, I'll acknowledge my values of honesty, authenticity and self-compassion'. Or I'll just go back to those three mantras: act with kindness (to me and the host), embrace curiosity (about the party and other people), seek joy (because it might be fun).

When thoughts and feelings show up, you have a choice about which direction to move in, but pausing to notice that you can choose how to react takes practice and you might feel you're in a liminal state (from *limin*, meaning 'threshold'). Transitioning from the known and instinctive to the unknown and new can feel uncomfortable. Letting go of old patterns and scripts is hard. This stuff is woven into us and is easily triggered when facing a novel, challenging situation. Untangling it takes awareness, engagement and lots of compassion.

The C-word

Ah, there's compassion again. Even I can struggle with the concept and I've written a 60,000-word thesis and published two academic papers on it. But defusing from self-criticism and moving towards self-compassion is the only way to handle anxiety. Because there are three options here. Option one is to fight it. Option two is to distract, disconnect and disengage from it. Option three is to stay with it, understand what your mind is trying to do, and try to make room for the pain by being kind to yourself. Options one and two hook us up and suck the life out of us. Option three gives us vitality and a sense of positive movement.

Dr Russ Harris says it's like motivating a donkey. Apparently, there are lots of donkeys in Australia. If you want your donkey to take your goods to market, you can beat it and whip it and it'll probably get there, but over time it will suffer and get ill. If you tell it that it's a good donkey and give it carrots, it'll also get there but you'll have a happy donkey with excellent night vision. Kindly acknowledging the suffering part of yourself is self-care. It's carrot, rather than stick.

Another C-word is 'control'. I once interviewed a sailor called Robin Elsey-Webb who had a life-changing experience while returning home from crewing a boat. He was attacked for no apparent reason and left for dead. Robin was lucky to survive – which he did, thanks to his girlfriend, Liz, who needed to make fast yet agonizing decisions about his care. He now has fifteen metal plates holding his head together. Is he giving up sailing? Not a bit of it. When I was interviewing him he was planning to complete the Vendée Globe yacht race – a single-handed, non-stop, non-assisted, round the world race where you sail alone for around 30,000 miles and up to 100 days. It'd be high stress on those high seas. How would he cope? I asked him. 'Control the controllables,' he replied, simply. He was right. Focusing our energy and attention on what we can influence, and letting go of what we can't, is the only way to get through the emotional storm.

Exercise: Dropping anchor

When the anxiety waves are high, when you feel like you are being battered by the salty slap of negative thoughts and the safety of the harbour is just out of reach, try to drop anchor. Think of it as a way of steadying the boat so you don't capsize. It's another Russ Harris metaphor and he suggests the acronym ACE might help with it.[4] Not the adverse childhood experiences we learned about earlier – this is an ACE that's grounding and positive.

A is *Acknowledge your inner experience.* Notice and name the difficult thoughts and feelings whipping through your mind. You don't need to get into a debate about whether they're true or false, just put the sensations into words, like 'here's anger' or 'I'm noticing worry again' or 'this is a painful memory showing up'.

C is *Connect and come back into your body.* Control your physical actions by standing up, stretching, moving around, changing your breathing, pushing your feet into the floor. Control the controllables.

E is *Engage with the world around you* by expanding your awareness to see, smell, hear and touch what is there – in addition to what you're experiencing internally. We are not trying to distract from the painful thoughts and feelings; we're seeing the bigger picture so we can refocus on where we want to go.

Dropping anchor is another way of being present so you can do what matters. Do it when the emotional weather is calm, or when the wind is getting up and your boat is starting to pick up speed – like if you're late for an appointment, or if you've made a silly mistake. Acknowledge, connect, engage. Open up, be present, and do what matters.

Don't let someone else drive your bus

When Philippa Perry and I were in her spare room, eating sponge fingers and drinking tea, we were chatting about all the techniques we use that we've found helpful with clients who are anxious with a strong self-critical voice. She tells it to take a back seat. I do something similar with an Acceptance and Commitment Therapy tool originally developed by Dr Steven C. Hayes and colleagues, called 'Passengers on the Bus'. Doing what matters means teasing out our values and turning them into an action plan. Values guide us and we need them to move us towards where we want to go. At the risk of mixing my metaphors, now we've dropped anchor, I'm jumping off the ship and getting on a bus.

Exercise: Passengers on the Bus[5]

Imagine you're the driver of a bus.

It's your bus and you've been driving it for as long as you can remember. You set the speed and the direction and you want to drive it towards the things that are important to you, where you feel things sit well with you and everything feels aligned with your values.

Have a think about what makes life rich and meaningful down that road. You may see yourself spending more time with family and friends, finding joy in embracing new things, exploring your creativity and learning, focusing on your personal growth. It may be developing connections with others, looking after your health, developing more compassion. What are the things that make your eyes sparkle – and if you could orientate your life around them – what would that look like?

Here you are, driving this bus, and you become aware of your passengers – some are lovely, kind, funny passengers but one is your self-critical passenger. Take a minute to really think about this self-critical passenger and the kinds of things they say to you.

This passenger has got on to your bus at some point in your life, maybe early childhood, maybe your teenage years, but here you are as a grown-up and here they still are with you, on the bus.

Imagine your self-critical passenger is standing or sitting close to you. Can you describe them? What do they look and sound like? A mean girl, a monster, a parent? Do they look like you or someone else? Do they have a name, a smell, a shape?

Notice there's you, driving your bus, and then there's your self-critical passenger, right next to you. Notice what they're saying. Perhaps it's that you're going the wrong way or are a bad driver. Maybe they're telling you that you're driving too fast or too slowly and it's the wrong destination anyway. They might tell you that everyone is watching how badly you're driving this bus and noticing how worthless you are and sniggering to all the other passengers about you. Notice all the familiar sensations that come up when this critic speaks to you and where you feel them in your body. It might be annoyance, frustration, sadness, panic. Just acknowledge and connect with them.

Before we deal with this self-critical passenger, let's have a think about how we've dealt with them in the past. Answer this question:

When I have a self-critical thought, I…

If you answer that you agree with it, argue with it or avoid it, you have stopped moving. Dealing with the self-critical passenger in these ways forces you to stop the bus and take your hands off the wheel so you can fight with it. Or it makes you block out what they're saying and grit your teeth to white-knuckle it down the road. Or just turn round and go home.

Any of those tactics are exhausting, and while you're engaging in them, how much real progress are you making to get towards that place where your eyes start sparkling again? Exactly.

Now, I know what you're thinking. Just throw the damn passenger off the bus. The trouble is, they'll get on at the next stop anyway. You've tried all these strategies and still they are here, nagging and spitting out insults and generally being unpleasant.

How you respond to them makes perfect sense. You want to keep them quiet. You want to ignore them. Completely understandable. The problem is that while you're doing this, either your bus isn't moving or you're hurtling down the road so fast, you're highly likely to crash.

What would it be like to allow the self-critical passenger to come along for the ride? Underneath that appalling behaviour is a good intention. Self-critical thoughts are there to tell us to be safe, to avoid suffering, to try harder so we can achieve good things. They just go about them in the wrong way. You could talk to your self-critical passenger a bit differently. 'I hear what you're saying,' you could say. 'Thank you for alerting me. Thanks for trying to help. I know you have good intentions for me. I know you want to protect me and, to do that, you think you have to talk nastily to me.'

Try to recognize why they're there and then talk to them in a caring way. Show compassion to your self-critic. Say they can stay on the bus, but they have to take their place alongside everyone and everything else. You may even want to invite your quieter, self-compassionate passenger to sit beside you. There they are, at the back.

You don't hear from them much when the self-critical passenger is shouting. It's too loud for them to be heard. But they are there.

It might be hard to show compassion to your critic, and it feels odd at first, because we are bullied and made fearful by them, but you can start to do so. You're saying to yourself that the arguing, ignoring and agreeing with the negative, self-critical thoughts have not worked up until now, so you're going with something else.

Try it the next time the self-critic shows up. However you respond, it's useful information about what you usually do to quieten it.

Here's the choice: you either FEAR it: Fawn – agree. Be Enraged – argue. Avoid – block. Or Run – escape.

Or you are CALM with it: Curiosity – be interested.

Allow – accept it. Let go – of the struggle. And Move – forward.

Psychological flexibility is a willingness to try to meet your anxiety, your harsh self-critic, as a compassionate observer, rather than a combatant.

Finally, when calming anxious thoughts – there are four As to remember

1. Acknowledge anxious thoughts without judgement or a fight. Allow them to be there even if you don't like them and don't want them.

2. Accommodate those thoughts, let them make themselves at home if needs be.

3. Appreciate what they have to offer, if they're alerting you to important stuff you need to deal with or reminding you of values you may be neglecting.

4. Act in a way that moves you towards behaving like the person you believe you can be.

We are all just doing our best in situations that keep testing us, but as that great sage Winnie the Pooh once said, 'You are braver than you believe, stronger than you seem, and smarter than you think.'[6]

Yes, we are.

Chapter 8: A quick refresher

- Accept unpleasant thoughts without suppression; they're trying to help.
- Show compassion to them, then unhook from them and move towards the direction you want to go in.
- Always have your values at the heart of what you do. They are your internal compass.
- Sometimes, anxious thoughts are priming you for a challenge – relabel them as excitement or anticipation.
- Self-doubt does not mean stop – have faith in your ability to manage tough things.

9

How to Manage Our Anxious Behaviours

'Tell me, what is it you plan to do with your one wild and precious life?'

Mary Oliver[1]

Do what matters

Henry has prostate cancer. He's in his sixties and is funny and self-effacing, despite telling me about his depressive, spiralling thoughts. Not surprising that he's got those. Henry was diagnosed in 2017, had surgery and radiotherapy to get rid of the tumour, and then two years later, the disease came back. Now, he tells me, the cancer is advanced, incurable and he's been given six years to live.

I already knew about the devastating effects of this disease. My lovely friend and *BBC Breakfast* colleague Bill Turnbull also lived with prostate cancer. Both men regretted not getting checked sooner. But I have learned another valuable lesson from them too, which I want to share with you. And their words, uttered to help others, should be tattooed on my own cancer-scarred body – which, through sheer bloody good luck, is still standing, when many are not.

Seize the life you have left and live it to its fullest, with the people you love. Hold the things that are important to you close. Behave like the person you believe yourself to be. Do what matters.

The quote from Mary Oliver at the start of the chapter is from her poem called 'The Summer Day'. It was used on an eight-week group mindfulness course that Henry attended, which transformed the life he had left. I am talking to him for that research project I spoke about earlier, looking at developing self-compassion and how hard that can be with constant worry, negative thinking and a strong, self-critical voice. The poem comes up when we are talking about how best he can manage 'all that shit flying round my brain'. He has already 'tried to use all my breathing and rationalization and evidence-based things like CBT'. But Henry says that 'nothing, nothing touched it at all... I couldn't even get into a place where I could think straight.' So he took action and signed up to the mindfulness course as 'the last throw of the dice'. There, he met people who understood what he was experiencing and showed him kindness. He did gentle movement, went on a silent retreat and gathered the courage to talk to his church community about his disease.

Cancer had threatened to isolate him. Instead, he opened up to an increased connection with others, developed self-compassion and committed himself to living his life with meaning, however much there was left of it. 'I think what Mary Oliver was saying to me at the end of that poem, is something about positivity,' he tells me. 'And don't waste the time that you've got in front of you. Use it to good effect.'

Bill was the same. In 2018, he invited me to his home in Suffolk that he shared with his wife Sesi, their three children and their two dogs. Family and a few friends knew about his cancer but he wanted to make it public to raise awareness of the disease. I was to interview him for the *Radio Times* magazine. I would be asking the questions, he'd be answering them. Very different to our *BBC Breakfast* days when we used to lark about – and do the news – on the red sofa. Not roles either of us welcomed, but I was privileged to be asked.

I knock on Bill's front door and he opens it with a smile and a hug. Sesi's just made tea, so we go into the sitting room and sit on another, different sofa to have another, weirder conversation. Bill has already told me about his regime of hormones and steroids, and as we settle in, he references his uncharacteristically swollen face. 'It leaves me not looking quite the young Adonis that you remember from a few weeks ago,' he laughs.

There is a lot of laughing in the hours we spend together. There are other, more complex emotions too. 'The contract I thought I had with life has been rather shortened,' he says, with typical understatement. The doctors had suggested he might live for another five or ten years. In the end, it will be less than that. As we chat, we aren't to know how long his 'contract' with life is, but he reminds me of a phrase coined by our friend and *BBC Breakfast* editor Alison Ford when she was diagnosed with incurable cancer. 'I don't want to die dying,' she said. Bill doesn't either. He wants to spend it living, surrounded and sustained by the love of his family, doing the things that matter.

'You have to be positive, don't you?' he says. 'I know I'm not going to get cured and I'm realistic about the long-term prospects, but they're not bad. Most importantly, I really do think I've had a wonderful life, with amazing experiences as a reporter and a presenter. And if it was all to end tomorrow, I couldn't have any complaints. I've had a really marvellous time.' As we come to the end of our recorded chat, we joke about going back on telly to present *Bill and Sian's Cancer Club* – a club, he says, with lots of members that no one wants to join.

On *BBC Breakfast*, we'd have this routine at the end of a showbiz interview if it felt like it had run its course. One of us would ask a cringe-worthy question, alerting the other that it was time to wrap up. Bill smiles as he remembers his: 'Is there one last message you'd like to give to your fans?' I follow up with mine: 'What's next for you?'

He is thoughtful for a moment and then answers both. 'To plan to make sure that my time is spent well. It's easy to let a day drift by, doing the usual sorts of things, and it's important to make sure that they all count. A determination to make the most of the time that you have left, however short or long that may be.'

A deep appreciation too, of those who love him, including his wife Sesi, who's waiting to have lunch with us. He will, he says, 'carry on doing the things that I enjoy doing' – like spending time with family and commentating for his beloved English Football League One club, Wycombe Wanderers, the team he's supported for two decades. After his death, players, staff and fans will remember him as humble, generous and warm. Someone who made others 'feel like a million dollars'.[2]

Bill died at the age of sixty-six, not knowing the profound impact he made on those he met and those he never knew. Those who got checked for cancer, because of him. Who are living, because of him.

The most common regret of those who are dying

The thinking and the feeling in life is crucial, but it's the doing which makes the difference. How we choose to behave, even in the face of suffering, can be transformative. But many of us only do that life audit towards the end of it. Bronnie Ware, an American palliative care nurse, says the most common regret among those who are dying is 'I wish I'd had the courage to live a life true to myself, not the life others expected of me'.[3] If you had to live the life which was true to you, how would it be different to the one you are living now? What would you do if you weren't frightened of what other people might think? Think back to your values exercise from the previous chapter. Can you allow yourself to follow a path guided by the things which are meaningful to you, behaving like the person you believe yourself to be?

Behaviour that is driven by our values makes for a better, less anxious life. Scientists analysed those with generalized anxiety disorder (GAD) who worried excessively and uncontrollably. Those who were most anxious, and often also depressed, were less likely to describe themselves as living and acting according to their values than those who did not have anxiety.[4] Why? Because if you are fused with your critical and internal judgements, you may avoid situations and experiences, despite wanting to do them. Like that work party I'm going to tomorrow. The discomfort of possible judgement or failure seems to outweigh the connection, engagement and joy you might find in those moments. Withdrawing adds to anxiety and keeps us isolated.

But that study of generalized anxiety disorder suggested that many of those who learned to become more aware of their thoughts and feelings reduced their avoidance strategies. They started making changes which felt consistent with their values too – in other words, doing more of the things that felt meaningful to them. And they said they were more accepting, less worried and distressed, and that the quality of their life had improved. It's a small study, but research elsewhere backs it up. Change comes when you are present, open up to difficult thoughts and feelings, and then act on what's really important to you.

HOW TO MANAGE OUR ANXIOUS BEHAVIOURS

Living a life true to you

Changing behaviours to manage anxiety is not a one-time fix, it's a lifelong process. And in a way, it feels less intimidating if we appreciate the to and fro of it: that there is no 'ta-da!' moment when it's all fixed. It's never fixed. We are all just doing our best, with what we know, now. I've learned to live with anxiety by making peace with it and with myself, and trying to do the things that evidence tells me will work. Which is what I'm passing on to you. It's your choice to do them or not. None of us needs to follow a life plan so exacting that it adds to our anxiety.

I remember chatting with the ex-Buddhist monk Andy Puddicombe, who created the meditation app Headspace. I knew mindfulness helped with anxiety, because I'd written academic papers on it. I'd been taught how to do it, had researched its beneficial effects on excessive worrying, and used mindful breathing with my clients. Yet some days, it just didn't work for me. It was too hard. My brain was scattered and resistant. Andy told me I was holding on too tightly, trying to be successful at being mindful yet making myself more anxious in the process. 'See it as a goalless path,' he said. It doesn't have to be forty-five minutes, cross-legged, trying to reach a Zen-like state.

Bring it into your day, lightly. After the mindfulness course, Henry started weaving. That's right, on a loom. Watching the bobbin go back and forth over the cloth was his way of bringing a mindful moment to his day.

Tanya, living with bowel cancer, found her mindful moment outside. 'Mindful gardening,' she says with a laugh. 'I love weeding because I've always found it quite meditative. You're pulling things up. It's so fulfilling.' Connecting with the earth, with nature, clearing away the weeds to make a space for things to bloom. It's an active metaphor for what is going on in her head.

Finding the stuff that you love, whether it's being creative or spending time in nature or connecting with others – it all helps with the tumult of uncertainty. For Henry, as well as mindfulness, it's faith and friends and self-compassion that help. He got in touch recently to say how valuable they all were and how fortunate he felt to still be here, five years and ten months after being told he had six years to live. He also wanted to tell me how much admiration he had for Bill after he spoke out about the cancer they both shared. Turns out they'd been at school together, too.

Doing something soothing and showing self-kindness lowers our threat response and our anxiety too.[5] But if we make nourishing activities a chore, or something we need to succeed at, it becomes yet another stick to beat ourselves with. Understanding and being kind towards our difficult thoughts and feelings makes us more likely to be able to do something about them. As the self-compassion researcher Kristin Neff says, you can't heal what you can't feel.[6]

Thinking, feeling and doing

We are all thinking, feeling and doing people, but those of us with anxiety tend to live in our minds. We try to out-think our problems. Sometimes the strategy works and the feared situation doesn't happen, or it changes. Our clever brain decides that thinking is the best way to handle challenging, frightening or unpredictable situations and it becomes the preferred way of coping.

As psychotherapist Philippa Perry says, 'People that think all the time, overthink and go around in circles because they never get to doing. And they don't know the feeling behind the thinking. They're just intellectualizing. It's a great way of becoming anxious.'

Remember how some of the people we've met in this book learned to take the power back from anxiety? They noticed and named the anxious thoughts. Knew when to use nervous energy as a performance enhancer. Saw negative emotions as useful messengers of important information but understood, with kindness, when their brilliant brain misfired and told them to be anxious and fearful of a situation that didn't deserve it. They registered the impact of sensations and signals on their body.

And then, instead of feeling stuck or hooked up on memories, fears and emotions, they were willing to accept them and move towards a different way of living with them. In other words, observing when anxiety threatened to make them avoid or withdraw or punish, and then thanking anxiety for looking out for them and doing different, values-based actions instead.

After a period of social anxiety, Philippa forced herself to 'flex the social muscle' and went out to reconnect with the people, places and parties that she'd previously enjoyed before she got out of the habit. It took up to a year to feel comfortable again, because she felt awkward and self-conscious – had forgotten 'how to do the give and take of dialogue'. What helped was knowing, deep down, that she has a curiosity about others and a 'conviction that I *do* enjoy this'.

Newsreader Nina Hossain felt the same: she didn't want to miss out on social interaction, even though she found it hard, so she learned to recognize when she was avoiding situations and would 'push myself out of the comfort zone and do them. Just jazz hands my way through it.' Philip Selway, Radiohead's drummer, kept getting back on stage, even after experiencing such terror that he couldn't feel his limbs, or hit his bass drum properly. Doing so meant acknowledging the gremlins, reframing anxiety as a source of positive energy, and building up 'a backlog of good experiences. The moments that define who you are. It may not completely look like you'd like it to look in your head. But you're always moving towards that point.'

For Daisy Goodwin, it was noticing the harsh self-critic who warned her every day as she settled down to write her play *By Royal Appointment* that 'no one's going to read it', but writing 1,000 words anyway. Knowing that 'everything you do has to come from a position of passion'. That although any failure feels like the sinking of the *Titanic* to you, to everyone else 'it's a tiny model boat capsizing'. Of course, the play was far from a failure, described as having insight, humour and heart. Tickets sold well and the lead actress was word-perfect.

But talking of being hit by an emotional storm, remember yachtsman Robin Elsey-Webb, training for the Vendée

HOW TO MANAGE OUR ANXIOUS BEHAVIOURS

Globe round the world race after a life-changing injury? He put it another way. Learn to 'control the controllables'. Let go of the things you can't do anything about, and take possession of the things you can. And use your anchor if the waves of anxiety threaten to tip your boat over.

Self-doubt and micro-ambitions

What unites everyone we've met in this book is they kept going, despite the questions, doubts and fears. They learned to live alongside their anxiety, grow with it, be kind towards it – but it wasn't enough just to understand it more deeply, they also had to *do*. That meant reminding themselves of their values in challenging times, to steer them towards the direction they wanted to go in. Whether those values were connection, community, friendship, creativity, exploration, they all showed up in the actions they took. And they kept doing them.

In the autumn of 2024, I was asked by Australian songwriter Tim Minchin whether I'd interview him for the first date of his UK book tour. Tim does so much more than write songs. He sings, he acts, he makes us laugh and cry and think. There's the record-breaking musical *Matilda*, of course, and the award-winning adaptation of *Groundhog Day*. A TV comedy *Upright*, as well as countless songs and albums and sell-out tours. He is also a poet-philosopher, using creativity to talk about love, success, rejection and thriving in a meaningless universe.

At the Albert Hall in Manchester, in front of a packed crowd, we talk for two hours about all those ideas. His book *You Don't Have to Have a Dream* is based on life lessons from his speeches, including one to the University of Western Australia which went viral, amassing tens of millions of views. Watch it; it'll make you think and laugh. One of the key messages that's stuck with me is this: be micro-ambitious. Have little dreams and short-term goals. Be careful of long-term ones because good things are often on the periphery and you might miss them. Do the small things, even when – especially when – you doubt yourself. And Tim does. Despite all that success. Self-belief yes, but also self-doubt. He works hard, he's authentic, he's kind. Those are good values to live by.

After our talk, he posts a picture of the two of us with a message that reads: 'My first book tour interview seemed to go down pretty damn well. Was a huge pleasure to chat with Dr Sian Williams, who is a brilliant, thoughtful, generous human.' And yes, not to toot my own horn, but that'll be one of those comments I'll remind myself of when I have my own self-doubt. You will have yours too, I'm sure. Like Philip Selway and his 'backlog of good experiences'. Store them all up so you have access when you need them.

And after all this, you may still be anxious. You may still hear the other voice that tells you that you'll screw up. You may feel that racing heart and churning stomach, want to run away and hide because it seems so powerful. None of this work you are doing eliminates anxiety. But it will shift the power balance. It will help you notice the trips and triggers that keep you trapped and then inform the choices you take, the values you live by, the environments you feel best in, the people and places that make your heart sing.

Anxiety has the power to alert us to what's wrong, so we can do something about it. And it also reminds us of one of our key strengths – our sensitivity. Because remember, it's your capacity to feel this intensely that makes you who you are. Makes you notice the others who are hurting and the things that need changing. I don't want to get rid of that – do you?

Action points

The key points in shifting the anxiety power balance are:

- Drop the struggle with it.
- Stand back and observe the anxious thoughts, feelings and sensations.
- Focus on the present, rather than past memories or future fears. Be here, now.
- Notice what people, places and opportunities your anxiety is making you avoid or escape from.
- Listen to what it's telling you which might be useful. Drop what isn't.
- Tune in to your values like courage, resilience, self-care and compassion for others – whatever they are.

- Think about small, workable actions to take you towards the life you want. And keep doing them.
- Remember the good things you've done and the person you know you can be.

A lot of these ideas come from acceptance and commitment therapy (ACT). ACT is a therapeutic approach based on something called relational frame theory – which seeks to explain how we derive meaning, relate and respond to the world. The psychologist behind both is Dr Steven C. Hayes (he of the Passengers on the Bus exercise from earlier) and recently he reminded me of a little ditty to summarize how the theories work: 'Learn it in one, derive it in two; put it in networks that change what you do.'[7] Understand it, relate to it differently, apply it and then keep doing it.

My own little ditty on managing anxiety would be: *Notice in one, name it in two, and make it a habit to change what you do.*

Yes, but...?

I know what you might be thinking. Yes, but... I've been living with this anxiety for decades and nothing I've tried works. Yes, but... what if I try and fail yet again? Yes but... I hardly know you, Sian, why should I trust what you say? Yes, but... if you still feel anxiety and haven't sorted yourself out, how are you going to help me? Yes, but... accepting my anxiety sounds like passive bullshit, why should I just accept what it's doing to me?

Add whatever 'Yes, but...' statements you're thinking and how they make you feel helpless and hopeless and get in the way of change. Notice how quickly your brain jumps in to judge you when you try something new. Understand that it's doing this to protect you from failure. I'm never going to convince you that your 'yes, but...' thoughts are wrong, or argue the true or false of them, because it's natural for our mind to do this when faced with something difficult. I bet you've tried incredibly hard to rid yourself of your anxiety, and I'd like to suggest if the previous habits haven't worked out, that you try something different. I know it takes courage and I know it's frightening. I have this stuff too. No one is exempt from pain, uncertainty and vulnerability, and none of those things go away, but actively being willing to accept that they're there makes them easier to live with.

The man in the arena

Try not to worry about how others will judge you on this path towards understanding your body, brain and behaviour and your new ways of thinking, feeling and doing. We are hardwired to care about what people think, but you don't have to care about what everyone thinks – especially not those who are not brave enough to do this themselves.

More than 100 years ago, US president Theodore Roosevelt told an audience in Paris: 'It is not the critic who counts; not the man who points out how the strong man stumbles, or where the doer of deeds could have done them better. The credit belongs to the man who is actually in the arena, whose face is marred by dust and sweat and blood; who strives valiantly; who errs, who comes short again and again, because there is no effort without error and shortcoming.'[8]

Roosevelt suggested that even if the man in the arena fails, he 'at least fails by daring greatly'. Dr Brené Brown took inspiration from his speech to write about vulnerability in her books, including *Daring Greatly* and *Rising Strong*. If you step into that arena, she says, get out of the habit of catching and holding on to the stuff from the cheap seats. Don't take feedback from those who are not courageous in their own lives; who are not in the arena getting their arse kicked.[9]

Being willing to get your arse kicked

If you choose to enter the arena, equip yourself with the tools to help you strive valiantly. There are more than 1,000 research papers which suggest the techniques shared with you in this book work, but they are ideas which may be new and strange and I can't give you guarantees that they will. Acceptance, commitment and self-compassion might feel unfamiliar if your life has been fraught with doubt and judgement, and it takes time to learn new habits.

That word 'acceptance' is a tough one too, because it can sound like giving up, giving in. Why should we accept anxiety, you may be thinking – isn't there good reason to be on edge, remembering what's happened in the past and what might face us in the future? But 'acceptance' doesn't mean resigning yourself to suffering or liking or approving it. It means acknowledging it and allowing it to be there. You know the Serenity Prayer? 'God, give me the courage to accept things I cannot change'? Whatever you believe, peace comes with accepting what we cannot control and acting on what we can. It's a willingness to stop struggling with things in our difficult past or letting them dominate our future. Insight on what has happened to us is important, but at some stage we have to focus on what we want to do differently. This is radical, active acceptance. It's not passive at all. It's more open-hearted than that.

Using our head, our heart, our hands

In Chapter 4, we heard about compassion focused therapy (CFT), designed for those with high levels of shame and self-criticism. I have lived with both. Many years ago, someone broke into my bedroom in a shared house while I was sleeping, did what he wanted to do and left. I have not slept in a bed which is against a wall since. My husband says I wake in 'muted fear' if he comes to bed late and stirs me, however hard he tries not to. I carried shame for freezing when it happened, then for not telling anyone. I have forgiven myself for what I did to survive and I am kind when instinctive reactions play out again. I am not alone. You too may have past experiences that render you voiceless, or frozen – and it can feel like a lifetime's work, this permission to feel pain, to open and expand around it, to hold it softly, breathe into it, bring a compassion to it. It's taken me a long time, but it is doable.

Think of it like this. Shifting the power of anxiety involves our head, our heart and our hands. The head is the noticing, naming, accepting part. It's not accepting that past hurts are OK, it's accepting that they happened and it's why you react the way you do. The heart is the commitment to change your behaviour to do things that are deeply important to you, to locate the bit in your soul where your values lie. To not let the bad things define you. The hands are what you do to take you towards the life you want to lead. Not trapped in the past, not frightened of the future.

Life improves with change, not by chance. Don't wait for the good things to happen to you. Don't think you don't deserve them. Don't keep beating yourself up. Support yourself as you grow; uncertainty can be painful. While you are taking the small, positive, realistic steps towards the life you want, be kind and be patient. You have faced worse. You are still here.

Exercise: Being willing to accept and commit to change

This exercise might help clarify the idea of willingness, when anxiety comes calling. Think about how you would complete the following sentences:

HOW TO MANAGE OUR ANXIOUS BEHAVIOURS

- My anxiety is like… – e.g. a judge, a critic, a bully
- It makes me feel… – e.g. frightened, sad, worthless, lonely
- It makes me want to… – e.g. avoid, punish, distract, withdraw
- I react to it by… – e.g. panicking, dissociating, overworking, procrastinating

Then think about what you are willing to do when it shows up next:

- I'll meet it with… – e.g. tolerance, patience, softness, curiosity, openness
- I'll say to it…. – e.g. here's the 'not good enough' story, the 'shame' narrative
- I'll act on it by…. – e.g. taking a breath, being kind, doing something with meaning

Action steps (and goals)

I've put goals in brackets above, because I'm mindful of Andy Puddicombe's 'goalless path'. Goals are a direction of travel, not a destination. There's no nod of approval for reaching them. They are yours, flexible and to be held lightly. A 'might', not a 'should'. Not about what you want to get rid of, but what you'd like to invite in. How might you act differently? What would you do less or more of?

How will you treat yourself and others, and engage with the world around you? Any activities you'd like to start or resume? Any people that you'd like to reconnect with or take a painful decision to give up on, to keep faith with yourself? Go back to your Bull's Eye exercise on page 240 to remind yourself of the life domains and personal values which could do with some focus.

Hopefully, you now understand more about who you are, how your mind works and why you do what you do. You've thought about what's important to you and where anxiety has got in your way. This is how to put that knowledge into action.

Values, goals and actions in practice

Remember Sophia from Chapter 2? She had anxiety and panic and had experienced physical, emotional and sexual abuse. Sophia lived with feelings of blame and shame, which were easy to hold – and frustration and anger, which were not. She binged on crap food and isolated herself. Sophia didn't believe she deserved good things. She had feelings of self-disgust, worthlessness and worried about what other people thought of her. The way she coped was by avoiding people altogether, withdrawing from difficult feelings, procrastinating and getting angry with herself.

When I asked Sophia what she wanted to stand for in the big picture, what qualities she wanted to develop based on her values, she was clear. She wanted to make

HOW TO MANAGE OUR ANXIOUS BEHAVIOURS

her family proud, to have a loving, long lasting relationship, and she said she wanted to be 'useful.' My final question asked what action she'd take to get there. More daily activity like walking, she replied. Making healthier food choices. Learning how to express emotions in a safe way and 'doing what I like, as well as what I must'.

We worked together for over a year. Sophia would talk and write or draw when the words wouldn't come. Re-authoring her story helped her reclaim her sense of power. Not just from those who had taken it originally, but from the anxiety which had exerted such a strong pull over her life since. She became kinder to herself, started taking responsibility for her health, did breathing exercises regularly and began helping others who'd gone through similar experiences. She knows she is not the finished article, none of us are. Or will be.

In our last session Sophia told me she'd bought me a gift. It was a beautiful, hardbacked gratitude journal. It was broken into sections. Level one was noticing, level two was reflecting and appreciating, and level three was practising gratitude. I have the diary in my hands now. This is my first entry from May 2021. In answer to the question *What happened today?* I wrote: 'I had my second vaccine, I submitted my psychology case study. I didn't hate working.' The next question: *Did something good happen to you today?* 'Fun conversation with colleagues. I tried meditating on the train. Not good, but I tried.' And the last one. *What could you be grateful for today?* 'I'm grateful that I'm feeling less pressure now the case study is submitted. Maybe I <u>can</u> do this job.'

Doubts, questions, fears. We all have them. Do it anyway. Keep going. Have faith.

Nourishing attachments

While you're going through all this, think about who you have in your corner who has faith in you too. In Chapter 7, we discovered the importance of attachment. When we are babies, having someone to care for us is crucial – and if it's not there, or is inconsistent, it feels dangerous, a feeling we learn to internalize as anxiety.

Dr Andrea Oskis is a therapist, a cook and a food writer who talks about the two key ingredients we need to sustain life: someone who takes care of us and something to eat. It's not just about physical sustenance – both bring good feelings and promote connection. And we get anxious if they aren't there. 'Anxiety is just our clue that something is wrong in our environment and we need to fix it,' she says.

Our attachment history can show up in our relationship with food. Think about yours. Perhaps you were nurtured and felt safe enough to venture from your secure base and take risks with new experiences and different foods. Or you might be more insecure in those attachments, feel anxious or avoidant. 'Someone who has been insecure in a more anxious way will get anxious over their food,' Andrea says. 'They're worried. Do they have enough of it? Is it there? Can I control it? And on the opposite side, the avoiding people will be the people that just think, "Ohh, I wish I had a pill to pop every day and that would give me my breakfast, lunch and dinner." They have a distance to it. It's a way of navigating the world, because then you don't have to stray into any grey areas, you don't have to go there with complexity.'

Food is never just something to eat. It can tell you about relationships, too. Because if you are anxious or avoidant with nourishment, she says, 'if you notice people are doing that in their food lives, my question would always be, where else in life are you doing that?'

I've read Andrea's book, marvellously titled *The Kitchen Shrink*,[10] and it rang true because I'd just been on a course and sat next to a food coach from Kuwait, who shared home-made snacks with me, unprompted. The following day she brought a bigger bag for us to eat together. 'That's so generous!' I said. 'You're lovely to have thought of me like that.' 'No,' she laughed. 'I'm just Arab. It's deeply ingrained to share what we have. It's a blessing.' It is also care and thoughtfulness and we are still in touch. It attached us.

Food can cut the loneliness out of life. When I worked at Maggie's Cancer Care centres, at the end of the day we sat round the kitchen table and shared what people brought. It opened the door to feelings that might not have been expressed before. It was powerful, emotional nourishment. I know that, when I had cancer, I was comforted by those who showed their love by cooking for me. Andrea says, 'In a crisis, it's the emotional help that gets you through it, but practical help can be a real stepping stone to letting someone in, and food can be a really nice way of getting there.'

The building blocks of trust, connection and compassion

Our attachment categories are not fixed in stone. Philippa Perry notes that 'we form in relationships and can reform in them'. She did. Her first attachment figure was not a parent, but her nanny. Philippa was sent off to boarding school, and when she came home, Nanny was gone. 'My secure attachment figure, the person that knew me the most and the best wasn't there anymore because apparently, I didn't need her anymore. I wasn't allowed to ask about her. And I wasn't allowed to grieve for her. So, I sort of just shut it all down.' She was ten years old. 'I think they would call it a nervous breakdown in those days. I couldn't stop crying for three days.'

I ask how she coped. Playing the class fool, making everyone laugh, she replies. 'But nothing deeper. I didn't have very close friends. Then I got married really quickly because I didn't think anybody would ever marry me.' It wasn't a happy relationship. 'Mostly it was him being unfaithful and me thinking I deserved that. And it was horrible. Him going "you're not good enough" and me kind of believing it.'

Philippa says she 'didn't think anyone could ever like me. Was very needy, didn't trust that anyone was ever going to stay around.' What moved her from an insecure attachment to a secure one? Meeting Grayson. 'There is nothing like being married to a loving man for thirty-five years to make you feel like "I'm OK, other people are OK. My friends stay around." It was reforming an attachment again.'

HOW TO MANAGE OUR ANXIOUS BEHAVIOURS

If you are thinking 'but I don't have anyone to connect with', then look beyond. It might not be your partner, or your family, or friends. It might be a neighbour down the road, someone you play online games with, someone in your faith community, or at the gym, or work, or college. I know an amazing woman, a Holocaust survivor called Trude Silman, who escaped from the Nazis at nine years old and came to the UK as a child refugee with nothing but fear, anxiety and bad memories. Now in her nineties, she spent most of her adult life trying to find her parents. She discovered that her father had been murdered at Auschwitz, but her mother remained missing. She has spent a lifetime searching for her. 'How did you survive with no one?' I asked her. 'The kindness of strangers,' she said. 'I reached for the outstretched hands.' Those outstretched hands are there, but sometimes we are reluctant to take them, frightened to show our vulnerability. And that can keep us stuck and rigid.

Connect with someone who is sensitive, reliable and consistent as you do this. Preferably more than one person. Look for places where that can happen, safely. You may be hesitant to start with, but it'll bring rewards and add some colour into your life, expanding it until, as Andrea Oskis says, we can experience 'the whole rainbow of feelings'.

When you're struggling, it can be hard to see the rainbow or reach for the outstretched hand. To move from self-criticism to feel deserving of love and self-compassion. Those who are sensitive might have spent so long pleasing other people they can't remember what they like or want.

To you, I'd say this. It's important to give kindness to others, but not to be worn out in the giving.

Dr Bessel van der Kolk says the question that often gets missed in therapy is the most important. It's this one: 'Who was there for you?' If you have a hard time answering it, think about where and when you have felt safe to feel what you feel. There will be someone, maybe even a community of people, who is there for you as you reconnect with the brain, the body and the behaviour, and establish different patterns of thinking and being and doing. To start living here, and not there.

How to nourish

Connections and relationships nourish and nurture us, just like food. They give us the energy to explore. But think back to the Three Circles from Chapter 4. If we are stuck on Threat, Drive or both, the Soothe – or nourish – gets lost. When we are anxious, we tend to reduce the number of activities that give us pleasure and nurture us: the ones that lift our mood, increase our energy and keep us calm. We may know that going out for a walk will make us feel better, but we don't have the will, or we feel tied to our work.

The number of depleting activities can rise too when we are on Threat, so we may turn to overeating, or overworking, or endlessly scrolling through social media or checking and rechecking emails.

It helps to ask ourselves honestly, 'How many nourishing

and how many depleting things do I do in a day?' Research suggests that even in small doses, doing more nurturing, values-led activities makes us feel better about ourselves, disrupts anxious or avoidant behaviour and jump-starts us towards something more joyful.

Exercise: Nourishing and depleting activities[11]

Start by asking yourself these general questions:

1. What nourishes me, increases my sense of wellbeing and makes me feel like I'm really living in the present moment?

2. What drains me and decreases my sense of being alive and present?

3. Accepting that there are things that I can't change, am I consciously choosing enough activities in my daily life that truly nourish me?

Some activities don't fit in either category. Paying bills and doing shopping may feel depleting, but there may be a sense of satisfaction or completion once they're done. You may not have any choice over doing them, but might reframe them differently.

Write a list of what you do in a typical day.

N = nourishing or nurturing – activities that lift, inspire or soothe you

D = depleting or draining – activities that drain energy, sink and smother you.

Activity	Nourishing/ Depleting (N, D)	Comments

When you look at the nourishing activities, perhaps ask yourself how you can change things, to have more time to do more of them.

HOW TO MANAGE OUR ANXIOUS BEHAVIOURS

And with the depleting or draining activities – can you do these less often, or if you can't, can you relate to them differently? Is there another way of looking at them? Is how you feel about them fact or opinion? Is this your self-critical, perfectionist voice speaking?

Here's an example. My black lab-cocker cross Molly is shedding all over the house. Big clumps of dark hair. And despite there being four people that live here, the tangled dog hair in every corner of every room only seems to bother me. I need to vacuum again and, because we all have better things to do, I know I will noisily and resentfully work my way around the house, huffing and cursing with no one noticing or caring. I can of course delegate, while recognizing that my perfectionist voice will begin as soon as I notice they have missed bits. Or I can accept that we have a shedding dog and ditch the drama. I can make a temporary commitment to do some of it, rather than waste time thinking how time-wasting it is. I can feel OK about not loving it, but will find satisfaction in it being gone. I can reward myself while doing it – tea in one hand, vacuum in the other, listening to a podcast.

Here's a more serious one. I need to go into hospital for an operation soon, which will involve general anaesthetic, surgery and recovery time. As I mentioned earlier, I died once on an operating table. Well, my heart stopped for a few minutes, then they restarted it, obviously. There's anxiety around that. And annoyance that I've had to pull out of the half marathon I was training for. The operation will deplete me, both physically and mentally. But I've been on a waiting list for eighteen months and I am grateful it's finally happening. I trust the surgeon wielding the knife. I am going into it healthy and strong, which means I'll recover faster. I am preparing by talking it through with the doctor, asking the physio which post-op exercises are safe, deferring my run until next year, booking a weekend away with a friend. I'm an impatient patient and I know my self-critical voice will tell me I'm not getting better quickly enough. I know there'll be anxiety beforehand too. But I can do things to minimize the impact of all that.

There are actions you can take now, even if they seem insignificant, which can make a real difference in reducing anxiety's power and reasserting your own. But also, making the most of the time you have left and not wasting it hooked up by everything anxiety says and does and makes you feel. As Steven C. Hayes says, 'Life is a choice. Anxiety is not a choice. Either way you go, you will have problems and pain. So, your choice here is not about whether or not to have anxiety. Your choice is whether or not to live a meaningful life.'[12]

And what will the meaningful life look like? The questions that Mary Oliver ends 'The Summer Day' with ask this: 'Doesn't everything die at last, and too soon? Tell me, what is it you plan to do with your one wild and precious life?'[13]

Chapter 9: A quick refresher

- It's not enough to think and feel, we must do. We need an action plan.

- The doing is anything that gets you unstuck and moves you towards the life you believe you can lead and the person you think you can be.

- Actions are based on values. Use them as a lighthouse to stay off the rocks and guide you.

- Notice in one, name it in two, make it a habit to change what you do – small actions can result in big change.

- Trust the voice that tells you you're doing OK, even if it's just a whisper.

10

And Finally... Four Extra Tips for Tending the Orchid

At the end of an evening news bulletin, there tends to be the '... and finally' story. After all the dark, depressing news is done, it's usually something uplifting and thought-provoking. It's meant to give you hope and send you off to bed smiling. By this point in the book, you may already be feeling a bit more positive after getting to know yourself better, understanding what anxiety makes you do and how hard you've tried to manage it, and developing new, more workable ways of living your life based on your values. In short, dropping the struggle with anxiety and learning new skills to live life better. But for all the orchids out there who need a bit of extra nurturing, here are some tips to keep you blooming.

Before we get there, a recap on what it means to be an orchid. Being anxious does not necessarily make you an orchid, and being sensitive does not necessarily make you anxious. But orchids, or highly sensitive people – often called HSPs – are more likely to experience stress, anxiety, depression, burnout and health complaints than those lower in sensitivity, according to a study of adults in their thirties.[1] Women typically score higher on sensitivity, but it affects all genders. Tom Falkenstein has written a book called *The Highly Sensitive Man*, and he says having a very sensitive nervous system means you process thoughts, feelings and sensations more deeply, become overstimulated more quickly, react more emotionally and sense subtle changes in your environment more intensely.[2]

He's sensitive, as many of us who gathered at a recent conference on the subject are. Including Australian researcher and lecturer Dr Becky Black, who was told in her childhood that she was 'too sensitive', believed it to be a fault and only felt understood in her fifties when she read a book on sensitivity by American psychologists Elaine and Arthur Aron.[3] She tells us that the brain of an HSP is unlike others – it's more active, receives more information but filters out less of it. 'There is simply more stuff that the HSP registers in the world.'

Here's the good news. Experiencing and registering 'more stuff' means sensitive people can get more joy out of the positive parts of life. Sensitive people also have a strong connection to nature.[4] They can experience music and art intensely.[5] They can be adaptive and creative because they are alert and ready to respond, and their increased awareness and empathy means they care, deeply[6] – which makes them excellent ambassadors, leaders and drivers of change. Rather than oppressing and overwhelming their lives, their sensitivity can be the very thing that helps them flourish and thrive.

How, though? I'm sure you've thought of your own action plan to help with anxiety, but here are some additional tips if you're also an orchid.

1. Give it light and keep it green

Because highly sensitive people are affected by nature, it's a vital daily requirement for orchids who feel they are wilting. It restores and calms them. Preferred environments tend to be by the sea, or in forests,[7] but being in a small green space or garden can help. Even small-scale greenery, like pot plants or a green colour on your walls, can affect stress levels for those who are anxious.[8] And those recovering from surgery who see some sort of nature, like a tree outside their window, recover faster and experience less anxiety too.[9]

Being in nature is called 'soft fascination',[10] because of the way it effortlessly helps our mind to wonder and wander, activating a part of the brain called the 'default mode network', which helps soothe us, lets our mind run free and puts us in a more creative state.[11] It's why you can get your best ideas when you're outside and moving. If you're walking, there's a burst of oxygen, increased blood flow, and areas in your brain like the hippocampus – responsible for memory, context, planning and ideas – are firing up too. A burst of nature dials the anxious, threat state right down.

If you're heading out, try to go in the morning to experience the benefits of early morning light; it'll boost the immune system and help you sleep better later.[12] When we wake, we have a burst of the stress hormone cortisol to help us get up and about, but it needs to vary throughout the day before dropping at night so we can rest. If it's too high, too low or too flat, that's not good for us physically or mentally.

Here's an example of how this stress response can impact those who worry. More than 100 UK primary and secondary school teachers were asked to write down their work-related thoughts in the evening and give a sample of their saliva to measure their cortisol levels. Then, in the morning, they were tested again. Those who worried and ruminated about work went to bed with high cortisol and woke with lower, flatter levels. In other words, they went to bed anxious, had a disturbed night and had difficulty waking up.[13] They were tired and wired.

Early morning light can help balance these stress levels, clarify our thinking and give us energy. Many years ago, I was part of an experiment at the University of Westminster.[14] I went to bed with an eye mask on, woke in the dark and had my saliva samples taken throughout the day to measure my cortisol. I was given a series of brain games to test my memory and thinking, too. The next day, I woke to naturally occurring morning light and the same tests were done. When I woke in the dark, my cortisol stayed high and flat during the day and my responses to the tests were poor. Waking to naturally occurring morning light made my cortisol levels nice and varied and I was better at the brain quizzes. It works with the right kind of artificial light too. Students given blue-enriched, LED short-wave light said they felt better and more alert.[15] So bring the light in and seek out green spaces. It's a wellbeing double whammy for those who are sensitive and anxious.

One last but huge point on nature. Eco- or climate-anxiety is affecting many of us. A study of 10,000 young people aged between sixteen and twenty-five in ten countries said they felt anxious, sad, angry, helpless, guilty or powerless about climate change; and three-quarters were frightened about the future.[16] But there's a ray of light here, too. College students in the US who recognized and sensed the huge challenges we face used it as a motivating force to inspire lifestyle changes or develop even small-scale climate activism.[17] Concern means you care. I firmly believe that climate ambassadors are the ones most sensitive and alert to the need for change. The orchids will help make the world a better place.

2. Feed your orchid well

Gut health is very important for highly sensitive people. So says a young Japanese psychologist and lecturer, Dr Shuhei Iimura, who was also at the sensitivity conference. It was his first time in the UK and his English was limited, so he was nervous. He told us when he feels stressed, he has stomach problems. 'I am experiencing that right now,' he said. I felt his pain.

You may, too. We know that digestion shuts down when we are anxious. The body doesn't need to digest

AND FINALLY...

breakfast if it's detected a threat. It either says *evacuate!* – in which case you need the loo, fast. Or it says *tighten up!* – in which case nothing moves, for ages. These symptoms are typical of the pain and discomfort caused by irritable bowel syndrome, or IBS, which occurs more frequently in those with anxiety. Research suggests they may even have a shared genetic origin. The study, which looked at 50,000 people with IBS across the world, found that those who experienced anxiety were likely to have had repeated courses of antibiotics in childhood, which affected their gut microbiome.[18] Which brings me back to the nervous Japanese psychologist. Because he is one of the few to have investigated the relationship between sensitivity and gut health.

Dr Iimura works with microbiologists to establish the link between the sensitive mind and an inflamed gut. You'll remember from Chapter 7 that inflammation fights infection, allows injuries to heal and we wouldn't survive without it. But too much of it can lead to disease. The sensitive tend to have higher gut inflammation and lower diversity in their microbiome, and when Dr Iimura tested nearly 900 Japanese adults, those who were highly sensitive also reported increased acid reflux, indigestion, abdominal pain, constipation and diarrhoea.[19]

More than 100 trillion bacteria live in our gut and there are over 1,000 different types of them.[20] We are unique, and so too is our microbiome, as it's influenced by what we eat, how old we are, our ethnicity and what medication we're on. Our poo reveals a lot about us, including our physical and mental health. If you are stressed and depressed with high gut inflammation, it'll show up in the toilet bowl.[21] Not literally, but when stool samples were taken from people who were depressed and put into otherwise healthy mice, the poor mice developed anxious and depressive-like symptoms, including reducing how much they moved about.[22] Mice given so-called healthy bacteria in another study saw those symptoms reduce.[23] We are not mice. But what we eat can have a big impact on how we feel, and improving gut health might be especially effective for those with high sensitivity.

If you changed your diet, would your mood improve? That was the question asked by an Australian study called SMILES – Supporting the Modification of Lifestyle in Lowered Emotional States.[24] Over twelve weeks, a group of volunteers with depression were given a Mediterranean-style diet. A second group received social support. Those who ate more fruit, vegetables, whole grains and fish saw improvements to their mental health, mostly in their depressive symptoms, but also in their anxiety levels. They had a poor diet to begin with, but the authors say that when they did the research, fewer than 6 per cent of Australians were eating an adequate amount of fruit and veg anyway.

If you're thinking of tweaking what you eat to improve your mood, probiotics might help too, according to a comprehensive review, which says that most research shows good effects on anxiety, low mood and stress.[25] These live microorganisms containing beneficial bacteria are found in fermented foods like yoghurt, kefir, kimchi, miso, sauerkraut and tempeh. Prebiotics – fibre-rich compounds which feed those gut-healthy bacteria – are in some of these foods too. People have been eating fermented foods for many millennia and there are thought to be thousands of different kinds.[26] The impact on physical health has been known for a while, but now scientists are looking at mental health too. About 700 young adults in the US were asked to note how many of these foods they ate over a month. Those eating more fermented foods likely to contain probiotics had less social anxiety, even if they were at a high genetic risk of it.[27]

What you eat will affect your brain, and ultimately your mood. Cutting back on ultra-processed foods, red meat, sugar and saturated fat, and increasing your fruit, veg and fibre is a no-brainer if you have anxiety. But don't wear yourself out trying to eat the 'right' foods and punishing yourself if you transgress. I have done this – as well as taking so many supplements that my dad said that I had 'started rattling'. He told me in front of an audience of millions, on an ITV primetime show I presented called *Save Money: Good Health*. Dad had never taken a vitamin, I had a supermarket Bag for Life stuffed full of them. In a television experiment, he went on the supplements, I came off them, and at various points over a month we had our blood and urine tested. The results? No difference. 'All you are doing, Sian,' said the scientist supervising the supplement swap, 'is producing very expensive wee.' We both had a decent diet to start with and maybe there was little to gain from taking them. But if you have a deficiency – and check with your doctor – they may help. Some supplements, like vitamin D for those in northern climes with not enough sun, or folic acid for those who are pregnant, might be important. But check the latest health advice.

And that review of studies into probiotic supplements I mentioned earlier says, although they have largely positive effects, you need to factor in the severity of the mental health condition, the quality of the supplement, the length of time you take it and the strain of bacteria within it. As you're asking, the research suggests *Clostridium butyricum* MIYAIRI 588, NVP-1704 and *Bifidobacterium longum* NCC3001 may help with mood, but the authors say there's still a knowledge gap about the 'best' probiotics and a lack of consensus on how to use them for mental wellbeing.[28] Give your orchid the right nutrients but don't overdo it. They need careful feeding.

3. Change its environment

There are two orchids on my mantelpiece, both birthday gifts. One is thriving, one has died. Why? Because not all orchids work well in new environments. My little purple orchid may have been overwatered, didn't get enough light or was wilting in the heat. Who knows. But I am now vigilant with the blooming, beautiful white one. Silver roots? Time to water. Floppy leaves? Too much sun. No flowers? Needs a feed.

AND FINALLY...

Highly sensitive people are acutely aware of subtle changes to the things around them. Negative and vulnerability-provoking environments will affect them deeply, but positive, resilience-enhancing ones will help them thrive.[29] Around half of our sensitivity is down to genes, but the other half has been shaped by the environment we grew up in. If it was challenging, we're more responsive to threat; if it was supportive, we feel the positive benefits.

But just as your environment can change, so can you. You have the awareness to reflect on who, what and where works best for you. As the highly sensitive person expert Professor Michael Pluess says, 'Maybe a job that comes with lots of demands and tight deadlines is simply not a great fit. Or maybe it can be managed well if there's a good level of autonomy. The question is, what is the environment's role in your anxiety and how can you change it so that you experience less anxiety – while also developing adaptive and effective coping strategies that help with your heightened sensitivity?' Go back to those exercises in Chapter 1 and see how you scored on the section that asked about sensitivity to detail in your environment. It might help when you look around yours.

Professor Pluess says believing you can reshape your environment if you are feeling overwhelmed is empowering. I ask him how to start that reshaping. 'Small things,' he replies, 'It might be making sure that you have time throughout the day where you have sufficient control over how much stimulation you have. It might be a daily walk in the park. Or rather than having non-stop meetings each day, having a few times a week where you have less. Some highly sensitive people are also extroverted and love being around people, but they can get overstimulated by others. They need to have breaks too, where they are with fewer people and exposed to less stimulation.'

Meaning, motivation, purpose and balance all play a part in this. Just because you're highly sensitive, Pluess says, does not mean you need to be 'wrapped in a blanket. You can still be tough. You can still be a CEO. You can still be outgoing, but you need to carefully look after yourself to get the right mix.'

Ah yes, let's talk about how we protect ourselves in the working environment. A few years ago, I was asked to speak at a wellbeing conference on providing 'psychological stability to staff in a turbulent world'. As I've mentioned, I help people in high-stress jobs who are experiencing anxiety, stress and trauma – mainly police officers, firefighters, ambulance staff, journalists and government officials working on public inquiries. I love it, but there is nothing more frustrating than helping someone reach a place of balance and calm, only for them to return to a job where the system fails to support them. Around a third of the population are HSPs with high emotional intensity and responsiveness, and they are more likely to experience burnout.[30] According to the World Health Organization, this is an 'occupational phenomenon' where you are exhausted and depleted, feel distanced, negative or cynical about your job, and see a decline in your professional performance.[31]

Burnout doesn't just affect the highly sensitive, but it

is frequently reported in caring professions, like front-line healthcare workers, emergency workers and teachers.[32] The top complaint driving burnout in more than fifteen countries is a toxic workplace,[33] with the main signs being a working environment which is disrespectful, non-inclusive, unethical, cut-throat and abusive.[34] And add to that being on call, unfair treatment, heavy workloads, low autonomy and a lack of support. It's not surprising people get sick or quit.[35]

You are not at fault, the system is. But you can't fix it alone, and you need to look after yourself while you seek out allies. Ask yourself these questions: What's my emotional load – what else am I carrying as well as this workplace stress? What are my firebreaks – how do I create boundaries, routines and structures to recharge? Who is in my support system – who is my buddy, my mentor, my champion?

Dr Elaine Aron, who wrote the influential book *The Highly Sensitive Person*[36] more than a quarter of a century ago, says HSPs make 'intuitive visionaries' and 'ideal employees'. They are great at awareness, empathy and connection. They think and feel deeply and innately, are attentive to subtle cues that others may miss, and spend time processing information rather than talking about it – all top skills in the workplace.

But Dr Aron says sensitive people can also overthink, misinterpret feedback and get anxious because they see everything that might go wrong. When asked what she'd write on a billboard to help, she said this: 'Step back, sink in, and look at the bigger picture.'[37]

If you're feeling ambushed, take time away from stimuli to pause and recharge. Develop your own personal protection plan, because being sensitive can be challenging. The thinking, brooding and internalizing, the self-doubt and feeling different, the sensory overwhelm at work and home – you'll need a space where you can escape and do some quieting.

Solitude is good for the sensitive. It's different to loneliness. Typically, the highly sensitive person doesn't feel socially lonely, but they can feel *emotionally* lonely if they don't find enough deep, intimate, meaningful relationships,[38] and that's important for close friends and family to know. Solitude, though, is a choice and can support wellbeing in the highly sensitive person.[39] If your orchid is starting to shrivel, it's a sign of stress. Change and shape the environment to keep it healthy.

4. Show it love

Being attentive to how your orchid is feeling is key to helping it thrive, and that means listening to its signals. You may have heard of 'interoception'. This is our ability to sense what's going on in our body and the shifts in our internal environment. When we perceive a real or imagined threat, the brain sends messages to our adrenal glands, prompting the heart to pump faster and send oxygenated blood rushing to our muscles to get ready to fight, or run, or play dead. The stress hormones increase blood sugar and release fat stores to give us energy to deal with the danger. When the stressor has gone, the body returns to normal. Except when it doesn't and causes ill health. Those who are anxious and highly sensitive can often feel on high alert.

Here's where interoception comes in. One review suggests the anxious mind not only registers but can *over*-interpret bodily sensations.[40] In one German study, people with and without social anxiety were asked to count their heartbeats during a series of sessions. Then an experimenter came in and told them they suddenly and unexpectedly had to deliver a live, three-minute presentation about a local music festival, as if they were applying for a job as a reporter. They would be on camera and in front of an audience who would assess their speech and their appearance. I know. I'm getting anxious – and I do this for a living. The individuals rated how they thought they would perform and their levels of anxiety, tension and nervousness. All were anxious, all saw their heart rates rise. But those who were socially anxious were more aware of their heartbeats, more accurate at counting them, and more fearful of how they would be judged than those who were not.[41] Interoception can be a good thing unless the fixation on the sensation is so negative that it takes you away from the task at hand. None of them had to do the presentation in the end. Back to Hitchcock's anticipation being worse than the bang. The participants each got twelve euros and their experiences were added to the ever-growing research on interoception and anxiety. For which we thank them.

The highly sensitive, with their increased interoceptive powers, tend to report more physical health problems.[42] Those experiencing chronic pain also report being highly responsive to internal sensations – but again, they tend to be less accurate when those signals are measured objectively.[43] They may misinterpret what they think they're feeling. Even if we know our own heart, we may not be right when we try to interpret what it's saying.[44]

But we can recognize, pause, step back, and bring in some love or self-compassion. That goes for all the highly sensitive overthinkers, the self-critics, avoiders, withdrawers and perfectionists. And those experiencing pain, too. One of my high-functioning, sensitive, anxious friends is currently experiencing acute back pain and asked me this question: 'Does anxiety cause pain, or does pain cause anxiety?' It can be a bit of both. There's certainly an overlap of anxiety and pain in some chronic conditions like fibromyalgia, lower back pain, headaches and, as above, irritable bowel syndrome.[45] The body and mind are inextricably interwoven, and sometimes it's hard to say this is psychological anxiety, that is physical pain.

Part of the reason could be that anxiety and pain trigger similar areas of the brain: the amygdala, which scans for danger; the hypothalamus, the body regulator, managing our hormones, temperature, heart rate and sleep; and the anterior cingulate gyrus, the decision-maker, affecting our thoughts and emotions. These regions are responsible for our perception of pain *and* our experience of anxiety. Two neurotransmitters, serotonin and norepinephrine – the chemical messengers sending signals throughout our body and brain – are also present in pain and anxiety. Chronic pain is complex but, put simply, the way we register pain in our body and the way we experience anxiety come from the *same parts of our brain*.[46]

This is not to doubt the severity of pain and the anxiety that comes with it, but the two share similar pathways and when we're trying to work out what we are sensing, we don't always get it right. Human errors apart, noticing – or interoception – is so much better than ignoring. In a study of studies, those experiencing pain who feared it, blocked it or catastrophized over it, experienced greater pain intensity – along with symptoms of anxiety and depression – than those who did not.[47]

What can make a difference to the severity of pain and the anxiety that comes with it? Acceptance, kindness and psychological flexibility. Living with pain is horrible, but like anxiety, trying to ignore and avoid it doesn't work. Being willing to accept it, and lean into it with some self-compassion, can help. In a study of those with pain, the ones who adopted a strategy of acceptance and developed coping mechanisms reduced both the pain and the anxiety.[48] Diffusing from the pain, being an observer of it rather than caught up in it or struggling with it, worked for both pain and anxiety. Inflexible thinking, trying to avoid difficult thoughts, feelings and sensations connected with the pain, made anxiety symptoms worse.

I'll give you an example from my own study with people living with a cancer experience, because if you are highly sensitive and in chronic pain, their stories may resonate. In Chapters 4 and 9, I introduced you to some people I met while researching the effects of a group mindfulness course on the self-critical, negative, judgemental mind. They told me what kinds of thoughts had been running through their heads and how they dealt with them before they started. Emma was living with stage 2 uterine cancer, just out of surgery and waiting for the results of further tests. 'Every time the post would come, I'd be shaking because I'd think that it's going to be bad news,' she says. 'Sometimes you just get almost covered with this paralyzing fear, and the fear would write its own narrative. I'm very good at the narratives. They are sort of long, involved and always end up with the doom and gloom scenario.' 'Which is what?' I ask. 'A very early death,' she replies. 'That they're going to find a lump and I'm going to have two cancers in two places.'

One way she unhooked from anxiety and fear was to pay attention to her 'little voice' of uncertainty. 'If you don't recognize it, then it's doing its thing without you actually acknowledging that it could be making you more worried and more stressed,' she says. Same with Lucy, whose cancer was in remission but who struggled with back pain. She thinks suppressing her thoughts and emotions made her pain worse. 'That stuff at the back of your head, nagging at you, or going "listen to me" and you say, "No. No, I'm not ready for you yet. Go away." But eventually it'll force its way through somehow. I suppressed the anger for so long, it made me ill, my body turned on me. And it's only after I accepted that, that

AND FINALLY...

I looked at the anger and I understood it, that I started healing. I got better.'

Before they started the course, their anxiety was sky-high and their self-compassion was rock-bottom. Afterwards, it was the other way around. It might have been the group, having time to themselves, the sharing of experiences, learning breathing exercises or the mindfulness itself. It's hard to know. But they all said mindfulness helped them manage both the pain and the anxiety because it allowed them to accept and bring a kindness to what they were experiencing.

Maya was living with chronic pain following cancer surgery. 'The pain was still there, but it didn't seem to affect everything that I did anymore.' What made a difference was 'concentrating on it, instead of trying to push it away, just being with it, accepting, being kind to myself and saying, "It's OK, it's there."' Maya was caught up in a 'tsunami of emotion or fear or just helplessness and before, there would be the sense of drowning, I'm definitely going to drown. Whereas now, yes, there is the tsunami of this. But it's going to wash over me and I'm going to bob up to the surface.' Mindfulness helped them become more aware of their body and the sensations it was producing, but they had to become kinder towards themselves too.

The creator of mindfulness-based stress reduction, Jon Kabat-Zinn, says mindfulness is 'paying attention, on purpose, in the present moment and non-judgmentally'.[49] Dwelling on pain doesn't help. Judging it, or your response to it, doesn't either. But noticing and accepting what is – rather than what is to be got rid of – makes a difference. Being steady, focusing inwards, noticing the rise and fall of your breath. That is enough for now.

All this is micro-level to start with. Think back to the nourishing and depleting exercise from Chapter 9. As well as mindful moments, there are other nurturing activities that can be especially helpful to replenish the depleted resources of highly sensitive people. As we heard in Chapter 1, HSPs respond well to uplifting movie clips.[50] Gratitude diaries before bed can aid sleep. HSPs are responsive to talking therapies, but if they can't access them, then being with close friends and family is vital. Because HSPs are often creative, and emotionally more reactive, the arts can give their mood a boost, too.

I present a daily music show called *Classical Unwind* on BBC Radio 3 Unwind, tailored to those who want a soothing, calming place to be. Music can lower cortisol, boost the reward neurotransmitter dopamine, encourage the strengthening of our immune system, regulate the heart rate and blood pressure,[51] and tap into memory, connecting us to times, people and places that matter to us. Students with depression saw their symptoms drop if they listened to classical music every day, just before bed.[52] Listening to music is a balm to the soul, giving us pause to sink into a different space.

Animals can be highly sensitive, just as we are, and HSPs show increased affinity with them too.[53] Being around animals gets us out of ourselves for a while and one study suggests a walk with a dog is better for those with anxiety than a walk without.[54]

AND FINALLY...

Moderate activity or exercise works for HSPs, increasing wonder chemicals like GABA and BDNF. GABA – or gamma-aminobutyric acid – is a neurotransmitter that acts like the brake in your car. It can slow a hyped-up nervous system and keep you from spiralling. GABA helps you remain calm, regulates sleep, improves memory function and reduces the brain's inflammatory response. In one study, people doing an hour of yoga three times a week showed an increase of GABA and a decrease in anxiety.[55] You can also get a boost of it by doing up to twenty minutes of vigorous exercise. Brain-derived neurotrophic factor – or BDNF – increases after exercise too, enhancing mental abilities and acting against anxiety.[56] This letting go of tension and stress using the body and breath is called 'somatic release' and it can help reset the nervous system.

You can choose to do all, some or none of this. It's your life – and your path through this will be different to everyone else's. Another Mary Oliver poem that I love is called 'The Journey', and I urge you to read the whole thing, because I won't do it justice here, but the essence is this. As you walked on your journey, she writes, there were voices around you who gave you bad advice, who shouted, 'Mend my life!' But on that road 'full of fallen branches and stones' there came a new voice, which was your own, which kept you company 'as you strode deeper and deeper into the world, determined to do the only thing you could do— determined to save the only life you could save'.[57]

Yours is the only life you can save. It's what I told myself a few years ago. When I'm anxious, I write. Not for anyone else to see, although a publisher encouraged me to include some of my excruciatingly honest diary entries in my book *Rise: Surviving and Thriving after Trauma*.[58] Writing can help us see ourselves. It reflects our present fears, future dreams, past hurts. One of the trauma techniques we sometimes use in clinic is called narrative exposure therapy (NET).[59] After assessing the client and hearing the story of what's going on for them, some props are introduced to illustrate their lifeline – flowers, stones and a string or ribbon. The flowers are the happy events, the stones the traumatic or fearful ones, and they are placed along this string or ribbon, starting with the earliest memory and ending with the most recent.

Seeing our history mapped along a line, with the solidity of the dark, troubling stones and the fragility of the colourful, joyful flowers, brings a sense of perspective. These things are there and you own them as part of your experience. My ribbon will wind, with different stones and flowers, as will yours, but seeing both reminds us not to become dominated by one or the other. We can see the wholeness of it, together with the bit of ribbon that stretches into the future with nothing on it yet. We look at it all, curiously, and we keep on our river-ribbon and after the last crappy, stoney thing happens, maybe a flower blooms from nowhere. That's how all this works. We are in forward motion and need to pay attention to the quiet blossoming of something good and not get tripped up on the pebbles. It's harder, because the good is whispering and delicate, like the orchid, and doesn't demand attention like the hard, cold solidity of something heavy.

AND FINALLY...

You can write your own narrative, to plot your own course on the ribbon. Some things have happened and may happen again, which you can't control and which will cause suffering. Others bring joy. Write about failure, write about vulnerability, write about pain and uncertainty. Write about awe and humour and love and purpose, too. All this connects you to the truthfulness about your life and to other people, because it's like a bridge. It's saying – I have this stuff, like you, to a greater or lesser extent, and I'm trying to make sense of it all so I can try to manage better when the next thing happens. There are feelings attached, and some of them hurt. Shame, embarrassment, fear, anxiety, they are human emotions – and by feeling and expressing them, we are connecting. Our story melds into other stories of other people. We are all struggling and trying to understand and make meaning of that river-ribbon.

I have a diary entry from a couple of years ago entitled 'Another January list of intentions'. I don't do resolutions but it's helpful to think about the year gone by, the stones and flowers. It's four pages long. I'll spare you. But the anxiety and sensitivity that show up in my diaries at twelve years old are still there in these older, wiser ones. I ask myself a question in this diary entry – *what's different from a year ago?* 'I like myself a little bit more,' I write. 'I take fewer shits (metaphorically). That's not to say I no longer worry, I do. But somehow over the last year of churn and change, there's been a shift in how I see life.'

I reflect on the TV job I had just left, the loved ones that I lost that year, the car crash I'd escaped from, the fact that time seemed to 'skitter away, our hold on it more tentative'. And then, I write this:

> Well, that's cheery. Make the most of it then, Sian. Embrace everything, stop worrying, take a leap, push yourself, get stronger, faster, fitter. Find joy and adventure. Laugh more at life and yourself. Breathe deeply. Stretch often. Eat well. Write. Tell people you love them. Find time to be with them. Prioritize family and friends over everything. Say yes more but say no when your gut speaks for you. Lean into the unpredictability of the following decades. There may be twenty, even thirty years left. Eke them all out. Don't waste days, revel in them. Don't punish yourself for what you did or did not do, have or have not done. The decision taken is always the right one because you will never know what the alternative was, but make sure it isn't governed by the judgement – or fear of judgement – of others. Keep it simple. Do the things that spark enjoyment with the people that enhance your life. Look forwards, rather than back.

The year before and the year that followed had both stones and flowers. As they all will. And yet the ribbon still winds, waiting for me to put my life on it. But doing so softly, gently, with care and kindness.

AND FINALLY...

Chapter 10: A quick refresher

- The highly sensitive person is hyperaware of their environment – they think more deeply, feel more strongly, sense more subtlety, empathize more intensely.

- HSPs respond well to nature, animals, exercise, rest and solitude, close social support, spirituality and regular breaks.

- Connection, awareness, balance and compassion work for most anxious people but especially the HSP.

- To help an orchid that's wilting, give it light, feed it well, change its environment and show it some love.

- When we do, an orchid blooms. When it blooms, it is magnificent. When it's magnificent, it is strong and powerful. It is the flower the others wish they were.

Ten Top Takeaways from Part Three

1. Trauma is a wound to the soul which can take a long time to heal. Soften the scar by finding your own soothing balm.

2. Panic is like being caught in a storm. If it comes, drop anchor, steady yourself and slow your breath until the winds pass.

3. Anxious feelings can imprison you behind fences of fear and shame. Use them to power and propel you instead.

4. Listen to the wisdom of your body when it's trying to tell you something you need to hear. Learn the difference between helpful and harmful.

5. Distinguish between tricky and sticky anxiety. Caffeine, sugar and hormone imbalances trick us, but can be fixed fast. Sticky takes longer but the work is worth it.

6. When stress strikes, don't let it make you small. Adopt a high-power pose to take up space and give you strength.

7. You can't out-think anxiety. You have to do, you need to act. Life improves with change, not chance.

8. The highly sensitive can thrive in green spaces, with light, the right food and knowing when they need time out. If your environment is wrong, adapt it.

9. Values help you navigate but don't let your passengers dictate your direction. You are the driver of your own bus.

10. Don't let the days drift by – make sure they all count. Be with the people you love. Behave like the person you know you can be.

Epilogue

Anxiety is not a thing to fix, to fight. It's not something we can hide from, ignore, or avoid. It's an essential part of who we are, it thrums within us. If we listen to its vibrations, feel them resonate in our body, hear what anxiety is saying to us and notice what it tells us to do, we can use it. This sensitivity can be a tool to help us – a powerful, motivating force for good. We are the ones who feel the emotion in the air, when others may not. Our nerve endings twitching with a high pitch of alertness, telling us something's not right, that we've become disconnected from our values or are not living in a way that feels true and authentic.

Sometimes, the noise of anxiety gets too loud, even when the horizon seems free from danger. We scan and we scan, we try to find reasons for feeling unsettled. The body becomes tense as we prepare to run, or fight, or play dead; the stress hormones course, the heart pumps faster, our immune system responds with inflammation to defend us from this unknown attacker. Our mind races through every possible worst-case scenario to find the reason behind this feeling of unease, but still we come up with nothing. The difficulty of sitting with this means we might stop going to places, being with people, trusting ourselves. We may question our worth and our reason for being.

The questioning, the isolation and the nervousness play into a familiar script which reminds us that, yet again, we are not doing it properly, this life we're living. And that if we just worked harder, achieved a bit more, hauled ourselves towards the perfect that we know we can be, that we believe other people are – well then, we will burn brighter, and all those insecurities will vanish. We will, at last, become the finished object. And so, we work, and we strive and we drive and we push harder and harder.

Or we retreat and we hide, and we become small in the darkness and, eventually, we find our body and brain have grown tired, we have used up all our strength and resources in this endless battle for survival, this tug of war as we try to wrest the power back from anxiety. And then, depleted, knowing we have lost the fight, we chastise and criticize.

But anxiety isn't our enemy; we can stop the struggle. In our tug-of-war battle with it, we can just drop the rope. And then, when we do, we can see that it's not a thing to go into combat with. Because it lives inside us, trying to help, occasionally getting it wrong. We can learn to live better with it.

As Sarah Wilson says in her wonderful book *First, We Make the Beast Beautiful*, we really have to *be* with our anxiety. 'By going down to the dark depths, we finally find the connection. Because anxiety, eventually and inevitably, makes us sit in our shit. It takes us there, to the darkness. It forces us to do the journey. And only then can we see what we were looking for. We can see the truth. We see it all as it is.'[1]

I once talked to a journalist called Patrick Howse who was forced to go to the depths. He was the head of a team in Iraq during the war in 2003, and he'd witnessed a rocket flying overhead and landing in the very building he was about to walk into. The building where he thought his team were. The rocket exploded, the building was damaged, he thought he'd lost colleagues and friends. Luckily, they were elsewhere, and no one was hurt. But when he came back to the UK to work on domestic politics, his acute anxiety and hypervigilance came with him, resulting in panic attacks and outbursts of frustration and rage. His marriage broke down, he couldn't do his job anymore, and everything changed except his anxious thoughts and feelings, which came with him everywhere. Until, he says, he was forced into 'the labyrinthine sewers of my mind. And when I went there it was mucky and difficult, but what I found there was interesting and helpful. And I learned to live with it.'

The philosopher Ludwig Wittgenstein told his students, when they were looking for a quick and easy solution, to 'go the bloody hard way'.[2] It can sometimes feel nasty and messy, but then, he said, that is when it's most important. That is when we find ourselves, our flawed, imperfect selves. And that is when we can start to heal – as long as we bring a curiosity and a compassion to it. We don't go the bloody hard way to beat ourselves up again. We already know how to do that, and it hasn't served us very well.

EPILOGUE

It is hard, as the Danish philosopher Søren Kierkegaard said, to see anxiety as 'an adventure that every human being must go through',[3] but we can do it. It's like Bilbo Baggins in *The Lord of the Rings*, leaving his safe little Hobbit house in the Shire to venture into a land which seems treacherous, where he's faced with many choice points and ways to turn. He could go home, he could take the whispering One Ring which promises the easy way, but he doesn't. He summons up courage in the face of doubt, and lives the adventure, even though he doesn't know where it will lead. As author J. R. R. Tolkien wrote in one of his later books, 'A man that flies from his fear may find that he has taken a shortcut to meet it.'[4] Face it, don't flee from it.

It's an adventure that's yours, and perhaps you can learn to thrive with the anxiety that comes with you. It's like that passenger on the bus. You can choose to have the self-critic next to you, telling you you're going the wrong way, or driving too slowly, or are just stupid, failing, worthless. If you argue with it, you need to stop the bus, take your hands off the wheel – and that means you're not heading to the place you want to get to. Is the self-critic saying anything useful and helpful? Is it alerting you to something you need to pay attention to? If so, listen to it, take action on it, thank it and then tell it to take its seat. If it's not helpful, don't argue, rationalize, fight or ignore. Tell it to sit down because you have somewhere to get to.

The other voice is there too, the one we usually ignore – the self-compassionate one. Maybe in the past you've been told to 'be kind to yourself' but didn't really know how to. Perhaps it's felt too self-indulgent, too 'self-help'-selfish. Perhaps you've told yourself that there's no time for that, there's stuff to be getting on with – and besides, when you've tried to follow a routine involving some kind of meditative, yoga-based, journal-writing activities, it's always seemed like so much effort when you feel so tired. And then, when you stop, when the daily habits become weekly or not at all, there's that familiar sense of failure that starts creeping in and, hello, here's self-criticism again. Self-compassion doesn't mean doing self-compassion perfectly. It means acknowledging the imperfection. The knowing that some days, most days, you're at least willing to try.

Dan Harris, host of the *10% Happier* podcast and author of *Meditation for Fidgety Skeptics*, has a couple of great slogans for when we feel the act of being mindful is too heavy and unattainable. They are 'one-minute counts' and 'dailyish'. He says, 'One minute is enough for you to pull out of the momentum of your day for a second, so that you're not just toppling forward all the time. It's not going to be magic, but it's still a little bit of calm.' The other slogan – 'dailyish' – 'provides enough elasticity so that if you fall off the wagon for a day or two or three, you can still start up again, and that's totally fine.'[5]

Explore, experiment, and learn to be comfortable with not doing it perfectly, not striving to do it well or how you think others must be doing it. Whether it's meditation, or writing, or any nurturing, nourishing thing that you do just for yourself, stop feeling guilty about not doing it, or doing it badly. Just pop it lightly into your week, more days than not. 'Dailyish'. For a moment, a minute, perhaps longer. It's acknowledging the small voice that tells you it's OK to look after yourself, that you are going the right way and are good enough with all your frailty and vulnerability. And that those very sensitivities might help you rather than hinder you, because they bring your attention to changes in your environment and subtleties in mood and tone, guiding your intuition towards the things that might be good to look after and pay attention to.

The adventure won't end, and as Oliver Burkeman so wonderfully points out in his email newsletter 'The Imperfectionist', you will never get to the point where you've finished with the problems and 'real life' starts. Your real life is *in* the problems. And, he says, the thought of being stuck with them forever initially brings a bit of peevishness in response:

> 'Wait, I'm never going to get to the problem-free phase? That's not what I signed up for!' But then comes the sense of a heavy burden having been lifted. The pressure's off. I get to unclench, relax, and fall back into the life I'm living. Far from this being dispiriting, I find myself much more motivated to get stuck in. It turns out my really big problem was thinking I might one day get rid of all my problems, when the truth is that there's no escaping the mucky, malodorous compost-heap of this reality. Which is OK, actually. Compost is the stuff that helps things grow.[6]

Growth is in the mucky stuff in the 'compost heap' of reality and the 'labyrinthine sewers' of the mind. There will never be a time when you exist comfortably with it all the time, because happiness, hope, contentment, whatever you call it, always comes with a big dose of something else – the car to fix, the job that's not going well, the kids that are having issues at school. Very rarely does life go well, in a long unbroken streak of good luck and fortune, where you smile on your ability to have finally mastered it. It's the same with anxiety. Some days will be a bit more rubbish, a bit darker, than others.

Let me tell you about the potatoes in the basement theory. It comes from Carl Rogers, a psychologist in the 1940s and a proponent of the person-centred school of therapy – one of the first types of counselling I was trained in. The key tenets are bringing an empathic, non-judgemental sense of inquiry to the person sitting in front of you, listening and then reflecting what they are saying back to them. The client, let's say you, is the expert. The psychologist, let's say me, is not.

As Rogers put it, 'It is the client who knows what hurts, what directions to go, what problems are crucial, what experiences have been deeply buried.'[7] He believed we all have a need to flourish, and here's where we get to the potatoes. They were growing in a bin in his parents' basement, which was dark and gloomy, with very little light. But he noticed the potatoes were growing tubers. Thin, spindly things, but growing towards the only available light, which was coming in through a small window. In all the darkness, they were trying to grow – or as

Rogers says, 'under the most adverse circumstances, they were striving to become'.[8]

The potato tubers didn't become potatoes, but they were trying to move towards the light, and Rogers called this the 'self-actualising potential'. Your life is unique, no one else can tell you how to live it, but even when there seems to be little available light, there is always the potential to grow. You are the expert in your experiences and what has stood in your way up until now. You are the one to make the choice to grow, to reach towards the light, taking your anxiety with you.

We are so afraid to show the world who we really are, and that can stunt our growth. I'll give you an example. It's taken me many years to write this book. *Rise* was about coping after adversity, including my own breast cancer experience, along with the emerging science about resilience. I was still writing after it came out, but suddenly, once it was in the world, I became aware that other people would have opinions and judgements on it. The reviews were nice, as it happens, and so were readers, but this felt new. I'd got some degree of public recognition when I was on the TV, but I had never spoken about myself, my experiences, my fears and failings. Now, here they were, in diary form, in a book, on the shelves, for all to see. An author once said to me that writing a book is like 'showing your bum in a shop window'. I told her that for me, it is like 'baring my breasts outside BBC Broadcasting House'.

It is such a vulnerable thing to do – to say 'I think this. What about you?' in the hope that it'll help. What egotism! Who would ever put something out there that comes from their own fallible mind, that could possibly resonate with others? How very *dare* they? I have never had the certainty of self-appointed social media gurus, who talk with such confidence about how to solve the lives of others. If I pop my head over the parapet, even with learning and research and experience as my armour, I'm still me, 'a small girl with thin powers of concentration, who tries hard and is keen to please'. Of course, it's bonkers to think that the teacher who said that to me over forty-five years ago would know I'd still carry it with me, let alone that I should let it somehow define me. It is not the whole of who I am. I am so much more than that. YOU are so much more than whatever anyone has said about you, or whatever opinion they may or may not hold. We all are. We can't be reduced to a sentence, or a label, or a judgement. As Walt Whitman would say, we contain multitudes.

And yet. My anxiety about publishing a book about anxiety almost stopped me writing the book. Or at least, putting all the learning together, for you. In 2023, I was a guest on BBC Radio 4's *Saturday Live*, a programme I used to host with my co-presenter, the Reverend Richard Coles. He was leaving and I was on to chat with him for his final show, along with other guests, one of whom was the author Harlan Coben. Harlan is a force of nature. A multiple award winner who has sold more than 80 million books and written thirty-six novels, many of which have been turned into huge TV series. He is a lovely, funny, self-deprecating man to boot. A quick aside to prove the point. He went to a liberal arts college with other soon-to-become authors, including Dan Brown, his fraternity brother, who he said 'sold more than me. I wasn't even the best-selling author in my own fraternity'.[9]

Harlan writes about what happens in the ripples when a stone is cast into a lake, those moments when something changes in an instant and how the past plays into the present. That's the thriller – someone who is caught in a moment when everything is suddenly upended. But the researching, he told us on the programme, is so much more fun than writing. 'I'll paint my house to avoid that moment when I need to write.' Well, that's a relief. And this from a man who has written scores of books.

He and I spent a good couple of hours before transmission in the green room, sampling dry BBC croissants. When he talked about the writing process, and because he's generous and kind and interested in other people, he asked me if I was writing too. 'I did write a book,' I said, 'and some articles and I write for myself, in diaries and in notebooks dotted around the house.' He asked me if I intended to do another book and I replied 'maybe'. 'What's stopping you?' he said. *Fear of judgement, of not having All The Knowledge, being laughed at, rejected*, I didn't say. 'Just write,' he told me. 'Doesn't matter what. You can edit a bad page, you can't edit a blank one.'

Harlan says he writes longhand at first, page after page, so he can cross things out, and write anywhere and not worry about it. He's written a whole book in the back of Uber cars because he wrote well in one of them and thought it was the thing to help his writing. 'Anything that makes you write is good, anything that makes you stop is bad,' he says. 'We all have paralysis. I have paralysis. Stephen King still has it. Insecurity, doubt, that imposter syndrome. If you don't have it, you're probably not a good writer. Only bad writers think they're good. So, push through and write what you need to write and then worry how good it is... Every day is a torture, every day there's a lot of self-hatred.'

This from a man who's sold millions and millions of books. Those same self-doubting thoughts, that same self-criticism, is within all of us, however successful someone seems on the outside.

Thank you, Harlan, because I started writing, and I thought, this is a story about anxiety. Storytelling is something I understand, because as a journalist I've been telling stories for ages. Anxiety is something I understand because I live alongside it and have spent a long time helping others to manage it. As a psychologist, you can be in a relationship with someone for weeks or months, sometimes even years, trying to understand their anxiety alongside them. We navigate it, together. Even though we are not in the same room, I hope you've felt something of that relationship in this book.

I know it can be hard and painful, and I've no doubt you've been to places that felt uncomfortable. But together, maybe we've uncovered some things, found an understanding and moved towards something else. It's an adventure, and we are all trying to make sense of a mucky, sometimes mean, unpredictable, uncontrollable world. Perhaps you have become more of a curious observer of yourself, and started to become more interested in what your brain and body and behaviour does in anxiety.

Remind yourself of the skills you've learned. And the 4 As:

1. Acknowledge – or notice – without judgement, or a fight. Name the feeling – 'here's anxiety' or 'I'm noticing anxiety' or 'that familiar feeling of anxiety is back again'.

2. Accommodate, open up and make room for the difficult thoughts and feelings. Invite anxiety in. You are no longer frightened of it. You are the one with the power.

3. Appreciate what anxiety has to offer. Sometimes it gives you the energy to channel into a performance, or it alerts you to stuff you need to deal with.

4. Act with your values to move towards the person you want to be and the life you deserve to have.

Russ Harris says it's about letting your thoughts chatter away like the murmuring on a radio channel you're not paying attention too. Don't engage with it unless it's telling you something you need to hear. Anxiety sometimes says, 'This matters. This is important,' he explains. 'Are you prepared? Does this need to be addressed? Is there something you need to do differently? And it's also very often intimately connected to your values, it's reminding you of your values around self-care or self-protection or caring for others. Can I, instead of seeing this as the enemy, can I see this as a source of information? What has it got to tell me that's useful?'

And do all this with self-compassion. It's hugely important but it's so much quieter than self-criticism. Make that whisper louder. And then keep practising it all.

Remember too, the Four Pillars of CARE that we touched on in the book.

C is *curiosity*. Be an interested observer when anxiety shows up.

A is *acceptance*. Know it's part of you and your sensitivity to the world.

R is *relating*. Develop a new relationship so it's no longer the enemy.

E is *empathy*. Allow for kindness. Other people's, yes, but your own too.

These skills get easier with practise. You will get to the point where you can employ them quickly, but that takes a while. Don't expect instant results. Be patient. Remain curious. Stay kind. And when the power of anxiety feels like the buffeting waves are about to engulf you, remember. You know how to ride them. You have learned to surf.

Good luck.

Acknowledgements

Although no longer here to read this, I want to firstly thank my parents. My dad, John Price Williams, a brilliant journalist who taught me and my brothers the value of hard work, being kind and lifelong learning. A man who 'didn't do emotion' but who showed it, in the end. My mum Kathy, a fiercely caring nurse and a loyal friend to many, whose passionate moods protected a tender heart. Thanks also to my beloved uncle, Dr David Price Williams, an adventurer and archaeologist who helped me dig into our own family history but who died before seeing it in print. To my brothers, Dave and Pete, who, like me, have pushed and drove and strove and who carry all the sensitivity and emotion that we're finally allowing ourselves to feel.

Thank you to those who gave so much wisdom and time to this book: Philippa Perry, Daisy Goodwin, Philip Selway, Nina Hossain, Dr Russ Harris, Professor Oliver Robinson, Professor Michael Pluess and Dr Andrea Oskis. To those who I've been privileged to walk alongside in therapy as we navigate anxiety – you may not recognize yourself in these pages, but thank you for being willing to go to difficult places together. To all who agreed to talk to me about the impact of anxiety, including those with cancer who replaced a self-critical voice with a compassionate one; to Angela Tilley, Robin and Liz Elsey-Webb, Hazel Ellis-Saxon and everyone who opens bruised souls to a broadcast audience on *Life Changing* and to producer Tom Alban for encouraging them to do so; and to Trude Silman and Patrick Howse. Thank you for sharing your stories.

There are many who have contributed their thinking, been supportive and given feedback to sections of this book including Lord Richard Layard, Dr Mark Williamson, Dr Steven C. Hayes, Dr Stephen Porges, Dr Thomas Curran, Dr Sarah Blainey, Dr Gina Rippon, Dr Chris Irons, Professor Paul Gilbert, Dr Jennifer Kemp, Dr Alex King, Dr Shane Ford, Dr Ed Burns, Sue Gerhardt, Sarah Wilson, Joanna Nylund, Nick Witchell and Tim Minchin. Thanks too, to Sesi Turnbull for welcoming reflections on Bill.

To my friends in psychology especially Dr Ana Draper, Dr Trudi Edginton, Dr Sarah Heke and Annie Billing. And to Professor Catherine Loveday for bringing her brilliance to our adventures with music and the mind.

A lifesaving thanks to the amazing medical teams at University College, The Royal Free, and Guy's and St Thomas' Hospitals, especially Shirley Day, Joanna Franks, Dr Glen Blackman, Dr Mary Burgess and Paul Roblin. I am grateful for your expertise and continual watchfulness.

Thank you to my kind, loyal, amazing friends for being there to ride the waves together – including Lizzy, Zöe, Brett, Dixi, Jude, Sam, Sophie, Jane, Alice, Josie, Alison

ACKNOWLEDGEMENTS

and Kevin, Nicky and Nick, and Dean and Andy. Also, to Lauren and Anna, forever yoga pals and first readers.

To my agents Sue Ayton and Nick Hulme and everyone at Knight Ayton for navigating the tricky waters of broadcast, always being encouraging yet protective. To Annabel Merullo, my literary agent, for finding the very best berth for this book and working on the next.

To Ed Faulkner, at Atlantic Books, for wholeheartedly loving this book from the off (and even making his own Worry Tree). The awesome Atlantic team, including Gemma Wain, the fastest, most efficient copyeditor, Felice McKeown on marketing, Alice Latham on rights and Kirsty Doole in publicity, who came up with a brilliant phrase for addressing the self-critic after reading the book: 'Stand down, soldier'. And thanks to Anna Morrison, who took one quote and made a beautiful cover out of it.

And thank you to my family for their continued encouragement. My sisters-in-law, Louisa, Katy, Marianne, Michaele and Cherine and my brother-in law Jeremy.

To my incredible children, Joss and Alex, my stepdaughter Emily, and Seth and Eve. Wise and funny, kind and warm – you are my 'pockets of happiness'. And to my husband, Paul. Who gave me space, time and tea. Who read every word, more than once. Who found the 'surf' quote. And who has always given me the courage to step onto the board and ride the waves. I couldn't have done this without you.

Appendix

These two common screening tools are indicative only and, as with all questionnaires in this book, cannot replace a clinical assessment or diagnosis.

Generalized Anxiety Disorder Questionnaire (GAD-7)[1]

Over the last two weeks, how often have you been bothered by any of the following problems?

1. **Feeling nervous, anxious or on edge?**

    Not at all
    Several days
    More than half the days
    Nearly every day

2. **Not being able to stop or control worrying?**

    Not at all
    Several days
    More than half the days
    Nearly every day

3. **Worrying too much about different things?**

    Not at all
    Several days
    More than half the days
    Nearly every day

4. **Trouble relaxing?**

    Not at all
    Several days
    More than half the days
    Nearly every day

APPENDIX

5. **Being so restless that it is hard to sit still?**

   Not at all
   Several days
   More than half the days
   Nearly every day

6. **Becoming easily annoyed or irritable?**

   Not at all
   Several days
   More than half the days
   Nearly every day

7. **Feeling afraid as if something awful might happen?**

   Not at all
   Several days
   More than half the days
   Nearly every day

The GAD-7 score is calculated by assigning scores of 0, 1, 2 and 3, to the response categories of 'not at all', 'several days', 'more than half the days', and 'nearly every day', respectively, and adding together the scores for the seven questions for a total anxiety severity score.

Anxiety severity scale:

- **0–4:** No anxiety
- **5–9:** Mild anxiety
- **10–14:** Moderate anxiety
- **15–21:** Severe anxiety

Scores of 5, 10 and 15 are taken as the cut-off points for mild, moderate and severe anxiety, respectively. When used as a screening tool, further evaluation is recommended when the score is 10 or greater.

Patient Health Questionnaire (PHQ-9)2

Name: .... Date: ....

Over the last 2 weeks, how often have you been bothered by any of the following problems?	Not at all	Several days	More than half the days	Nearly every day
1. Little interest or pleasure in doing things	0	1	2	3
2. Feeling down, depressed or hopeless	0	1	2	3
3. Trouble falling or staying asleep, or sleeping too much	0	1	2	3
4. Feeling tired or having little energy	0	1	2	3
5. Poor appetite or overeating	0	1	2	3
6. Feeling bad about yourself – or that you are a failure or have let yourself or your family down	0	1	2	3
7. Trouble concentrating on things, such as reading the newspaper or watching television	0	1	2	3
8. Moving or speaking so slowly that other people could have noticed? Or the opposite – being so fidgety or restless that you have been moving around a lot more than usual	0	1	2	3
9. Thoughts that you would be better off dead or of hurting yourself in some way	0	1	2	3

For office coding: Total Score _____ = _____ = _____ = _____

If you checked off any problems, how difficult have these problems made it for you to do your work, take care of things at home, or get along with other people?

☐ Not difficult at all ☐ Somewhat difficult ☐ Very difficult ☐ Extremely difficult

Helpful Reading

I've used these books with clients and recommended them to friends too.

Workbooks: ways to tackle anxiety using ACT, CBT, CFT and mindfulness

Greenberger, D., & Padesky, C. A. (2016). *Mind over mood: Change how you feel by changing the way you think* (2nd ed.). Guilford Publications.

Forsyth, J. P., 1965, & Eifert, G. H. (2016). *The mindfulness & acceptance workbook for anxiety: A guide to breaking free from anxiety, phobias & worry using acceptance & commitment therapy* (Second ed.). New Harbinger Publications.

Harris, R. (2019). *ACT made simple: An easy-to-read primer on acceptance and commitment therapy* (Second ed.). New Harbinger Publications.

Hayes, S. C., & Smith, S. (2005). *Get out of your mind and into your life: The new acceptance and commitment therapy.* New Harbinger Publications.

Hayes, S. (2020). *Acceptance and commitment therapy. Principles of becoming more flexible, effective, and fulfilled.* Audiobook. Sounds True.

Irons, C., & Beaumont, E. (2017). *The compassionate mind workbook.* Robinson.

Neff, K., & Germer, C. K. (2018). *The mindful self-compassion workbook: A proven way to accept yourself, build inner strength, and thrive.* The Guilford Press.

Tirch, D. D., Schoendorff, B., & Silberstein, L. R. (2014). *The ACT practitioner's guide to the science of compassion: Tools for fostering psychological flexibility.* New Harbinger Publications, Inc.

Williams, J. M. G., & Penman, D. (2011). *Mindfulness: A practical guide to finding peace in a frantic world.* Piatkus.

General: if you want to know more about the body-brain connection

Damasio, A. R. (2000). *The feeling of what happens: Body, emotion and the making of consciousness.* Vintage.

Jarrett, C. (2015). *Great myths of the brain.* Wiley Blackwell.

Swaab., D. (2014). *We are our brains. A neurobiography of the brain, from the womb to Alzheimer's.* Spiegel & Grau.

Siegel, D. J. (2011). *Mindsight: Transform your brain with the new science of kindness* (2011th ed.). Oneworld.

Thubten, G. (2020) *A Monk's Guide to Happiness.* St Martin's Essentials.

Classics: if you haven't got them already

Grosz, S., 1952. (2014). *The examined life: How we lose and find ourselves.* Vintage Books.

Haidt, J. (2025). *The anxious generation: How the great*

rewiring of childhood is causing an epidemic of mental illness. Penguin Books.

Kahneman, D. (2012). *Thinking, fast and slow*. Penguin.

Layard, R., & Clark, D. M. (2014). *Thrive, the power of psychological therapy*. Allen Lane.

Maté, G. &. (2003). *When the body says no: Understanding the Stress–Disease connection*. J Wiley.

Seligman, M. E. P. (2011). *Flourish: A new understanding of happiness and well-being – and how to achieve them*. Nicholas Brealey.

Servan-Schreiber, D. (2012). *Healing without Freud or Prozac: Natural approaches to curing stress, anxiety and depression*. Pan Macmillan.

Van der Kolk, B. A. (2015). *The body keeps the score: Mind, brain and body in the transformation of trauma*. Penguin Books.

Memoirs: if you want a helpful, funny, personal take

Pritchett, P. (2021). *My mess is a bit of a life: Adventures in anxiety*. Faber & Faber.

Wilson, S. (2019). *First, we make the beast beautiful: A new journey through anxiety*. Penguin.

Minchin, T. (2024). *You don't have to have a dream: Advice for the incrementally ambitious*. Ebury Publishing.

Notes

Preface

1. Mental Health Research. (2023). Anxiety or anxiety disorder? Retrieved from https://mentalhealth-uk.org/help-and-information/conditions/anxiety-disorders/what-is-anxiety/.

Before we dive in. Or the Introduction.

1. Everett, F. (2023). I'm 52 and I've struggled with anxiety all my life. *The Times*. Retrieved from https://www.thetimes.com/article/im-52-and-ive-struggled-with-anxiety-all-my-life-jf5zjzvdt.
2. Halliwell, L. (ed.) (1984). *Halliwell's Filmgoer's Companion*.
3. Truffaut, F. (1989). *Letters* (Jacob, G., de Givray, C. & Adair, G., Eds, p. 589). Faber.
4. Ackroyd, P. (2016). *Alfred Hitchcock: A Brief Life*. Doubleday.
5. Wilson, F. (2015). How Hitchcock instilled his own anxieties in his audience. *Newsweek*. Retrieved from https://www.newsweek.com/2015/04/10/hitchcock-artist-anxiety-who-instilled-fear-his-actresses-and-audience-319302.html.
6. Holley, D., Varga, E. A., Boorman, E. D., & Fox, A. S. (2024). Temporal dynamics of uncertainty cause anxiety and avoidance. *Computational psychiatry*, 8(1), 85–91. https://doi.org/10.5334/cpsy.105.
7. King, S. (1986). *It* (p. 14). Viking Press.
8. American Psychological Association. (2022). What's the difference between stress and anxiety? Retrieved from: https://www.apa.org/topics/stress/anxiety-difference,
9. Kessler R. C., Sampson N. A., Berglund P., Gruber M. J., et al. (2015). Anxious and non-anxious major depressive disorder in the World Health Organization world mental health surveys. *Epidemiology and Psychiatric Sciences*, 24, 210–226.
10. Seltzer, L. F. You only get more of what you resist – why? *Psychology*

Today. Retrieved from https://www.psychologytoday.com/gb/blog/evolution-the-self/201606/you-only-get-more-what-you-resist-why.

1. Dandelion or Orchid?

1. Ellis, B. J., & Boyce, W. T. (2008). Biological sensitivity to context. *Current Directions in Psychological Science, 17*(3), 183–187. https://doi.org/10.1111/j.1467-8721.2008.00571.x.
2. Pluess, M., Aron, E., Kähkönen, J. E., Lionetti, F., et al. (2024). Sensitivity Research. Retrieved from https://sensitivityresearch.com/.
3. Pluess, M., Aron, E., Kähkönen, J. E., Lionetti, F., et al. (2025). Evolution of the concept of sensitivity and its measurement: The highly sensitive person scale revised. (Preprint) Retrieved from https://osf.io/preprints/psyarxiv/w7bqu.
4. Aron, E. N., & Aron, A. (1997). Sensory processing sensitivity and its relation to introversion and emotionality. *Journal of Personality and Social Psychology, 73*(2), 345–368.
5. Jarrett, C. (2018). New 'highly sensitive child' test identifies three groups: Orchids, dandelions and tulips. *The Psychologist*. Retrieved from https://www.bps.org.uk/research-digest/new-highly-sensitive-child-test-identifies-three-groups-orchids-dandelions-and.
6. Lionetti, F., Aron, A., Aron, E. N., Burns, G. L., et al. (2018). Dandelions, tulips and orchids: Evidence for the existence of low-sensitive, medium-sensitive and high-sensitive individuals. *Translational Psychiatry, 8*(1), 24. https://doi.org/10.1038/s41398-017-0090-6.
7. Kagan, J., Snidman, N., Arcus, D., & Reznick, J. S. (1994). *Galen's prophecy: Temperament in human nature*. Basic Books.
8. Assary, E., Zavos, H. M. S., Krapohl, E, Keers, R, Pluess, M. (2021). Genetic architecture of Environmental Sensitivity reflects multiple heritable components: a twin study with adolescents. *Mol Psychiatry, 26*(9), 4896–4904. https://doi.org/10.1038/s41380-020-0783-8.
9. Gerhardt, S. (2025). *1001 days. How our first years shape our lifelong health* (pp. 139–141). Penguin.
10. Felitti, V. J., Anda, R. F., Nordenberg, D., Williamson, D. F., et al. (1998). Relationship of childhood abuse and household

dysfunction to many of the leading causes of death in adults. the adverse childhood experiences (ACE) study. *American Journal of Preventative Medicine, 14*(4), 245–58. doi:10.1016/s0749-3797(98)00017-8. PMID: 9635069
11. Barboza Solís, C., Kelly-Irving, M., Fantin, R., Darnaudéry, M., et al. (2015). Adverse childhood experiences and physiological wear-and-tear in midlife: Findings from the 1958 British birth cohort. *Proceedings of the National Academy of Sciences of the United States of America, 112*(7). https://doi.org/10.1073/pnas.1417325112.
12. Reis, D. L., Ribeiro, M. G., Couto, I., Maia, N., et al. (2024). Correlations between childhood maltreatment, anxiety and depressive symptoms, and risk behaviors in adolescent schoolchildren. *Trends Psychiatry Psychotherapy, 46*. https://doi.org/10.47626/2237-6089-2021-0456.
13. Hovens, J. G. F. M., Giltay, E. J, Wiersma, J. E., Spinhoven, P., et al. (2012). Impact of childhood life events and trauma on the course of depressive and anxiety disorders. *Acta Psychiatrica Scandinavica, 128*, 198–207. https://doi.org/10.1111/j.1600-0447.2011.01828.x.
14. Repetti, R. L., & Reynolds, B. (2011). Allostatic processes in the family. *Development and Psychopathology, 23*(3), 921–38. https://doi.org/10.1017/S095457941100040X.
15. Barboza Solís, C., Kelly-Irving, M., Fantin, R., Darnaudéry, M., et al. (2015). Adverse childhood experiences and physiological wear-and-tear in midlife: Findings from the 1958 British birth cohort. *Proceedings of the National Academy of Sciences of the United States of America, 112*(7). https://doi.org/10.1073/pnas.1417325112.
16. Lionetti, F., Aron, A., Aron, E. N., Burns, G. L., et al. (2018). Dandelions, tulips and orchids: Evidence for the existence of low-sensitive, medium-sensitive and high-sensitive individuals. *Translational Psychiatry, 8*(1), 24. https://doi.org/10.1038/s41398-017-0090-6.
17. Pluess, M., & Boniwell, I. (2015). Sensory-processing sensitivity predicts treatment response to a school-based depression prevention program: evidence of vantage sensitivity. *Personality and Individual Differences, 82*, 40–45. https://doi.org/10.1016/j.paid.2015.03.011.

NOTES

18. Jarrett, C. (2015). The ideal therapist doubts their professional skills but loves themselves as a person. *The Psychologist*. Retrieved from https://www.bps.org.uk/research-digest/ideal-therapist-doubts-their-professional-skills-loves-themselves-person; Nissen-Lie, H., Rønnestad, M., Høglend, P., Havik, et al. (2015). Love yourself as a person, doubt yourself as a therapist? *Clinical Psychology & Psychotherapy*, 24(10), 48–60. https://doi.org/10.1002/cpp.1977.
19. Pluess, M., Lionetti, F., Aron, E. N., & Aron, A. (2023). People differ in their sensitivity to the environment: An integrated theory, measurement and empirical evidence. *Journal of Research in Personality*, 104, 104377. https://doi.org/10.1016/j.jrp.2023. 104377.
20. Pluess, M., Lionetti, F., Aron, E. N., & Aron, A. (2023). People differ in their sensitivity to the environment: An integrated theory, measurement and empirical evidence. *Journal of Research in Personality*, 104, 104377. https://doi.org/10.1016/j.jrp.2023. 104377.
21. Harman, R. (2023). Why Jacinda Ardern's star waned in New Zealand. BBC News. Retrieved from https://www.bbc.co.uk/news/world-asia-64328433.
22. Alcee, M. (2023). What highly sensitive leaders can do. A personal perspective: The unexpected legacy of Jacinda Ardern. *Psychology Today*. Retrieved from https://www.psychologytoday.com/gb/blog/live-life-creatively/202304/what-highly-sensitive-leaders-can-do.
23. Howell, A. (2024). How the already anxious avoided global spike in Covid anxiety. *The Harvard Gazette*. Retrieved from https://news.harvard.edu/gazette/story/2024/03/how-the-already-anxious-avoided-global-spike-in-covid-anxiety/.
24. Doyle, G. (2016). Yes, I've got these conditions. Instagram post. Retrieved from https://www.instagram.com/p/BI_WZvEΛAYX/?hl=en.
25. American Psychiatric Association. (2022). *Diagnostic and Statistical Manual of Mental Disorders* (5th ed.). https://doi.org/10.1176/appi.books.9780890425787.
26. Biography.com editors. (2024). Frida Kahlo. Retrieved from https://www.biography.com/artists/frida-kahlo.
27. Almeida, L. (2020). Quotes from Frida Kahlo. Retrieved from https://www.denverartmuseum.org/en/blog/quotes-frida-kahlo.

28. Watt, G. (2005). Frida Kahlo. *British Journal of General Practice*, 55(517), 646–647.
29. Ratner, H., George, E., & Iveson, C. (2012). *Solution focused brief therapy: 100 key points and techniques*. Routledge. https://doi.org/10.4324/9780203116562.
30. Yu, F. (2019). Miracle Question in couple and family therapy. In Lebow, J. L., Chambers, A. L., & Breunlin D. C. (Eds.). *Encyclopaedia of couple and family therapy* (p. 219). Springer. https://doi.org/10.1007/978-3-319-49425-8_1072.
31. Singer, M. A. (2007). *The Untethered Soul: The Journey Beyond Yourself*. New Harbinger Publications.

2. Anxiety – a Life Sentence?

1. Carnegie, D. (1948). *How to stop worrying and start living*. Simon & Schuster.
2. Holt, G. (2011). When suicide was illegal. BBC News. Retrieved from https://www.bbc.co.uk/news/magazine-14374296.
3. Higginbottom, P. (2024). The workhouse: The story of an institution. Retrieved from https://www.workhouses.org.uk/intro/.
4. Grant-Smith, R., & Lomax, M. (1922). *The experiences of an asylum patient* (pp. 26, 136). George Allen & Unwin. Retrieved from https://archive.org/details/39002028421130.med.yale.edu/page/96/mode/2up.
5. Hilton, C., & Groves, C. (2021). "Petty tyranny and soulless discipline": Lunatic asylums in the headlines 100 years ago. Retrieved from https://www.rcpsych.ac.uk/news-and-features/blogs/detail/history-archives-and-library-blog/2021/06/08/women-in-psychiatry-100-years-ago.
6. Reid, F. (2007). Distinguishing between shell-shocked veterans and pauper lunatics: The ex-services' welfare society and mentally wounded veterans after the great war. *War in History*, 14(3), 347–371. Retrieved from https://www.jstor.org/stable/26070711; Hilton, C. (2021). *Civilian lunatic asylums during the First World War, A study of austerity on London's fringe*. Palgrave Macmillan. https://doi.org/.1007/978-3-030-54871-1.
7. McVean, A. (2017). The history of hysteria. Retrieved from https://www.mcgill.ca/oss/article/history-quackery/history-hysteria.

NOTES

8. Prentice, C. (2021). Lobotomy: The brain op described as 'easier than curing a toothache'. BBC News. Retrieved from https://www.bbc.co.uk/news/stories-55854145.
9. Calcaterra, N. E, & Barrow, J. C. (2014). Classics in chemical neuroscience: Diazepam (Valium). *ACS Chemical Neuroscience*, 5(4), 253–60. https://doi.org/10.1021/cn5000056.
10. The Lancet (editorial) (2025). 50 years of SSRIs: Weighing benefits and harms. *The Lancet*, 405(10490), 1641. https://doi.org/10.1016/S0140-6736(25)00981-X.
11. World Health Organization. (2023). Anxiety disorders. Retrieved from https://www.who.int/news-room/fact-sheets/detail/anxiety-disorders.
12. NHS England. (2021). Record high patient numbers completing NHS treatment for common mental illness. Retrieved from https://www.england.nhs.uk/2021/11/record-high-patient-numbers-completing-nhs-treatment-for-common-mental-illness/.
13. American Psychiatric Association (2024). Annual Mental Health Poll. Retrieved from https://www.psychiatry.org/news-room/news-releases/annual-poll-adults-express-increasing-anxiousness.
14. National Alliance on Mental Illness. Anxiety disorders (2017). Retrieved from https://www.nami.org/about-mental-illness/mental-health-conditions/anxiety-disorders/.
15. Australian Bureau of Statistics (2022). National study of Health and Wellbeing 2020–2022. Retrieved from https://www.abs.gov.au/statistics/health/mental-health/national-study-mental-health-and-wellbeing/latest-release.
16. Javaid, S. F., Hashim, I. J., Hashim, M. J., Stip, E., et al. (2023). Epidemiology of anxiety disorders: Global burden and sociodemographic associations. *Middle East Current Psychiatry*, 30, 44 (2023). https://doi.org/10.1186/s43045-023-00315-3.
17. Ruscio, A. M., Hallion, L. S., & Lim, C. C. W. (2017). Cross-sectional comparison of the epidemiology of DSM-5 generalized anxiety disorder across the globe. *JAMA Psychiatry*, 74(5), https://doi.org/10.1001/jamapsychiatry.2017.0056.
18. Haywood, D. C. D., & Hart, N. H. (2024). Avoiding the pitfalls of the DSM-5: A primer for health professionals. *General Hospital Psychiatry*, 90, 89–90. https://doi.org/10.1016/j.genhosppsych.2024.07.006.
19. National Health Service (2023). Social anxiety (social phobia).

Retrieved from https://www.nhs.uk/mental-health/conditions/social-anxiety/.
20. Kapp, S. K. (2019). *Autistic Community and the Neurodiversity Movement: Stories from the Frontline* (1st ed.). Springer Singapore. https://doi.org/10.1007/978-981-13-8437-0.
21. Santhouse, A. (2025). *No More Normal*. Granta Books.
22. Foa, E. B., McLean, C. P., Zang, Y., Zong, J., et al. (2016). Psychometric properties of the posttraumatic stress disorder symptoms scale interview for DSM-5 (PSSI-5). *Psychological Assessment*, 28, 1159–1165. https://doi.org/10.1037/pas0000259.
23. Cloitre, M., Shevlin, M., Brewin, C. R., Bisson, J. I., et al. (2018). The International Trauma Questionnaire: Development of a self-report measure of ICD-11 PTSD and complex PTSD. *Acta Psychiatrica Scandinavica*, 138(6), 536–546. https://doi.org/10.1111/acps.12956.
24. Spitzer, R. L., Kroenke, K., Williams, J. B., & Löwe, B. (2006) A brief measure for assessing generalized anxiety disorder: The GAD-7. *Archives of Internal Medicine*, 166(10), 1092–1097.
25. Kroenke, K., Spitzer, R. L., & Williams, J. B. W. (2001). The PHQ-9: Validity of a brief depression severity measure. *Journal of General Internal Medicine*, 16(9), 606–613.
26. Adapted from Butler, G., & Hope, T. (2007). *Managing your Mind: The Mental Fitness Guide*. Oxford University Press.
27. Ford, S & Gillanders, D. (n.d.). *Valued Living: A Self-Help Guide to Living Effectively with Emotional Pain*, University of Edinburgh. Retrieved from https://contextualscience.org/sites/default/files/Self-Help%20ACT%20Manual%20for%20Anxiety%20&%20Depression.pdf.

3. The Happy Trap

1. Gallup, *World Happiness Report 2025*. Retrieved from https://www.gallup.com/analytics/349487/world-happiness-report.aspx.
2. Finland Toolbox. Nature Relationship. Retrieved from https://toolbox.finland.fi/finland-in-stories/nature-relationship/.
3. Finland Toolbox. Finnish Forests. Retrieved from https://toolbox.finland.fi/business-innovation/finnish-forests-growing-ideas/.
4. Visit Finland, Finnish Everyman's Rights – The Right to Roam

NOTES

and Enjoy Nature. Retrieved from https://www.visitfinland.com/en/articles/finnish-everyman-rights-the-right-to-roam/.

5. Helliwell, J. F., Layard, R., Sachs, J. D., De Neve, J.-E., et al. (Eds.) (2025). *World Happiness Report 2025*. University of Oxford: Wellbeing Research Centre.

6. Lehti, M., & Kivivuori, J. (2005). Alcohol-related violence as an explanation for the difference between homicide rates in Finland and the other Nordic countries. *Nordic Studies on Alcohol and Drugs*, 22(1). 7–24. https://doi.org/10.1177/145507250502201S04.

7. Zashev, P. (2022). We must act upon the happiness as the happiest nation, *Helsinki Times*. Retrieved from https://www.helsinkitimes.fi/columns/columns/viewpoint/22619-we-must-act-upon-the-happiness-in-the-happiest-country.html

8. Sorkkila, M., & Aunola, K. (2020). Risk factors for parental burnout among Finnish parents: The role of socially prescribed perfectionism. *Journal of Child and Family Studies*, 29, 648–659 (2020). https://doi.org/10.1007/s10826-019-01607-1.

9. Gallup, Understanding how Gallup uses the Cantril Scale: Development of the 'thriving, struggling, suffering' categories. Retrieved from http://www.gallup.com/poll/122453/understanding-gallup-uses-cantr il-scale.aspx.

10. Cantril, H. (1965). *The Pattern of Human Concerns*. Rutgers University Press.

11. Nilsson, A. H., Eichstaedt, J. C., Lomas, T., Schwartz, A., & Kjell, O. (2024). The Cantril Ladder elicits thoughts about power and wealth. *Scientific Reports*, 14(1), 2642. Retrieved from https://doi.org/10.1038/s41598-024-52939-y.

12. Garner, H. (2023). Helen Garner on happiness: 'It's taken me 80 years to figure out it's not a tranquil, sunlit realm'. *The Guardian*. Retrieved from https://www.theguardian.com/culture/2023/feb/05/helen-garner-on-happiness-its-taken-me-80-years-to-figure-out-its-not-a-tranquil-sunlit-realm.

13. Helliwell, J. F., et al. (2025). Chapter 2: Caring and sharing. In *World Happiness Report 2025*. https://doi.org/10.18724/whr-31zp-ga37.

14. Whippman, R. (2016). *America the Anxious: How our pursuit of happiness is creating a nation of nervous wrecks*. St. Martin's Press.

15. Action for Happiness. https://actionforhappiness.org/.
16. Frayman, D., Krekel, C., Layard, R., MacLennan, S., & Parkes, I. (2024). Value for money: How to improve wellbeing and reduce misery. *CEP Reports*, 44. Retrieved from https://cep.lse.ac.uk/pubs/download/special/cepsp44.pdf.
17. Krekel, C., De Neve, J.-E., Fancourt, D., & Layard R., (2021). A local community course that raises wellbeing and pro-sociality: Evidence from a randomised controlled trial. *Journal of Economic Behavior & Organization*, 188, 322–336. https://doi.org/10.1016/j.jebo.2021.05.021.
18. His Holiness the 14th Dalai Lama of Tibet: Official website. Brief Biography Retrieved from https://www.dalailama.com/the-dalai-lama/biography-and-daily-life/brief-biography.
19. Hofmann, S. G., Grossman, P., & Hinton, D. E. (2011). Loving-kindness and compassion meditation: Potential for psychological interventions. *Clinical Psychology* Review, 31(7):, 1126–32. https://doi.org/10.1016/j.cpr.2011.07.003.
20. Aurelius, M. (2003). *Meditations: A New Translation* (Modern Library Classics) (G. Hays, Trans.). Random House.
21. Schneeberg, N. (2008). The medical history of Thomas Jefferson (1743–1826). *Journal Medical Biography*, 16(2), 118–25. https://doi.org/10.1258/jmb.2007.007036.
22. Frankl, V. E. (2006). *Man's Search for Meaning: An Introduction to Logotherapy*. Beacon Press.
23. Hillesum, E. T. (2011). *An Interrupted Life: The Diaries and Letters of Etty Hillesum 1941–43*. Persephone Books.
24. Ricard, M. (2015) *Happiness: A Guide to Developing Life's Most Important Skill* (2nd revised ed.) Atlantic Books.
25. Rozanski, A., Bavishi, C., Kubzansky, L. D., & Cohen, R. (2019). Association of optimism with cardiovascular events and all-cause mortality: A systematic review and meta-analysis. *JAMA Network Open*, 2(9). https://doi.org/10.1001/jamanetworkopen.2019.12200.
26. Scheier, M. F., Carver, C. S., & Bridges, M. W. (2001). Optimism, pessimism, and psychological well-being. In E. C. Chang (Ed.), *Optimism & Pessimism: Implications for Theory, Research, and Practice* (pp. 189–216). American Psychological Association. https://doi.org/10.1001/10.1037/10385-009.
27. Boehm, J. K., Qureshi, F., Chen, Y., Soo, J., et al. (2020).

Optimism and cardiovascular health: Longitudinal findings from the coronary artery risk development in young adults study. *Psychosomatic Medicine*, 82(8), 774–781. https://doi.org/10.1001/10.1097/PSY.0000000000000855.

28. Hood, B. (2024). Optimism and Health. Retrieved from https://www.bps.org.uk/psychologist/optimism-and-health.

29. Andersson, M. A. (2012). Dispositional optimism and the emergence of social network diversity. *Sociological Quarterly*, 53(1), 92–115; Lee, L. O., James, P., Zevon, E. S. et al. (2019). Optimism is associated with exceptional longevity in 2 epidemiologic cohorts of men and women. *Proceedings of the National Academy of Sciences*, 116(37), 18357–62.

30. Plomin, R., Scheier, M. F., Bergeman, C. S., Pedersen, N. L., et al. (1992). Optimism, pessimism and mental health: A twin/adoption analysis. *Personality and Individual Differences*, 13(8), 921–930. https://doi.org/10.1001/10.1016/0191-8869(92)90009-E.

31. Sweeny, K, S. J. (2010). The costs of optimism and the benefits of pessimism. *Emotion*, 10(5), 750–3. https://doi.org/10.1037/a0019016.

32. Hecht, D. (2013). The neural basis of optimism and pessimism. *Expermental Neurobiology*, 22(3), 173–99. https://doi.org/10.5607/en.2013.22.3.173.

33. The Finnish Happiness Institute. The secret to Finnish women's happiness: Nature, equality, and community. Retrieved from https://happinessinfinland.com/?page_id=243.

34. Nylund, J. (2018). *Sisu: The Finnish act of courage.* (1st ed.). Octopus Publishing Group. Reproduced with permission of the author.

35. Adapted from Nylund, J. (2018). *Sisu: The Finnish act of courage.* (1st ed.). Octopus Publishing Group. With permission from the author.

36. Edelman Trust Barometer. (2025). *Global Report: Trust and the crisis of grievance.* Retrieved from https://www.edelman.com/sites/g/files/aatuss191/files/2025-01/2025%20Edelman%20Trust%20Barometer%20Global%20Report_01.23.25.pdf.

37. Edelman. 2025 Edelman Trust Barometer reveals high level of grievance towards government, business and the rich (2025). Retrieved from https://www.edelman.com/news-awards/2025-edelman-trust-barometer-reveals-high-level-grievance.

38. Newman, N. (2024). Overview and key findings of the 2024 Digital News Report. Reuters Institute. Retrieved from https://reutersinstitute.politics.ox.ac.uk/digital-news-report/2024/dnr-executive-summary.
39. Gross, J. (2023). How Finland is teaching a generation to spot misinformation. *New York Times*. Retrieved from https://www.nytimes.com/2023/01/10/world/europe/finland-misinformation-classes.html.
40. IPSOS. (2025). IPSOS global opinion polls: The State of the World. Trustworthiness. Retrieved from https://www.ipsos.com/en/global-opinion-polls/trustworthiness; King's College. (2023). *Love thy neighbour? Public trust and acceptance of the people who live alongside us*. World Values Survey. Retrieved from https://www.kcl.ac.uk/policy-institute/assets/love-thy-neighbour.pdf.

4. Understanding the Inner Voice

1. Tolle, E. (2005). *A New Earth: Awakening to Your Life's Purpose*. Dutton/Penguin Group.
2. Maté, G. (2016). Be compassionate towards your stupid friend. Retrieved from https://beyondaddiction.ca/2016/07/05/your-stupid-friend/.
3. Harvard University. A Guide to Brain Architecture. Retrieved from https://developingchild.harvard.edu/resource-guides/guide-brain-architecture/.
4. Schimmenti, A., & Bifulco, A. (2015). Linking lack of care in childhood to anxiety disorders in emerging adulthood: The role of attachment styles. *Child and Adolescent Mental Health*, 20(1), 41–48. https://doi.org/10.1111/camh.12051.
5. Maté, G. (2016). Be compassionate towards your stupid friend. Retrieved from https://beyondaddiction.ca/2016/07/05/your-stupid-friend/.
6. Jakubowski, K. P., Barinas-Mitchell, E., Chang, Y., Maki, P. M., et al. (2022). The cardiovascular cost of silence: Relationships between self-silencing and carotid atherosclerosis in midlife women. *Annals of Behavioral Medicine*, 56(3), 282–290. https://doi.org/10.1093/abm/kaab046.
7. Emran, A., Iqbal, N., & Dar, I. A. (2020). 'Silencing the self'

NOTES

and women's mental health problems: A narrative review. *Asian Journal of Psychiatry*, 53, 102197. https://doi.org/10.1016/j.ajp.2020.102197.

8. Eyal, M. (2023). Self-silencing is making women sick. *Time*. Retrieved from https://time.com/6319549/silencing-women-sick-essay/.
9. Williams, S., Clarke, S., & Edginton, T. (2023). Mindfulness for the self-management of negative coping, rumination and fears of compassion in people with cancer: An exploratory study. *Cancer Reports*, 6(3), e1761–n/a. https://doi.org/10.1002/cnr2.1761.
10. Gilbert, P., Clark, M., Hempel, S., Miles, J. N. V., & Irons, C. (2004). Criticising and reassuring oneself: An exploration of forms, styles and reasons in female students. *British Journal of Clinical Psychology*, 43, 31–50. https://doi.org/10.1017/S1352465804002048.
11. Gilbert, P., Clarke, M., Hempel, S., Miles, J. N. V., & Irons, C. (2004). Functions of self-criticising/attacking scale (FSCS). *APA Psych Tests*. https://doi.org/10.1037/t54210-000.
12. Driscoll, R. (1989). Self-condemnation: A comprehensive framework for assessment and treatment. *Psychotherapy*, 26(1), 104–111. https://doi.org/10.1037/h0085394.
13. Gilbert, P., & Irons, C. (2005). Focused therapies and compassionate mind training for shame and self-attacking. In P. Gilbert (Ed.), *Compassion: Conceptualisations, Research and Use in Psychotherapy* (pp. 263–325). Routledge.
14. Gilbert, P. (2009). Introducing compassion-focused therapy. *Advances in Psychiatric Treatment: The Royal College of Psychiatrists' Journal of Continuing Professional Development*, 15(3), 199–208. https://doi.org/10.1192/apt.bp.107.005264.
15. Gilbert, P. (2009). *The Compassionate Mind: A New Approach to Life's Challenges*. Constable and Robinson. The Three Circles illustration here is adapted from Irons, C., & Beaumont, E. (2017). *The compassionate mind workbook*. London: Robinson. with kind permission of the author.
16. Gilbert, P. (2017). A brief outline of the evolutionary approach for compassion focused therapy. *EC Psychology and Psychiatry*, 3(6), 218–227. Retrieved from https://repository.derby.ac.uk/item/93885/a-brief-outline-of-the-evolutionary-approach-for-compassion-focused-therapy.
17. Gilbert, P., & Irons, C. (2005). Focused therapies and compassionate mind training for shame and self-attacking. In P.

Gilbert (Ed.), *Compassion: Conceptualisations, Research and Use in Psychotherapy* (pp. 263–325). Routledge.
18. Adapted from Irons, C., & Beaumont, E. (2017). *The compassionate mind workbook*. Robinson. With kind permission of the author.
19. Adams, T. (2001) Connolly on the couch. *The Observer Magazine*. Retrieved from https://www.theguardian.com/theobserver/2001/sep/23/features.magazine67.

5. High-Functioning Anxiety, Perfectionism and... Procrastination

1. O'Keefe Museum. Music for the eyes: A new Georgia O'Keeffe experience. Retrieved from https://www.okeeffemuseum.org/blog-publications/music-for-the-eyes/.
2. Savage, M. (2025). Singer Self Esteem: There were moments I considered giving up. BBC News. Retrieved from https://www.bbc.co.uk/news/articles/cx250z234n2o.
3. Verrico, L. (2025). Self Esteem: 'I'm political, I'm outspoken — and I'm terrified all the time'. *The Times*. Retrieved from https://www.thetimes.com/culture/music/article/self-esteem-interview-a-complicated-woman-m7fqtw90k.
4. Goodwin, D. (2022). Have you got high-functioning anxiety? *The Times*. Retrieved from https://www.thetimes.com/uk/politics/article/high-functioning-anxiety-signs-znpjz6mm7.
5. Egan, S. J., Wade, T. D., & Shafran, R. (2011). Perfectionism as a transdiagnostic process: A clinical review. *Clinical Psychology Review*, 31(2), 203–212. https://doi.org/10.1016/j.cpr.2010.04.009.
6. Shahar, G., Blatt, S. J., Zuroff, D. C., Krupnick, J. L., & Sotsky, S. M. (2004). Perfectionism impedes social relations and response to brief treatment for depression. *Journal of Social and Clinical Psychology*, 23(2), 140–154. https://doi.org/10.1521/jscp.23.2.140.31017.
7. Bieling, P. J., Israeli, A. L., & Antony, M. M. (2004). Is perfectionism good, bad, or both? Examining models of the perfectionism construct. *Personality and Individual Differences*, 36(6), 1373–1385. https://doi.org/10.1016/S0191-8869(03)00235-6.
8. Limburg, K., Watson, H. J., Hagger, M. S., & Egan, S. J. (2017).

NOTES

The relationship between perfectionism and psychopathology: A meta-analysis. *Journal of Clinical Psychology, 73*(10), 1301–1326. https://doi.org/10.1002/jclp.22435.

9. Burgess, A. M., Frost, R. O., & DiBartolo, P. M. (2016). Development and validation of the Frost Multidimensional Perfectionism Scale–Brief. *Journal of Psychoeducational Assessment, 34*(7), 620–633. https://doi.org/10.1177/0734282916651359.

10. Woodfin, V., Binder, P., & Molde, H. (2020). The psychometric properties of the Frost Multidimensional Perfectionism Scale–Brief. *Frontiers in Psychology, 11*, 1860. https://doi.org/10.3389/fpsyg.2020.01860.

11. Kemp, J. (2021). *The ACT Workbook for Perfectionism: Build Your Best (Imperfect) Life Using Powerful Acceptance and Commitment Therapy and Self-Compassion Skills* (1st ed.). New Harbinger Publications, Inc. Retrieved from https://go.exlibris.link/m83Fx7lf.

12. Curran, T., & Hill, A. P. (2019). Perfectionism is increasing over time: A meta-analysis of birth cohort differences from 1989 to 2016. *Psychological Bulletin, 145*(4), 410–429. https://doi.org/10.1037/bul0000138.

13. Curran, T., (2023). *The Perfection Trap: The Power of Good Enough in a World That Always Wants More.* London: Cornerstone Press. Retrieved from https://go.exlibris.link/TMycNx3Q.

14. Hewitt, P. L., & Flett, G. L. (1991). Perfectionism in the self and social contexts: Conceptualization, assessment, and association with psychopathology. *Journal of Personality and Social Psychology, 60*(3), 456–470. https://doi.org/10.1037/0022-3514.60.3.456.

15. Hamachek, D. E. (1978). Psychodynamics of normal and neurotic perfectionism. *Psychology, 15*, 27–33. https://doi.org/10.4236/psych.2014.59110

16. Flett, G. L., Hewitt, P. L., Nepon, T., Sherry, S. B., & Smith, M. (2022). The destructiveness and public health significance of socially prescribed perfectionism: A review, analysis, and conceptual extension. *Clinical Psychology Review, 93*, 102130. https://doi.org/10.1016/j.cpr.2022.102130.

17. Curran, T., & Hill, A. P. (2019). Perfectionism is increasing over time: A meta-analysis of birth cohort differences from 1989 to 2016. *Psychological Bulletin, 145*(4), 410–429. https://doi.org/10.1037/bul0000138.

18. Hewitt, P. L., & Flett, G. L. (1991). Perfectionism in the self and social contexts: Conceptualization, assessment, and association with psychopathology. *Journal of Personality and Social Psychology, 60*(3), 456–470. https://doi.org/10.1037/0022-3514.60.3.456.
19. Childs, J. H., & Stoeber, J. (2012). Do you want me to be perfect? Two longitudinal studies on socially prescribed perfectionism, stress and burnout in the workplace. *Work and Stress, 26*(4), 347–364. https://doi.org/10.1080/02678373.2012.737547.
20. Haimovitz, K., & Dweck, C. S. (2016). What predicts children's fixed and growth intelligence mind-sets? Not their parents' views of intelligence but their parents' views of failure. *Psychological Science, 27*(6), 859–869. https://doi.org/10.1177/0956797616639727.
21. Mohammadian, Y., Mahaki, B., Dehghani, M., Vahid, M.A., & Lavasani, F.F. (2018). Investigating the Role of Interpersonal Sensitivity, *Anger, and Perfectionism in Social Anxiety. International Journal of Preventive Medicine*, 9(2), 1–12. https://doi.org/10.4103/ijpvm.IJPVM_364_16.
22. Stoll, O., Lau, A., & Stoeber, J. (2008). Perfectionism and performance in a new basketball training task: Does striving for perfection enhance or undermine performance? *Psychology of Sport and Exercise, 9*(5), 620–629. https://doi.org/10.1016/j.psychsport.2007.10.001.
23. Hill, A. P., Witcher, C. S. G., Gotwals, J. K., & Leyland, A. F. (2015). A qualitative study of perfectionism among self-identified perfectionists in sport and the performing arts. *Sport, Exercise, and Performance Psychology, 4*(4), 237–253. https://doi.org/10.1037/spy0000041.
24. Cooper, A. (2024) Simone Biles: 'I thought America hated me.' *Call Her Daddy* podcast.
25. NBC Sports (2021). Simone Biles opens up about 'twisties', making best decision for team Tokyo Olympics. Retrieved from https://www.youtube.com/watch?v=t-4eJ2TZytY.
26. CNN Sports. (2024). Simone Biles tells CNN competing in Paris 'meant the world' after struggles in Tokyo. Retrieved from https://edition.cnn.com/2024/08/06/sport/simone-biles-cnn-olympics-spt.
27. Wei, J., Sze, I. N., Ng, F. F., & Pomerantz, E. M. (2020). Parents' responses to their children's performance: A process examination

NOTES

in the United States and China. *Developmental Psychology*, 56(12), 2331–2344. https://doi.org/10.1037/dev0001125.
28. Bouguettaya, A., Cruwys, T., Moulding, R., King, R., & Bliuc, A. (2019). Evidence that frame of reference effects can reduce socially prescribed perfectionism. *Frontiers in Psychology*, 9, 2703. https://doi.org/10.3389/fpsyg.2018.02703.
29. Frost, R. O., Marten, P., Lahart, C., & Rosenblate, R. (1990) The dimensions of perfectionism. *Cognitive Therapy and Research*, 14(5), 449–468. https://doi.org/10.1007/BF01172967; Umandap, J. D., & Teh, L. A. (2020). Self-compassion as a mediator between perfectionism and personal growth initiative. *Psychological Studies*, 65(3), 227–238. https://doi.org/10.1007/s12646-020-00566-8.
30. Hendriksen, E. (2025). *How to Be Enough: Seven Life Changing Steps for Self-Critics, Over-Thinkers and Perfectionists*. Bonnier Books.
31. Wohl, M. J. A., Pychyl, T. A., & Bennett, S. H. (2010). I forgive myself, now I can study: How self-forgiveness for procrastinating can reduce future procrastination. *Personality and Individual Differences*, 48(7), 803–808. https://doi.org/10.1016/j.paid.2010.01.029.
32. Blouin-Hudon, E. C., & Pychyl, T. A. (2017). A mental imagery intervention to increase future self-continuity and reduce procrastination. *Applied Psychology*, 66(2), 326–352. https://doi.org/10.1111/apps.12088.
33. Flett, G. L. (2025). *Mattering as a Core Need in Children and Adolescents: Theoretical, Clinical, and Research Perspectives*. American Psychological Association.
34. Hewitt, P. L., Flett, G. L., Sherry, S. B., Habke, M., Parkin, M., et al. (2003). The interpersonal expression of perfection: Perfectionistic self-presentation and psychological distress. *Journal of Personality and Social Psychology*, 84(6), 1303–1325. https://doi.org/10.1037/0022-3514.84.6.1303
35. Sohn, E. (2024). Perfectionism and the high-stakes culture of success: The hidden toll on kids and parents. Retrieved from https://www.apa.org/monitor/2024/10/antidote-achievement-culture; Wallace, J. B. (2023). *Never enough: When achievement culture becomes toxic—and what we can do about it*. Portfolio/Penguin.

6. Imposter syndrome, performance and social anxiety

1. Yorke, T. (1992). *Creep*. Radiohead. Slade, S., Kolderie, P. Q. (Prods). Chipping Norton Studios, Oxfordshire, England.
2. BBC Four Online. More dangerous songs: And the band played on. Retrieved from https://www.bbc.co.uk/programmes/articles/5R152hTbVPQdYjn29q5jt4/16-songs-banned-by-the.
3. Clance, P. R., & Imes, S. A. (1978). The imposter phenomenon in high achieving women: Dynamics and therapeutic intervention. *Psychotherapy (Chicago, Ill.)*, 15(3), 241–247. https://doi.org/10.1037/h0086006.
4. Anderson, L. V. (2016). Feeling like an imposter is not a syndrome. *Slate*. Retrieved from https://slate.com/business/2016/04/is-impostor-syndrome-real-and-does-it-affect-women-more-than-men.html.
5. Thompson, T., Foreman, P., & Martin, F. (2000). Impostor fears and perfectionistic concern over mistakes. *Personality and Individual Differences*, 29(4), 629–647. https://doi.org/10.1016/S0191-8869(99)00218-4.
6. Origins of the fear of success. (1981) *American Journal of Psychiatry*, 138(1), 95–8. https://doi.org/10.1176/ajp.138.1.95.
7. Thomas, M., & Bigatti, S. (2020). Perfectionism, impostor phenomenon, and mental health in medicine: A literature review. *International Journal of Medical Education*, 11, 201–213. https://doi.org/10.5116/ijme. 5f54.c8f8.
8. Blöte, A. W., Kint, M. J. W., Miers, A. C., & Westenberg, P. M. (2009). The relation between public speaking anxiety and social anxiety: A review. *Journal of Anxiety Disorders*, 23(3), 305–313. https://doi.org/10.1016/j.janxdis.2008.11.007.
9. Heiser, N. A., Turner, S. M., & Beidel, D. C. (2003). Shyness: Relationship to social phobia and other psychiatric disorders. *Behaviour Research and Therapy*, 41(2), 209–221. https://doi.org/10.1016/S0005-7967(02)00003-7.
10. Ruscio, A. M., Brown, T. A., Chiu, W. T., Sareen, J., et al. (2007). Social fears and social phobia in the United States: Results from the National Comorbidity Survey replication. *Psychological Medicine*, 38(1), 15–28. https://doi.org/10.1017/S0033291707001699.

NOTES

11. American Psychiatric Association. (2022). *Diagnostic and Statistical Manual of Mental Disorders: DSM-5-TR* (5th ed.). American Psychiatric Association Publishing. Retrieved from https://go.exlibris.link/Bpyr3qQ2.
12. Wilson, A. C., & Gullon-Scott, F. (2024). 'It's not always textbook social anxiety': A survey-based study investigating the nature of social anxiety and experiences of therapy in autistic people. *Autism: The International Journal of Research and Practice*, 28(11), 2923–2936. https://doi.org/10.1177/13623613241251513.
13. Gilovich, T., Medvec, V. H., & Savitsky, K. (2000). The spotlight effect in social judgment: An egocentric bias in estimates of the salience of one's own actions and appearance. *Journal of Personality and Social Psychology*, 78(2), 211–222. https://doi.org/10.1037/0022-3514.78.2.211.
14. Gilovich, T., Savitsky, K., & Medvec, V. H. (1998). The illusion of transparency: Biased assessments of others' ability to read one's emotional states. *Journal of Personality and Social Psychology*, 75(2), 332–346. https://doi.org/10.1037/0022-3514.75.2.332.
15. Gilovich, T., Medvec, V. H., & Savitsky, K. (2000). The spotlight effect in social judgment: An egocentric bias in estimates of the salience of one's own actions and appearance. *Journal of Personality and Social Psychology*, 78(2), 211–222. https://doi.org/10.1037/0022-3514.78.2.211.
16. Oren-Yagoda, R., Schwartz, M., & Aderka, I. M. (2021). The grass is always greener: Envy in social anxiety disorder. *Journal of Anxiety Disorders*, 82, 102445. https://doi.org/10.1016/j.janxdis.2021.102445.
17. Nishikawa, Y., Fracalanza, K., Rector, N. A., & Laposa, J. M. (2022). Social anxiety and negative interpretations of positive social events: What role does intolerance of uncertainty play? *Journal of Clinical Psychology*, 78(12), 2513–2524. https://doi.org/10.1002/jclp.23363.
18. Adapted from Gilbert, P. (2018). An introduction to the theory and compassion focused therapy and compassionate mind training for shame-based difficulties. The Compassionate Mind Foundation.
19. Craske, M. G., Treanor, M., Conway, C. C., Zbozinek, T., & Vervliet, B. (2014). Maximizing exposure therapy: An inhibitory learning approach. *Behaviour Research and Therapy*, 58, 10–23. https://doi.org/10.1016/j.brat.2014.04.006.

20. Craske, M. G., Treanor, M., Conway, C. C., Zbozinek, T., & Vervliet, B. (2014). Maximizing exposure therapy: An inhibitory learning approach. *Behaviour Research and Therapy*, 58, 10–23. https://doi.org/10.1016/j.brat.2014.04.006.
21. Rippon, G. (2025). *The Lost Girls of Autism: How Science Failed Autistic Women – and the New Research That's Changing The Story.* Pan Macmillan.
22. Russell, G., Stapley, S., Newlove-Delgado, T., Salmon, A., et al. (2022). Time trends in autism diagnosis over 20 years: a UK population-based cohort study. *Journal of Child Psychology and Psychiatry*, 63(6), 674–682. https://doi.org/10.1111/jcpp.13505
23. Murdoch, C. &., Cahill, T. & Worrall-Davies, A. (2025). Meeting the needs of autistic adults in mental health services. Retrieved from https://www.england.nhs.uk/long-read/meeting-the-needs-of-autistic-adults-in-mental-health-services/.
24. Moseley, R. L., Turner-Cobb, J. M., Spahr, C. M., Shields, G. S., & Slavich, G. M. (2021). Lifetime and perceived stress, social support, loneliness, and health in autistic adults. *Health Psychology*, 40(8), 556–568. https://doi.org/10.1037/hea0001108.
25. Roberts, K., & Rankin, P. M. (2025). A cognitive help or hindrance? A systematic review of cognitive behavioural therapy to treat anxiety in young people with autism spectrum disorder. *Clinical Child Psychology and Psychiatry*, 30(2), 419–435. https://doi.org/10.1177/13591045251314906.
26. Spain, D., Blainey, S. H., & Vaillancourt, K. (2017). Group cognitive behaviour therapy (CBT) for social interaction anxiety in adults with autism spectrum disorders (ASD). *Research in Autism Spectrum Disorders*, 41–42, 20–30. https://doi.org/10.1016/j.rasd.2017.07.005; Spain, D., & Blainey, S. H. (2015). Group social skills interventions for adults with high-functioning autism spectrum disorders: A systematic review. *Autism: The International Journal of Research and Practice*, 19(7), 874–886. https://doi.org/10.1177/1362361315587659.
27. O'Brien, A., Smith, J., Mantovani, N., White, S., et al. (2024). A controlled trial of a virtual reality experience to support wellbeing in healthcare students. https://doi.org/10.31234/osf.io/9jgp2.
28. Wilson, A. C., & Gullon-Scott, F. (2024). Social anxiety in

autistic people: Does the Clark and Wells model fit? *Journal of Autism and Developmental Disorders*, 54(10), 3908–3920. https://doi.org/10.1007/s10803-023-06108-1.

7. How to Soothe our Anxious Body

1. Nietzsche, F. W. (2006). *Thus Spoke Zarathustra: A Book for All and None*. Cambridge University Press.
2. Van der Kolk, B. A., 1943. (2015). *The Body Keeps the Score: Mind, Brain and Body in the Transformation of Trauma*. Penguin Books. Retrieved from https://go.exlibris.link/L3tdZZTS.
3. National Institute for Health and Care Research (NIHR). The Genetic Links to Anxiety and Depression (GLAD) study. Retrieved from https://gladstudy.org.uk/about.
4. Marshall, G. N., Miles, J. N. V., & Stewart, S. H. (2010). Anxiety sensitivity and PTSD symptom severity are reciprocally related: Evidence from a longitudinal study of physical trauma survivors. *Journal of Abnormal Psychology (1965)*, 119(1), 143–150. https://doi.org/10.1037/a0018009.
5. Marshall, G. N., Miles, J. N. V., & Stewart, S. H. (2010). Anxiety sensitivity and PTSD symptom severity are reciprocally related: Evidence from a longitudinal study of physical trauma survivors. *Journal of Abnormal Psychology (1965)*, 119(1), 143–150. https://doi.org/10.1037/a0018009.
6. Stec, A. A., Purser, D. A., & Hull, T. (2025). Grenfell Tower Fire: Firefighters' activities and their exposure to fire smoke and heat. *Journal of Occupational and Environmental Medicine*, 67(1), e1–e11. https://doi.org/10.1097/JOM.0000000000003271.
7. de Jonge, P., Roest, A. M., Lim, C. C. W., Florescu, S. E., et al. (2016). Cross-national epidemiology of panic disorder and panic attacks in the world mental health surveys. *Depression and Anxiety*, 33(12), 1155–1177. https://doi.org/10.1002/da.22572.
8. Williams, S. (2016). *Rise: Surviving and Thriving after Trauma*. Weidenfeld & Nicolson.
9. Nestor, J. (2020). *Breath: The New Science of a Lost Art* (p. 212). Penguin Life.
10. Nestor, J. (2020). *Breath: The New Science of a Lost Art* (p. 183). Penguin Life.

11. Röttger, S., Theobald, D. A., Abendroth, J., & Jacobsen, T. (2021). The effectiveness of combat tactical breathing as compared with prolonged exhalation. *Applied Psychophysiology and Biofeedback*, 46(1), 19–28. https://doi.org/10.1007/s10484-020-09485-w.
12. Porges, S. W. (2023). The vagal paradox: A polyvagal solution. *Comprehensive Psychoneuroendocrinology (Online)*, 16, 100200.
13. Porges, S. W. (2022). Polyvagal theory: A science of safety. *Frontiers in Integrative Neuroscience*, 16, 871227. https://doi.org/10.3389/fnint.2022.871227.
14. Neff, K., & Germer, C. K. (2018). The mindful self-compassion workbook: A proven way to accept yourself, build inner strength, and thrive. The Guilford Press. Retrieved from https://go.exlibris.link/YXVtKf2H.
15. The Center for Mindful Self-Compassion. https://centerformsc.org/pages/sc-resources.
16. The Compassionate Mind Foundation. https://www.compassionatemind.co.uk/.
17. Hannibal, K. E., & Bishop, M. D. (2014). Chronic stress, cortisol dysfunction, and pain: A psychoneuroendocrine rationale for stress management in pain rehabilitation. *Physical Therapy*, 94(12), 1816–1825. https://doi.org/10.2522/ptj.20130597.
18. Hare, O. A., Wetherell, M. A., & Smith, M. A. (2013). State anxiety and cortisol reactivity to skydiving in novice versus experienced skydivers. *Physiology & Behavior*, 118, 40–44. https://doi.org/10.1016/j.physbeh.2013.05.011.
19. Sullivan, R. M., Wilson, D. A., Ravel, N., & Mouly, A. (2015). Olfactory memory networks: From emotional learning to social behaviors. *Frontiers in Behavioral Neuroscience*, 9, 36. https://doi.org/10.3389/fnbeh.2015.00036.
20. A shot of anxiety and the world stinks: How stress can rewire brain, making benign smells malodorous. (2013). *Science Daily*. Retrieved from https://www.sciencedaily.com/releases/2013/09/130924174150.htm.
21. Kritsidima, M., Newton, T., & Asimakopoulou, K. (2010). The effects of lavender scent on dental patient anxiety levels: A cluster randomised-controlled trial. *Community Dentistry and Oral Epidemiology*, 38(1), 83–87. https://doi.org/10.1111/j.1600-0528.2009.00511.x.

22. Moss, M., Cook, J., Wesnes, K., & Duckett, P. (2003). Aromas of rosemary and lavender essential oils differentially affect cognition and mood in healthy adults. *International Journal of Neuroscience*, *113*(1), 15–38. https://doi.org/10.1080/00207450390161903.
23. Vigna, E., & Carli, V. (2024). Catalyst effect of human body odours in social anxiety treatment – a pilot study. *European Psychiatry*, *67*(1), S9. https://doi.org/10.1192/j.eurpsy.2024.48.
24. Bowlby, J. (1983). *Attachment & Loss: Volume 1: Attachment* (2nd ed.). Basic Books. Retrieved from https://go.exlibris.link/Dz1JmMQb; Bowlby, J. (1988). *Attachment and Loss: Volume 2: Separation, Anxiety and Anger*. Basic Books. Retrieved from https://go.exlibris.link/D7D1GrMC.
25. Ainsworth, M. D. S., Blehar, M., Waters, E., & Wall, S. N. (2015). *Patterns of Attachment: A Psychological Study of the Strange Situation*. Routledge, Taylor & Francis Group. https://doi.org/10.4324/9780203758045/.
26. Harlow, H. F., & Zimmermann, R. R. (1958). The development of affectional responses in infant monkeys. *Proceedings of the American Philosophical Society*, *102*(5), 501–509.
27. Carmichael, C. L., Goldberg, M. H., & Coyle, M. A. (2021). Security-based differences in touch behavior and its relational benefits. *Social Psychological & Personality Science*, *12*(4), 550–560. https://doi.org/10.1177/1948550620929164.
28. Dreisoerner, A., Junker, N. M., Schlotz, W., Heimrich, J., et al. (2021). Self-soothing touch and being hugged reduce cortisol responses to stress: A randomized controlled trial on stress, physical touch, and social identity. *Comprehensive Psychoneuroendocrinology (Online)*, *8*, 100091. https://doi.org/10.1016/j.cpnec.2021.100091.
29. Becklund, A. L., Rapp-McCall, L., & Nudo, J. (2021). Using weighted blankets in an inpatient mental health hospital to decrease anxiety. *Journal of Integrative Medicine*, *19*(2), 129–134. https://doi.org/10.1016/j.joim.2020.11.004.
30. Koole, S. L., Sin, M. T. A., & Schneider, I. K. (2014). Embodied terror management: Interpersonal touch alleviates existential concerns among individuals with low self-esteem. *Psychological Science*, *25*(1), 30–37. https://doi.org/10.1177/0956797613483478.
31. Amy Cuddy: TED speaker (2012). Retrieved from https://www.ted.com/speakers/amy_cuddy.

32. Carney, D. R., Cuddy, A. J. C., & Yap, A. J. (2010). Power posing: Brief nonverbal displays affect neuroendocrine levels and risk tolerance. *Psychological Science*, 21(10), 1363–1368. https://doi.org/10.1177/0956797610383437.
33. Siegel, D. J., (2011). *Mindsight: Transform your brain with the new science of kindness.* Oneworld. Retrieved from https://go.exlibris.link/Vf9B0RQk.
34. Vora, E. (2022). The Anatomy of Anxiety: Understanding and overcoming the body's fear response. Retrieved from https://nextbigideaclub.com/magazine/anatomy-anxiety-understanding-overcoming-bodys-fear-response-bookbite/32808/.
35. Kundakovic, M., & Rocks, D. (2022). Sex hormone fluctuation and increased female risk for depression and anxiety disorders: From clinical evidence to molecular mechanisms. *Frontiers in Neuroendocrinology*, 66, 101010. https://doi.org/10.1016/j.yfrne.2022.101010.
36. Baker, K. E., Wilson, L. M., Sharma, R., Dukhanin, V., et al. Hormone therapy, mental health, and quality of life among transgender people: A systematic review. *Journal of the Endocrine Society*, 5(4), bvab011. https://doi.org/10.1210/jendso/bvab011.
37. Bryant, C., Judd, F. K., & Hickey, M. (2012). Anxiety during the menopausal transition: A systematic review. *Journal of Affective Disorders*, 139(2), 141–148. https://doi.org/10.1016/j.jad.2011.06.055.

8. How to Calm Our Anxious Thoughts

1. Adapted from Harris, R. (2019). *Act Made Simple* (2nd ed.). New Harbinger Publications; Dahl, J. C., & Lundgren, T. L. (2006). *Living beyond your pain: Using Acceptance and Commitment Therapy to ease chronic pain.* New Harbinger Publications.
2. Adapted from Harris, R. (2019). *Act Made Simple* (2nd ed.). New Harbinger Publications; Dahl, J. C., & Lundgren, T. L. (2006). *Living beyond your pain: Using Acceptance and Commitment Therapy to ease chronic pain.* New Harbinger Publications.
3. Adapted from Carr, B. (2013). Live Your Core Values: 10-Minute Exercise to Increase Your Success. https://taproot.com/live-your-core-values-exercise-to-increase-your-success/.

NOTES

4. Harris, R. (2022). *The Happiness Trap: Stop struggling, start living* (New ed.). Robinson.
5. Hayes, S. C., Strosahl, K., & Wilson, K. G. (2012). *Acceptance and Commitment Therapy: The Process and Practice of Mindful Change* (2nd ed.). Guilford Press. Retrieved from https://go.exlibris.link/TgVxV6rX.
6. Geurs, K. & Crocker, C. *Pooh's Grand Adventure: The Search for Christopher Robin (*1997). [Motion Picture] Disney.

9. How to Manage Our Anxious Behaviours

1. Oliver, M. (2017). *Devotions: The Selected Poems of Mary Oliver* (p. 399). Penguin Press.
2. BBC News. (2022). Bill Turnbull was a 'fan with the mic' at Wycombe Wanderers. Retrieved from https://www.bbc.co.uk/news/uk-england-beds-bucks-herts-62763704.
3. Ware, B. (2012). The top five regrets of the dying – A life transformed by the dearly departing. Retrieved from https://bronnieware.com/regrets-of-the-dying/.
4. Michelson, S. E., Lee, J. K., Orsillo, S. M., & Roemer, L. (2011). The role of values-consistent behavior in generalized anxiety disorder. *Depression and Anxiety*, 28(5), 358–366. https://doi.org/10.1002/da.20793.
5. Neff, K. D., Rude, S. S., & Kirkpatrick, K. L. (2007). An examination of self-compassion in relation to positive psychological functioning and personality traits. *Journal of Research in Personality*, 41(4), 908–916. https://doi.org/10.1016/j.jrp.2006.08.002.
6. Neff, K. D. (2011). Self-compassion, self-esteem, and well-being. *Social and Personality Psychology Compass*, 5(1), 1–12. https://doi.org/10.1111/j.1751-9004.2010. 00330.x.
7. Hayes, S. C. (2019). *A Liberated Mind: The Essential Guide to ACT, Transform Your Thinking and Find Freedom From Stress, Anxiety, Depression and Addiction* (p. 80). Vermilion. Retrieved from https://go.exlibris.link/gbThbl78.
8. Roosevelt, T., 1858–1919. (2012). *In the Words of Theodore Roosevelt: Quotations from the Man in the Arena* (O'Toole P., Ed., p. 112). Cornell University Press. doi:10.7591/9780801465970.
9. Brown, B. (2015). *Rising Strong*. Vermillion.
10. Oskis, A. (2025). *The Kitchen Shrink: How the Food We*

Eat Reveals Who We Are – and How We Love. Bloomsbury Publishing.
11. Adapted from North Bristol NHS Trust. Taking care of myself. Retrieved from https://www.nbt.nhs.uk/sites/default/files/attachments/Session%207%20theory%20and%20practice%20combined%202020.pdf.
12. Hayes, S. C. (2005). Hard won wisdom in dealing with anxiety. Retrieved from https://stevenchayes.com/hard-won-wisdom-in-dealing-with-anxiety/.
13. Oliver, M. (2017). *Devotions: The Selected Poems of Mary Oliver* (p. 350). Penguin Press.

10. And Finally... Four Extra Tips for Tending the Orchid

1. Damatac, C. G., ter Avest, M. J., Wilderjans, T. F., De Gucht, V., et al. (2025). Exploring sensory processing sensitivity: Relationships with mental and somatic health, interactions with positive and negative environments, and evidence for differential susceptibility. *Current Research in Behavioral Sciences*, 8, 100165. https://doi.org/10.1016/j.crbeha.2024.100165.
2. Falkenstein, T. (2019). How to deal with overstimulation (and why it matters to the HSP man). Retrieved from https://highlysensitiverefuge.com/highly-sensitive-man-tom-falkenstein/.
3. ABC News. (2024). What it means to be a 'highly sensitive person' (and how to tell if you're one). Retrieved from https://www.abc.net.au/news/2024-10-15/what-it-means-to-be-highly-sensitive-person/104471154.
4. Carroll, S., O'Brien, A., Lionetti, F., O'Reilly, A., & Setti, A. (2025). Flourishing as a highly sensitive person: A mixed method study on the role of nature connectedness and chaotic home environment. *Frontiers in Psychology*, 16, 1480669. https://doi.org/10.3389/fpsyg.2025.1480669.
5. Lionetti, F., Pastore, M., Moscardino, U., Nocentini, A., et al. (2019). Sensory processing sensitivity and its association with personality traits and affect: A meta-analysis. *Journal of Research in Personality*, 81, 138–152. https://doi.org/10.1016/j.jrp.2019.05.013.
6. Acevedo, B. P., Aron, E. N., Aron, A., Sangster, M., et al. (2014).

NOTES

The highly sensitive brain: An fMRI study of sensory processing sensitivity and response to others' emotions. *Brain and Behavior*, 4(4), 580–594. https://doi.org/10.1002/brb3.242.

7. Carroll, S., O'Brien, A., Lionetti, F., O'Reilly, A., & Setti, A. (2025). Flourishing as a highly sensitive person: A mixed method study on the role of nature connectedness and chaotic home environment. *Frontiers in Psychology*, 16, 1480669. https://doi.org/10.3389/fpsyg.2025.1480669.

8. Gu, J., Liu, H., & Lu, H. (2022). Can even a small amount of greenery be helpful in reducing stress? A systematic review. *International Journal of Environmental Research and Public Health*, 19(16), 9778. https://doi.org/10.3390/ijerph19169778.

9. Ulrich, R. S. (1984). View through a window may influence recovery from surgery. *Science (American Association for the Advancement of Science)*, 224(4647), 420–421. https://doi.org/10.1126/science.6143402.

10. Kaplan, S. (1995). The restorative benefits of nature: Toward an integrative framework. *Journal of Environmental Psychology*, 15(3), 169–182. https://doi.org/10.1016/0272-4944(95)90001-2.

11. Beaty, R. E., Benedek, M., Wilkins, R. W., Jauk, E., Fink, A., et al. (2014). Creativity and the default network: A functional connectivity analysis of the creative brain at rest. *Neuropsychologia*, 64, 92–98. https://doi.org/10.1016/j.neuropsychologia.2014.09.019.

12. Blume, C., Garbazza, C., & Spitschan, M. (2019). Effects of light on human circadian rhythms, sleep and mood. *Somnologie: Schlafforschung Und Schlafmedizin = Somnology: Sleep Research and Sleep Medicine*, 23(3), 147–156. https://doi.org/10.1007/s11818-019-00215-x.

13. Cropley, M., Rydstedt, L. W., Devereux, J. J., & Middleton, B. (2015), The relationship between work-related rumination and evening and morning salivary cortisol secretion. *Stress Health*, 31, 150–157. https://doi.org/10.1002/smi.2538.

14. Clow, A., Hucklebridge, F., Stalder, T., Evans, P., & Thorn, L. (2010). The cortisol awakening response: More than a measure of HPA axis function. *Neuroscience and Biobehavioral Reviews*, 35(1), 97–103. https://doi.org/10.1016/j.neubiorev.2009.12.011.

15. Choi, K., Shin, C., Kim, T., Chung, H. J., & Suk, H-J. (2019). Awakening effects of blue-enriched morning light

exposure on university students' physiological and subjective responses. *Scientific Reports, 9*(1), 345. https://doi.org/10.1038/s41598-018-36791-5.

16. Hickman, C., Marks, E., Pihkala, P., Clayton, S., et al. (2021). Climate anxiety in children and young people and their beliefs about government responses to climate change: A global survey. *The Lancet Planetary Health, 5*(12), e863–e873.

17. Maduneme, E. (2024). Some slice of climate anxiety… is good: A cross-sectional survey exploring the relationship between college students, media exposure and perceptions about climate change. *Journal of Health Communication, 29*(sup1), 45–56.

18. Eijsbouts, C., Zheng, T., Kennedy, N. A., Bonfiglio, F., et al. (2021). Genome-wide analysis of 53,400 people with irritable bowel syndrome highlights shared genetic pathways with mood and anxiety disorders. *Nature Genetics, 53*(11), 1543–1552.

19. Iimura, S., & Takasugi, S. (2022). Sensory processing sensitivity and gastrointestinal symptoms in Japanese adults. *International Journal of Environmental Research and Public Health, 19*. https://doi.org/10.3390/ijerph19169893

20. Valdes, A. M., Walter, J., Segal, E., & Spector, T. D. (2018). Role of the gut microbiota in nutrition and health. *BMJ (Online), 361*, k2179. https://doi.org/10.1136/bmj.k2179.

21. Iimura, S., Takasugi, S., Yasuda, M., Saito, Y., & Morifuji, M. (2023). Interactions between environmental sensitivity and gut microbiota are associated with biomarkers of stress-related psychiatric symptoms. *Journal of Affective Disorders, 339*, 136–144.

22. Zheng, P., Zeng, B., Zhou, C., Liu, M., et al. (2016). Gut microbiome remodeling induces depressive-like behaviors through a pathway mediated by the host's metabolism. *Molecular Psychiatry, 21*(6), 786–796.

23. Ding, Y., Bu, F., Chen, T., Shi, G., et al. (2021). A next-generation probiotic: Akkermansia muciniphila ameliorates chronic stress–induced depressive-like behavior in mice by regulating gut microbiota and metabolites. *Applied Microbiology and Biotechnology, 105*(21–22), 8411–8426.

24. Jacka, F. N., O'Neil, A., Opie, R., Itsiopoulos, C., et al. (2017). A randomised controlled trial of dietary improvement for adults with major depression (the 'SMILES' trial). *BMC Medicine, 15*(1), 23–13.

NOTES

25. Merkouris, E., Mavroudi, T., Miliotas, D., Tsiptsios, D., et al. (2024). Probiotics' effects in the treatment of anxiety and depression: A comprehensive review of 2014–2023 clinical trials. *Microorganisms (Basel), 12*(2), 411.
26. Leeuwendaal, N. K., Stanton, C., O'Toole, P. W., & Beresford, T. P. (2022). Fermented foods, health and the gut microbiome. *Nutrients, 14*(7), 1527.
27. Hilimire, M. R., DeVylder, J. E., & Forestell, C. A. (2015). Fermented foods, neuroticism, and social anxiety: An interaction model. *Psychiatry Research, 228*(2), 203–208.
28. Merkouris, E., Mavroudi, T., Miliotas, D., Tsiptsios, et al. (2024). Probiotics' effects in the treatment of anxiety and depression: A comprehensive review of 2014–2023 clinical trials. *Microorganisms (Basel), 12*(2), 411.
29. Damatac, C. G., ter Avest, M. J., Wilderjans, T. F., De Gucht, V., et al. (2025). Exploring sensory processing sensitivity: Relationships with mental and somatic health, interactions with positive and negative environments, and evidence for differential susceptibility. *Current Research in Behavioral Sciences, 8*, 100165. https://doi.org/10.1016/j.crbeha.2024.100165.
30. Golonka, K., & Gulla, B. (2021). Individual differences and susceptibility to burnout syndrome: Sensory processing sensitivity and its relation to exhaustion and disengagement. *Frontiers in Psychology, 12*, 751350.
31. World Health Organization. (2019). Burn-out an 'occupational phenomenon': International classification of diseases departmental update. Retrieved from https://www.who.int/news/item/28-05-2019-burn-out-an-occupational-phenomenon-international-classification-of-diseases.
32. Edú-Valsania, S., Laguía, A., & Moriano, J. A. (2022). Burnout: A review of theory and measurement. *International Journal of Environmental Research and Public Health, 19*(3), 1780. https://doi.org/10.3390/ijerph19031780.
33. McKinsey Health Institute. (2022). Addressing employee burnout: Are you solving the right problem? Retrieved from https://www.mckinsey.com/mhi/our-insights/addressing-employee-burnout-are-you-solving-the-right-problem.
34. MIT Sloan Management Review, (2022). Why every leader needs to worry about toxic culture. Retrieved from https://

sloanreview.mit.edu/article/why-every-leader-needs-to-worry-about-toxic-culture/.
35. Society for Human Resource Management. (2019). The high cost of a toxic workplace culture. Retrieved from https://www.shrm.org/content/dam/en/shrm/research/SHRM-Culture-Report_2019.pdf.
36. Aron, E. (1998). *The Highly Sensitive Person: How to Thrive When the World Overwhelms You.* Turabian.
37. Forbes. (2020). Why highly sensitive people make the best leaders, according to a psychologist. Retrieved from https://www.forbes.com/sites/melodywilding/2020/04/13/why-highly-sensitive-people-make-the-best-leaders-according-to-a-psychologist/
38. Meckovsky, F., Novak, L., Meier, Z., Tavel, P., & Malinakova, K. (2025). Highly sensitive persons feel more emotionally lonely than the general population. *Scientific Reports*, 15(1). https://doi.org/10.1038/s41598-025-87138-w.
39. Black, B., & Kern, M. (2020). A qualitative exploration of individual differences in wellbeing for highly sensitive individuals. *Palgrave Communications*, 6(1), 1–11. https://doi.org/0.1057/s41599-020-0482-8.
40. Brewer, R., Murphy, J., & Bird, G. (2021). Atypical interoception as a common risk factor for psychopathology: A review. *Neuroscience Biobehavior Review*, 130–470. https://doi.org/10.1016/j.neubiorev.2021.07.036.
41. Stevens, S., Gerlach, A. L., Cludius, B., Silkens, A., et al. (2011). Heartbeat perception in social anxiety before and during speech anticipation. *Behaviour Research and Therapy*, 49(2), 138–143. https://doi.org/10.1016/j.brat.2010.11.009.
42. Benham G. (2006). The highly sensitive person: Stress and physical symptom reports. *Personality and Individual Differences*, 40, 1433–1440. https://doi.org/10.1016/j.paid.2005.11.021.
43. Horsburgh, A., Summers S. J., Lewis, A., Keegan, R.J., & Flood, A. The relationship between pain and interoception: A systematic review and meta-analysis. *The Journal of Pain*, 25(7). https://doi.org/10.1016/j.jpain.2024.01.341.
44. Garfinkel, S. N., Seth, A. K., Barrett, A. B., Suzuki, K., & Critchley, H. D. (2015). Knowing your own heart: Distinguishing interoceptive accuracy from interoceptive awareness. *Biological Psychology*, 104, 65–74. https://doi.org/10.1016/j.biopsycho.2014.11.004.

45. Harvard Medical School. (2021). Pain, anxiety and depression. Retrieved from https://www.health.harvard.edu/mind-and-mood/pain-anxiety-and-depression.
46. de Heer, E. W., Gerrits, M. M. J. G., Beekman, A. T. F., Dekker, J., et al. (2014). The association of depression and anxiety with pain: A study from NESDA. *PloS One*, 9(10), e106907. https://doi.org/10.1371/journal.pone.0106907.
47. Rogers, A. H., & Farris, S. G. (2022). A meta-analysis of the associations of elements of the fear-avoidance model of chronic pain with negative affect, depression, anxiety, pain-related disability and pain intensity. *European Journal of Pain*, 26(8), 1611–1635. https://doi.org/10.1002/ejp.1994.
48. McCracken, L. M., & Eccleston, C. (2003). Coping or acceptance: What to do about chronic pain? *Pain*, 105(1), 197–204. https://doi.org/10.1016/S0304-3959(03)00202-1.
49. Kabat-Zinn, J. (2005). *Wherever You Go, There You Are: Mindfulness Meditation in Everyday Life.* (p. 3–4). New York: Hachette. Retrieved from https://go.exlibris.link/sdRb3bqD.
50. Lionetti, F., Pastore, M., Moscardino, U., Nocentini, A., et al. (2019). Sensory processing sensitivity and its association with personality traits and affect: A meta-analysis. *Journal of Research in Personality*, 81, 138–152. https://doi.org/10.1016/j.jrp.2019.05.013.
51. de Witte, M., Spruit, A., van Hooren, S., Moonen, X., & Stams, G. (2020). Effects of music interventions on stress-related outcomes: A systematic review and two meta-analyses. *Health Psychology Review*, 14(2), 294–324. https://doi.org/10.1080/17437199.2019.1627897.
52. Harmat, L., Takács, J., & Bódizs, R. (2008). Music improves sleep quality in students. *Journal of Advanced Nursing*, 62(3), 327–335. https://doi.org/10.1111/j.1365-2648.2008.04602.x.
53. Setti, A., Lionetti, F., Kagari, R. L., Motherway, L., & Pluess, M. (2022). The temperament trait of environmental sensitivity is associated with connectedness to nature and affinity to animals. *Heliyon*, 8(7), e09861. https://doi.org/10.1016/j.heliyon.2022.e09861.
54. Wołyńczyk-Gmaj, D., Ziółkowska, A., Rogala, P., Ścigała, D., et al. (2021). Can dog-assisted intervention decrease anxiety level and autonomic agitation in patients with anxiety

disorders? *Journal of Clinical Medicine, 10*(21), 5171. https://doi.org/10.3390/jcm10215171.
55. Streeter, C. C., Whitfield, T. H., Owen, L., Rein, T., et al. (2010). Effects of yoga versus walking on mood, anxiety, and brain GABA levels: A randomized controlled MRS study. *The Journal of Alternative and Complementary, 16*(11), 1145–1152. https://doi.org/10.1089/acm.2010.0007.
56. Sleiman, S. F., Henry, J., Al-Haddad, R., El Hayek, L., et al. (2016). Exercise promotes the expression of brain derived neurotrophic factor (BDNF) through the action of the ketone body β-hydroxybutyrate. *eLife, 5*. https://doi.org/10.7554/eLife.15092.
57. Oliver, M. (2004). *New and Selected Poems, Volume One* (Rep. ed.) Beacon Press.
58. Williams, S. (2016). *Rise: Surviving and Thriving after Trauma.* Weidenfeld & Nicolson.
59. Schauer, M., Elbert, T., & Neuner, F. (2011). *Narrative Exposure Therapy: A Short-Term Treatment for Traumatic Stress Disorders* (2nd rev. ed.). Hogrefe. Retrieved from https://go.exlibris.link/4phwZcJY.

Epilogue

1. Wilson, S. (2018). *First, We Make the Beast Beautiful: A New Journey Through Anxiety* (1st ed., p. 299). Macmillan Australia. Retrieved from https://ebookcentral.proquest.com/lib/[SITE_ID]/.
2. Rhees, R. (1969). *Without Answers.* Routledge & Kegan Paul Ltd.
3. Kierkegaard, S. (2013). In Thomte R. (Ed.), *Kierkegaard's Writings, VIII, Volume 8: Concept Of Anxiety: A Simple Psychologically Orienting Deliberation on the Dogmatic Issue of Hereditary Sin.* Princeton University Press https://doi.org/10.1515/9781400846979.
4. Tolkien, J. R. R.. (2007). *The Children of Húrin* (1st ed.). HarperCollins.
5. Brinker, A. Meditation Advice for Beginners from Dan Harris. Interview. Retrieved from https://www.penguinrandomhouse.com/articles/interview-with-dan-harris.
6. Burkeman, O. The Imperfectionist: What if you never sort your life out? Retrieved from https://www.oliverburkeman.com/never.
7. Rogers, C. R. (1961). *On Becoming a Person: A therapist's view*

of psychotherapy. Constable. Retrieved from https://go.exlibris.link/KFXyfbg5.
8. Rogers, C. R. (1980). *A Way of Being.* Houghton Mifflin Company. Retrieved from https://go.exlibris.link/N05sm34C.
9. BBC Saturday Live (2023). Retrieved from https://www.bbc.co.uk/programmes/m001kgbv.

Appendix

1. Spitzer, R. L., Kroenke, K., Williams, J. B. W., & Löwe, B. (2006). A brief measure for assessing generalized anxiety disorder: The GAD-7. *Archives of Internal Medicine, 166*(10), 1092–1097.
2. Kroenke, K., Spitzer, R. L., & Williams, J. B. W. (2001). The PHQ-9: validity of a brief depression severity measure. *Journal of General Internal Medicine, 16*(9), 606–613.

Index

abuse, 32, 33, 57–8, 126
acceptance and commitment
    therapy (ACT), 36, 97, 103,
    117–18, 126–7, 249, 268,
    270–71
acceptance, 2, 82, 103, 228
ACE, 248
Action for Happiness, 80–84
acute stress, 214
adaptability, 24, 31, 35, 47
adrenaline, 10, 128, 180, 203
adverse childhood experiences
    (ACEs), 31–3, 107–11, 126
Afghanistan, 79
agoraphobia, 197, 225
Ainsworth, Mary, 220
alcohol, 46, 78, 173, 174–5, 226
America the Anxious
    (Whippman), 80
American Psychiatric
    Association, 53
amygdala, 174, 300
Anda, Robert, 32
anger, 64, 118–19, 133, 150
animals, 304
anticipation, 7–8
antidepressants, 53, 78
anxiety
    avoidance behaviours, *see*
        avoidance behaviours

behaviour and, 63–4, 255–85
childhood and, *see* childhood
as energy source, 179–80,
    193, 215, 263, 310
essential function, 6, 72,
    121–2, 123–6, 151
false vs true, 226
high-functioning, 46, 54, 71,
    122–3, 135–60
mental effects, 63–4, 230–53
neurodivergence and, 55–6,
    110, 165, 183–92
parasitic nature, 7
perfectionism, *see*
    perfectionism
performance anxiety, 108,
    162, 163–4, 165–6,
    177–80
physical effects, 63–4,
    197–229
power of anxiety, *see* power
    of anxiety
procrastination, 47, 108, 122,
    143, 145, 155–7, 160, 193
relationships and, *see*
    relationships
societal causes, 18, 290
social anxiety, *see* social
    anxiety
state anxiety, 218

INDEX

trauma and, 199–202
tricky vs sticky, 227–8, 310
anxiety disorders, 14, 15, 41, 50–68, 71
   diagnoses, 57–62
   DSM on, 41, 55
   generalized anxiety disorder (GAD), 15, 54, 61
   global prevalence, 53
Anxiety Lab, University College London, 1, 168, 207
Apollo 8 spacecraft, 99
Ardern, Jacinda, 39
Aron, Arthur, 287
Aron, Elaine, 287, 297
art, 27, 35
asylums, 50–51
attachments, 72, 199, 214, 220–22, 276–80
Attenborough, David, 99, 101
attention deficit hyperactivity disorder (ADHD), 55, 110, 191
aurora borealis, 74–7
Auschwitz concentration camp, 89, 90, 279
Australia, 53, 79, 292
autism spectrum disorder (ASD), 55, 165, 182–92, 194
autonomic nervous system (ANS), 128, 203, 210, 211
avoidance behaviours, xvi, 29, 46–7, 64, 66, 168–74, 260, 263–4, 281
   autism and, 183, 189
   busyness, 46, 119–21, 133, 143
   drug use, 46, 173, 174–5
   procrastination, 47, 108, 122, 143, 145, 155–7, 160, 193
   withdrawal, 47, 48–50, 260

backlog of good experiences, 177, 264, 266
Bala, Wales, 48–9
balance exercise, 129–30
behaviour, 63–4, 255–85
   action steps, 273–6
   attachments and, 276–80
   head, heart and hands, 271–2
   man in the arena, 269–71
   micro-ambitions, 265–7
   nourishing vs depleting activities, 280–84, 304
   thinking, feeling and doing, 262–5
   values and, 259–62, 274–6, 285
Biles, Simone, 151–3
Birds, The (1963 film), 8
Black, Becky, 287
Blackman, Glen, 14–15
blame, xvi, 59, 64, 153, 274
blood pressure, 92
blood sugar, xv, 10, 214, 298
Blouin-Hudon, Eve-Marie, 156
body, 63–4, 197–229
   breathing, 208–10
   fight-flight-freeze-faint-fawn, xiii, 11, 92, 128, 164, 211, 224, 298
   grounding and, 207–8
   hormones, 10, 128, 203, 214–19, 298–9
   interoception, 298–308

listening to, 226, 228, 229, 310
locating anxiety in, 204, 212
resculpting, 222–3
smell and, 219–20
soften-soothe-allow exercise, 212–14
touch and, 214, 220–22
vagus nerve, 210–11
Body Keeps the Score, The (Van der Kolk), 199
body language, 222–3
borderline personality disorder (BPD), 61
Bowlby, John, 220
box breathing, 209–10
Boyce, W. Thomas, 24
brain, 10–13, 63–4, 65, 68, 97, 113, 230–54
  comfort zone and, 235
  exercise and, 305
  fight response, xiii, 11, 92
  foetal development, 111
  frontal lobotomies, 51–2
  hormones and, 227
  interoception, 298–308
  nature and, 288–90
  negativity bias, 34, 68, 132
  neurodiversity, 55–6
  optimism and, 93
  panic and, 204
  perfectionism and, 154, 155
  plasticity, 155, 227
  social comparison and, 97
  spotlight effect, 159
  worry and, 13
brain-derived neurotrophic factor (BDNF), 305

Brazil, 54
Breath (Nestor), 209
breathing, 64, 174, 201, 202, 208–10, 212
  exercises, 37, 62, 190, 208–10, 228, 248, 261, 275, 303–4
British Broadcasting Corporation (BBC), xi–xvii, 135–6, 216, 218, 230, 319
  Breakfast, 157, 218, 231, 255, 257, 258
  Classical Unwind, 304
  'Creep' ban (1993), 161
  How to Have a Better Brain, 205
  Life Changing, 95, 107, 197
  One O'Clock News, 218
  Saturday Live, 320
  Science of Resilience, The, 23–4
  2000 Today, 99
Brown, Brené, 270
Brown, Dan, 321
Brown, Jeff, 23
Brühl, Annette, 205–7, 209
Buddhism, 82, 84, 88, 90, 261
Bull's Eye exercise, 237–41
bullying, 33, 126
Burgess, Alexandra, 141
Burkeman, Oliver, 317
burnout, 24, 41, 138, 141, 143, 145, 148, 160, 163, 287, 296–8
busyness, 46, 119–21, 133, 143
butterflies, 43, 64
By Royal Appointment (Goodwin), 137, 264

INDEX

caffeine, 226, 310
CALM, 252–3
Canada, 54, 147, 156
cancer, 4, 14–15, 23, 49, 59–65, 114–15, 255–60, 261, 277, 302, 319
Cantril Ladder, 78–80
cardiovascular health, 11, 93, 119
CARE, 2, 324
Carnegie, Dale, 48
catastrophizing, 40, 137, 214, 233
Center for Mindful Self-Compassion, 214
Charles III, King, xiii
childhood, 31–4, 72
   adverse experiences, 31–3, 107–11, 126
   attachments, 72, 199, 214, 220–22, 276–7
   inner voice and, 107–12, 114, 126, 133, 150
   perfectionism and, 140, 148, 149, 150, 153
China, 153
choice points, 235–6
Christchurch attack (2019), 39
chronic pain, 119, 300–308
chronic stress, 10–11, 215, 298–9
Clance, Pauline Rose, 162
Classical Unwind, 304
climate crisis, 11, 18, 101, 290
Coben, Harlan, 320–22
cognitive behavioural therapy (CBT), 35, 62–4, 126–7, 172, 256

Coles, Richard, 320
comfort zone, 233–6
community, 30, 55, 80, 82, 94, 101, 103
comparisons, 1, 97–8, 102, 104, 168
compassion, 3, 5, 12, 18, 38, 39, 47, 88, 90, 102, 103, 244, 246–7
   see also self-compassion
compassion-focused therapy (CFT), 126–30, 271
Compassionate Mind Foundation, 214
competitiveness, 145, 148
complex PTSD (C-PTSD), 58, 62
Complicated Woman, A (Self Esteem), 135
concentration camps, 89, 90, 279
confidence, 233–6
Connolly, Billy, 130, 132–33
control, 12, 15–17, 88, 103, 247, 248, 265
Cooper, Alex, 152
core beliefs, 115–17
Cornell University, 167
cortisol, 10, 128, 203, 214–19, 223, 288–9
Covid-19 pandemic (2019–23), 39, 40, 140, 169
cramps, 64
creativity, 26, 27, 34, 35
'Creep' (Radiohead), 161
critical thinking, 101
criticism, 28, 39, 43, 58, 107–11
   see also self-criticism

Cuddy, Amy, 223
curiosity, 2, 5, 12, 18, 37, 59, 84, 90, 102, 103, 244, 245
   social anxiety and, 174, 176, 181, 190, 192, 245–6, 264
Curran, Thomas, 145

dailyish, 316–17
Dalai Lama, 82, 84, 101
dare question, 46
dares, 215–18
default mode network, 288
depleting activities, 280–84, 304
depression, 13–14, 30, 31, 32, 33, 35, 40, 44, 61, 80, 199–200, 287
   autism and, 183
   gut health and, 292
   hormones and, 227
   imposter syndrome and, 163
   music and, 304
   perfectionism and, 88, 135, 137, 139, 142–3, 147, 153, 159
   self-criticism and, 123, 131
   values and, 260
depth of processing, 25, 34
details, sensitivity to, 25
diabetes, 57
diagnoses, 57–62, 71
Diagnostic and Statistical Manual of Mental Disorders, 41, 55
Diana, Princess of Wales, xiii–xv, 211
diazepam, 52
diet, 276–7, 292
digestive problems, 11, 64, 290–94
disinformation, 98, 101
disorder label, 55, 71, 73, 104
disordered eating, 141, 153
distractions, 46, 64
domestic violence, 78
don't think about exercise, 91–2, 120–21
dopamine, 222
doughnut experiment, 91–2, 120–21
Doyle, Glennon, 40
dropping anchor, 247–8, 310
drugs, 173

early morning light, 288–90
early-warning signalling, 38–41, 103
Earthrise, 99
eating disorders, 139, 141, 153
economics, 18
Edelman, 99, 100
education, 77, 107–11, 140, 148, 238
Egas Moniz, António, 52
electric shock treatments, 51
Elizabeth II, Queen, xiii
Elsey-Webb, Robin, 247, 264–5
embarrassment, 64, 110, 124, 125, 165, 168, 214
emergency workers, 200–202, 237, 297
emotional abuse, 32, 33, 57–8, 126
emotions, 25, 29, 37, 58, 204, 235, 263, 287

INDEX

body language and, 223
breathing exercises and, 37
empathy, 35
inner weather, 90, 176, 247, 248
reactivity, 29, 34
silencing of, 111, 119–20, 150
smells and, 219
empathy, 2, 25, 35, 39, 156
endorphins, 128
environment, 25, 29, 36–8, 288–90, 294–8, 309, 311
Escape to the Country, 135
eudaemonia, 88
Everett, Flic, 7
exercise, 38, 82, 211, 295, 305
exercises
   acceptance and commitment, 272–3
   balance exercise, 129–30
   Bull's Eye, 237–41
   don't think about exercise, 91–2, 120–21
   dropping anchor, 247–8
   feared situations, 171–3
   going deeper exercise, 69–71
   living values exercise, 241–4
   miracle question, 45–7
   nourishing and depleting activities, 281–4
   Passengers on the Bus, 249–53
   perfectionist type exercise, 141–3
   piece of paper exercise, 117–18
   power exercise, 65–8
   sculpture exercise, 42–4
   self-criticism function exercise, 123–6
   soften-soothe-allow exercise, 212–14
   thoughts and feelings exercise, 86–8
   Threat, Drive, Soothe exercise, 129–30
Experiences of an Asylum Patient, The (Grant-Smith), 51
exposure therapy, 167, 169–73, 263–4
external referencing, 85–6, 146–7
extraversion, 29
eye contact, 173, 183

failure, 143–4, 147, 149–50, 153, 154, 158, 194, 214
fainting, xiii–xvii, 211
fake news, 99
Falkenstein, Tom, 287
fatigue, 11
fear, 11, 64, 73, 310
FEAR, 252
fear, 73, 198
Felitti, Vincent, 32
fermented foods, 292–3
fibromyalgia, 300
fight-flight-freeze-faint-fawn, xiii, 11, 92, 128, 164, 211, 224, 298
financial worries, 11

Finland, 74–8, 79, 93–7, 101
Finnish Happiness Institute, 93–4
First, We Make the Beast Beautiful (Wilson), 313
Five Processes of Unhelpful Perfectionism, 143
fixed mindset, 149, 153
flow, 85, 102, 157–8
folic acid, 294
food, 276–7, 292
football, 85
Ford, Alison, 258
forests, 75
Frankl, Viktor, 89
frontal lobotomies, 51–2
future self, 156–7

gambling, 96
gamma-aminobutyric acid (GAMMA), 305
gardening, 261–2
Garner, Helen, 79
generalized anxiety disorder (GAD), 15, 54, 61, 260
Genetic Links to Anxiety and Depression (GLAD), 199
Gerhardt, Sue, 31
Germer, Christopher, 212–14
Gilbert, Paul, 126, 214
goals, 266, 273
going deeper exercise, 69–71
Goodwin, Daisy, 54, 122, 135–8, 144, 145, 149–50, 158, 182, 264
Google, 98–100
Grand Designs, 135
Grant-Smith, Rachel, 50–51

gratitude, 275
Great Celebrity Bake Off, The, 215
Greece, ancient, 88
Grenfell Tower fire (2017), 4, 200–202
grounding, 207–8
growth mindset, 149, 153
guilt, 110, 138, 144
gut health, 290–94

happiness, 74–102, 103
  Cantril Ladder, 78–80, 103
  comparison and, 97–8, 102, 104
  demand to be happy, 84–6
  nature and, 74–7, 94, 288–90, 309
  optimism vs pessimism, 92–3, 102
  pockets of happiness, 89–90, 102
  prosocial behaviour and, 80–84, 94, 103
  sisu, 94–7
  World Happiness Report, 74, 77–8, 79–80, 81
Harlow, Harry, 221
Harris, Dan, 316
Harris, Russ, 35–6, 97, 174–5, 180, 233, 237, 246–7, 248, 323
Harry, Duke of Sussex, xiii
Hayes, Steven, 249, 268, 284
headaches, 119, 300
headphones, 173, 225
Headspace, 261
healthcare, 77, 148, 297

heart health, 11, 93, 119, 300
Hendriksen, Ellen, 156
high-functioning anxiety, 46, 54, 71, 122–3, 135–60
    imposter syndrome, 108, 161–4, 232, 322
    perfectionism, 46, 71, 122, 138–60, 193
Highly Sensitive Man, The (Falkenstein), 287
highly sensitive people (HSPs), 23–42, 103, 286–309, 311
    animals and, 304, 309
    childhood and, 31–4
    creativity, 26, 27, 34, 35
    as early-warning signallers, 38–41, 103
    empathy, 25, 35
    environment and, 25, 29, 36–8, 288–90, 294–8, 309, 311
    exercise and, 305
    gut health and, 290–94
    heritability and, 30–31
    interoception and, 298–308
    nature and, 288–90, 309
    negativity and, 29, 31, 34, 103
    positive aspects, 34–6
    solitude and, 298, 309
    as superpower, 40–41
Highly Sensitive Person Scale, 25–30
Highly Sensitive Person, The (Aron), 297
Hillesum, Etty, 90
Hillsborough disaster (1989), 3
hippocampus, 288

Hitchcock, Alfred, 7–8, 216, 299
Holocaust (1941–5), 89, 90, 279
homicide, 78
hormones, 10, 128, 203, 214–19, 227, 298–9, 300, 310
Hossain, Nina, 182, 186, 264
hot coals, walking on, 216
How to Have a Better Brain, 205
Howse, Patrick, 314
humiliation, 32, 33, 110, 164, 165
Hyde Park, London, xiii–xv, 211
hypervigilance, 11, 14, 31, 33, 39, 137, 314
hyponatremia, 205
hypothalamus, 300
hysteria, 51

'I Do and I Don't Care' (Self Esteem), 135
Iimura, Shuhei, 290
illusion of transparency, 166
Imes, Suzanne, 162
immigration, 231, 232
immune system, 11, 92, 289, 312
imposter syndrome, 108, 161–4, 232, 322
inflammation, 34, 214, 291, 292, 312
inner voice, 107–33, 134, 193, 315–16
    childhood and, 107–12, 114, 126, 133, 150

chronic pain and, 302–3
compassion and, 112, 113, 120, 121, 126–9, 315–16
core beliefs and, 115–17
encouragement, 121–2, 125–6
functions, 121–2, 123–6
imposter syndrome and, 162–3
kindness and, 114, 126–7, 130–33, 193, 315
not good enough voice, 114–17
Passengers on the Bus exercise, 249–53, 315
perfectionism and, 122, 138, 141, 143, 145, 146, 150, 155, 157–8
self-silencing and, 119–20, 133, 150
shoulds, oughts and musts, 115–17, 119–20, 133, 235, 244
stupid friend, 111–12, 121, 130–33, 193
Threat-Drive-Soothe systems, 127–30, 137, 160, 193
values and, 237
inner weather, 90, 176, 247, 248
insider-outsider comparison, 1, 97–8, 102, 104
insomnia, 43, 119, 141, 200, 231
institutions, 80, 94, 100–101
internal referencing, 85–6, 146–7
interoception, 298–308
introversion, 164
Iran, 54

Iraq War (2003–11), 314
irritability, 11, 61, 154, 188
irritable bowel syndrome, 119, 291, 300
It (King), 9
ITN, 218

Japan, 132
Jefferson, Thomas, 88
journalism, 3–4
Journey, The (Oliver), 305
Jung, Carl, 17

Kabat-Zinn, Jon, 303
Kahlo, Frida, 44
Kapp, Steven, 55
Kemp, Jennifer, 143
Kierkegaard, Søren, 315
kindness, 82, 141, 242, 244, 245, 273, 279, 280
see also self-kindness
King, Stephen, 9, 322
Kitchen Shrink, The (Oskis), 277
Knock Down Ginger, 215–16
knowing through, 71–2, 73

labels, 55, 71, 73, 104, 107–11
Layard, Richard, 81, 83
Lebanon, 79
leisure, 239
Life Changing, 95, 107, 197
liminal states, 246
lobotomies, 51–2
London School of Economics, 81, 145
loneliness, 80, 111, 148, 184, 277, 298

INDEX

Lord of the Rings, The (Tolkien), 315
lost girls of autism, 185–6
lower back pain, 300
lunacy, 50–52
Lundgren, Tobias, 237

Maggie's Cancer Care, 277
mal-information, 98–9
Manilow, Barry, 167
Marcus Aurelius, Roman emperor, 88
Margaret, Countess of Snowdon, 219
Marley, Bob, 167
Marsh, Henry, 52
Maté, Gabor, 111, 112
maternity leave, 77
maximizers, 138–9, 146, 160
meaning, 82, 89, 116, 236–44
media
    misinformation, 98–100, 101
    social media, 85, 97, 100, 153, 181, 231, 280, 320
    trust in, 98–100, 101
medication, 1–2, 52
meditation, 156–7, 261–2, 275
Mental Health Awareness Week, 231
micro-ambitions, 265–7
microbiome, 226, 290–94
migraines, 119
millennium celebrations, 99
Minchin, Tim, 265–7
mindfulness, 120, 131, 211, 239, 243, 256, 261–2, 302–4
    dailyish, 316–17
    soften-soothe-allow, 212–14
miracle question, 45–7
misinformation, 98–100, 101
motherhood, 118–19
movement, 38, 82, 211, 295, 305
music, 26, 27, 35, 304

narrative exposure therapy (NET), 306
National Health Service (NHS), xii, 3, 13, 81, 191, 200
nature, 35, 38, 74–7, 94, 261–2, 288–90
Nazi Germany (1933–45), 89, 90, 279
Neff, Kristin, 212–14, 262
negativity, 17, 29, 31, 90, 103, 115, 119, 129, 131, 256
    cognitive behavioural therapy and, 126
    dropping anchor and, 247
    neural bias toward, 34, 68, 132
    perfectionism and, 144, 148
    piece of paper experiment, 117
    social identity and, 168, 174
neglect, 25, 31, 32, 112, 126
nerve rest cures, 50
nervous system, 128, 203, 210, 211, 287, 305
Nestor, James, 209
neurodivergence, 55–6, 183–92
    attention deficit hyperactivity disorder (ADHD), 55, 110, 191

autism spectrum disorder (ASD), 55, 165, 182–92
neuroplasticity, 155, 227
neuroticism, 29
neurotransmitters, 300, 305
New York Marathon, 205–6
New York Times, 40
New Zealand, 54, 79, 203
Nietzsche, Friedrich, 197
Nin, Anaïs, 230
No More Normal (Santhouse), 56
non-binary people, 227
norepinephrine, 300
Northern Lights, 74–7
Northumbria University, 216
not good enough voice, 114–17
noticing, 54, 63, 69, 92, 101, 112, 193, 215, 235, 245, 248, 263, 267
  body, 213, 222, 224
  safety behaviours, 173–4
nourishing activities, 280–84, 304
Nylund, Joanna, 94

O'Keeffe, Georgia, 134
obesity, 32
obsessive compulsive disorder, 141
oestrogen, 227
Oliver, Mary, 256–7, 284, 305
Olympic Games, 151–3
One O'Clock News, 218
oppositional defiant disorder (ODD), 61
optimists, 92–3, 102

orchid hypothesis, 24–5, 29, 38, 200, 286–309
orthorexia, 141
Oskis, Andrea, 276–7, 279
other-orientated perfectionism, 145–6
overstimulation, 25, 27, 188, 287
overthinking, xii, 39, 86, 135, 138, 149, 157, 215, 231, 263, 297
oxytocin, 128, 222

Pablo Honey (Radiohead), 161
pain, 214, 299–308
panic, 6–7, 11, 54, 57, 64, 66, 71, 125, 152, 197–229, 310
  breathing and, 208–10
  global prevalence, 203
  grounding, 207–8
  parasympathetic nervous system, 128, 203, 210, 211
parents, *see under* childhood
Passengers on the Bus, 132, 249–53
paternity leave, 77
Patient Health Questionnaire (PHQ-9), 61
people pleasing, 17, 41, 112, 116–17, 138, 150–51, 193, 279–80
perfectionism, 17, 46, 71, 88, 108, 122, 138–60, 193
  burnout and, 138, 141, 143, 145
  childhood and, 140, 148, 149, 150, 153
  external referencing and, 146–7

INDEX

failure and, 143–4, 147, 149–50, 153, 154, 158, 194
function of, 151
good and bad, 141–5
high standards and, 138, 143, 144, 145–6, 154–5
imperfection, embrace of, 153–4, 160, 194
imposter syndrome and, 162
other-orientated, 145–6
people pleasing, 150–51
procrastination and, 122, 143, 145, 155–7, 160
rise in, 145–8, 153
self-orientated, 145
socially prescribed, 146–8, 153, 159
spotlight effect and, 153–4, 159
performance anxiety, 108, 162, 163–4, 165–6, 177–80
bigger picture, 177–9
fuel to the fire, 179–80, 215
Perry, Grayson, 30, 278
Perry, Philippa, 12, 169–70, 190, 263–4
on childhood, 72
on disorders, 56–7
on happiness, 84–6
on perfectionism, 155
on relationships, 278
on self-criticism, 131–2, 249
on sensitivity, 29–30
on shoulds, 86, 116
on social anxiety, 169–70, 190, 263–4
personal growth, 239, 249
pessimists, 92–3, 102

physical abuse, 32, 57–8, 126
physical activity, 38, 82, 211, 295, 305
physical conditions, 57
piece of paper exercise, 117–18
playing dead, 210
Pluess, Michael, 23–4, 29, 34–5, 295–6
pockets of happiness, 89–90, 102
politics, 18, 77, 99–100, 101
polyvagal theory, 211
Porges, Stephen, 210, 211
Portugal, 54
positive experiences, 25
positivity, 257
post-traumatic stress disorder (PTSD), 58, 62
potatoes in the basement, 318–19
poverty, 48–9, 140
power of anxiety, 5, 6, 12, 18, 65–8, 104, 193, 214, 234, 266–7, 272, 284, 313, 324
acceptance and commitment and, 103, 125
compassion-focused therapy and, 125
exercise on, 66–8
as fuel, 179–80, 215, 263, 310
noticing/naming and, 263, 272
values and, 238
power poses, 223
prebiotics, 293
prefrontal cortex, 204
Press Association, 219

377

probiotics, 293–4
problem solving, 12
processing, depth of, 25, 34
procrastination, 47, 108, 122, 143, 145, 155–7, 160, 193
prostate cancer, 255–9
Psycho (1960 film), 8
psychology, 3, 139–40
Puddicombe, Andy, 261, 273

Radio Four, 95, 107, 197, 205, 320
Radio Three, 304
Radio Times, 257
Radiohead, 54, 122–3, 158, 161–2, 163, 165–6, 177–81, 215, 264, 266
rage rooms, 150
regrets, 259–60
rejection, 11, 54, 57, 61, 64, 107–11, 149, 165, 168, 192
  neurodiversity and, 184–5
relational frame theory, 268
relationships, 11, 38, 45, 56, 58, 60, 61, 82, 239, 276–80
  childhood, 31–4, 72, 126
  food and, 276–7
  happiness and, 78, 82
resilience, 23–4, 82
Ricard, Matthieu, 90
Rippon, Gina, 185
Rise (Williams), 205, 306, 319
Robinson, Oliver, 1, 6, 11, 168, 207, 217
Rogers, Carl, 318–19
Rome, ancient, 88
Roosevelt, Theodore, 269

rumination, 10, 34, 62, 64, 66, 93, 214, 233, 289

Saariselkä, Finland, 74–7
safety behaviours, 64, 72, 127, 171–4
  see also avoidance behaviours
San Diego, California, 32
Santhouse, Alastair, 56
Saturday Live, 320
saunas, 94
Save Money: Good Health, 293
schools, 77, 107–11, 148
Science of Resilience, The, 23–4
screens, 46
sculpture exercises, 42–4, 222–3
Self Esteem, 135
self-absorption, 83
self-compassion, 2, 36, 59, 72, 84, 228, 246–7, 254, 256–7, 262, 270
  attachments and, 279
  chronic pain and, 303
  inner voice and, 112, 113, 120, 121, 126–9, 315–16
  perfectionism and, 132, 154–5, 316
  social anxiety and, 174
  soothing and, 212, 228
self-criticism, 1, 17, 36, 40, 46, 66, 67, 107–33, 134, 246–7, 256, 264, 271, 315
  attachments and, 279
  childhood and, 107–12, 114, 126, 133, 150
  chronic pain and, 302–3
  compassion and, 112, 113, 120, 121, 126–9, 315–16

INDEX

core beliefs and, 115–17
functions of, 123–6, 193
imposter syndrome and, 162–3
kindness and, 114, 126–7, 130–33, 193, 315
not good enough voice, 114–17
Passengers on the Bus exercise, 249–53, 315
perfectionism and, 122, 138, 141, 143, 145, 146, 150, 155, 157–8
self-silencing and, 119–20, 133, 150
shoulds, oughts and musts, 115–17, 119–20, 133, 235, 244
Threat-Drive-Soothe systems, 127–30, 137, 160, 193
values and, 237
self-doubt, 265–7
self-esteem, 56, 80, 117, 146, 148, 163
self-kindness, 36, 62, 68, 84, 114
behaviour and, 262, 263, 265, 275
body and, 212, 213, 225
inner voice and, 114, 126–7, 130–33, 193, 315
perfectionism and, 141, 154–5, 194
thoughts and, 235, 246, 250
self-orientated perfectionism, 145
self-sacrifice, 119
self-silencing, 119–20, 133, 150

self-soothing, 33, 114, 129, 133, 144, 155, 160
Selway, Philip, 54, 122–3, 158, 161–2, 163, 165–6, 177–81, 215, 264, 266
sensitivity, 23–42, 103, 267, 286–309
childhood and, 31–4
creativity and, 26, 27, 34, 35
early-warning signalling, 38–41, 103
empathy and, 35
environment and, 25, 29, 36–8
heritability, 30–31
Highly Sensitive Person Scale, 25–30
interoception and, 298–308
negativity and, 29, 31, 34
positive aspects, 34–6, 267
superpower, 40–41, 267
Serenity Prayer, 271
serotonin reuptake inhibitors (SSRIs), 53
serotonin, 300
sexual abuse, 32, 58
shame, 49, 59, 64, 73, 96, 168, 198, 202, 205, 207, 224, 271, 273, 310
high-functioning anxiety and, 138, 143, 144, 147, 148
inner voice and, 110, 113, 126, 131
short-term goals, 266
shoulds, oughts and musts, 115–17, 119–20, 133, 235, 244
shyness, 164

Siegel, Dan, 224
Sierra Leone, 79
Silman, Trude, 279
Singer, Michael, 47, 108
sisu, 94–7
skydiving, 216–18
sleep insomnia, 43, 119, 141, 200, 231
sleep, 38, 43, 214, 226, 227, 300
small talk, 177, 183, 186–7
smells, 219–20
SMILES, 292
smoking, 32
social anxiety, 25, 54, 56, 108, 164–5, 168, 193, 263–4
   acknowledgment of, 174–6
   autism and, 182–92, 194, 264
   avoidance behaviours, 168–74
   exposure therapy, 167, 169–73, 263–4
   gut health and, 293
   spotlight effect, 153–4, 159, 166–7, 193
   spotlight shifting, 176–7, 190, 192
social anxiety disorder (SAD), 164–5
social comparison, 1, 97–8, 102, 104, 168
social connections, 80–84, 94, 103
social media, 85, 97, 100, 153, 181, 231, 280, 320
social phobia, 141
social welfare, 77
socially prescribed

perfectionism, 146–8, 153, 159
soft fascination, 288
soften-soothe-allow exercise, 212–14
solitude, 37, 75, 298, 309
somatic release, 305
soothing body, 207–29
soothing, 33, 114, 129, 133, 144, 155, 160
speedboats, 85–6
Spencer, Charles, 9th Earl Spencer, xiii
sports, 151–3
spotlight effect, 153–4, 159, 166–7, 193
St Andrews University, 109
state anxiety, 218
statue exercise, 42–4
Stoicism, 88
stories, 2–4
stress, 10–11, 32, 65, 141, 148, 150, 151, 203, 210, 211, 286
   chronic, 10–11, 215, 298–9
   cortisol, 10, 128, 203, 214–19, 223, 288–9
   early morning light and, 288–90
   interoception, 298–9
Strictly Come Dancing, 215
sugar, 46, 226, 293, 310
suicide, 48, 61, 147
'Summer Day, The' (Oliver), 256–7, 284
superbikes, 216
survivor stories, 94–7
suspense, 7–8, 299

INDEX

sweating, 64, 175
sympathetic nervous system, 128, 203, 210, 211

Taylor, Rebecca Lucy, 135
teachers, 37, 101, 148, 289
TED, 223
Tenzin Gyatso, 14th Dalai Lama, 82, 84, 101
testosterone, 223
Thatcher, Margaret, 218
therapy, 1–2, 14–15, 81, 139–40
   acceptance and commitment therapy, 36, 97, 103, 117–18, 126–7, 249, 268, 270–71
   cognitive behavioural therapy, 35, 62–4, 126–7, 172, 256
   compassion-focused therapy, 126–30, 271
   exposure therapy, 167, 169–73, 263–4
   narrative exposure therapy, 306
thinking, 230–53
   values, xvii, 16, 46, 71, 72, 104, 236–53
   choice points, 235–6
   comfort zone, 233–6
   depth of, 25, 34
thoughts and feelings exercise, 86–8
Threat-Drive-Soothe systems, 127–30, 137, 160, 193, 212, 280
Tibet, 82
Tilley, Angela, 197–8, 224, 225

Tolkien, John Ronald Reuel, 315
Tolle, Eckhart, 107, 108
Toseland, James, 216
touch, 214, 220–22
transgender people, 227–8
trauma, 199–202, 306, 310
tricky vs sticky anxiety, 227–8, 310
Truffaut, François, 8
trust, 77, 80, 94, 99–100, 111
tuberculosis, 48, 49
Turnbull, Bill, 255–259
twisties, 151–3

United Kingdom, 74, 79, 147
United States, 53, 54, 74, 88, 147, 153, 164, 203, 293
   UK trade deal (2025), 231, 232
United States Navy Seals, 209–10
University College London, 1, 14, 168, 207
University of Cambridge, 205
University of Western Australia, 266
University of Westminster, 289

vagus nerve, 210–11
Valium, 52
values, xvii, 16, 46, 71, 72, 104, 236–46, 259–62, 265, 274–6, 285
Van der Kolk, Bessel, 199, 280
Vendée Globe yacht race, 247, 264–5
Victoria, 135

video clips, 38
virtual reality, 191
vitamin D, 294
Vora, Ellen, 226–7

wallet test, 77, 80
Ware, Bronnie, 259
Wax, Ruby, 176, 190
wear and tear, 34
weaving, 261
welfare, 77
Whippman, Ruth, 80
Whitman, Walt, 320
William, Prince of Wales, xiii, 109
Williamson, Mark, 82
Wilson, Sarah, 313
Winnie the Pooh, 253
Witchell, Nick, xiv–xv

withdrawal, 47, 48–50, 260
Wittgenstein, Ludwig, 314
women's rights, 77
work, 86, 146, 164, 200–202, 237, 238, 295–8
World Happiness Report, 74, 77–8, 79–80, 81
World Health Organization (WHO), 296
worry, 10, 12–13, 65, 103, 233, 256, 261, 289
  Worry Tree, 62–4
worst case scenarios, 64, 66, 116, 128, 169, 214
writing, 305–8, 316, 319–20
Wycombe Wanderers, 259

YK2 computer bug, 99
yoga, 210, 211, 305, 316